Copyright 2019. All rights reserved.

Limit of Liability/Disclaimer of Warranty

Neither we nor any third parties provide any warranty or guarantee as to the accuracy, timeliness, performance, completeness or suitability of the information and materials found or offered in this study guide for any particular purpose. You acknowledge that such information and materials may contain inaccuracies or errors and we expressly exclude liability for any such inaccuracies or errors to the fullest extent permitted by law.

Free Extra Practice Exam

We'd love to hear from you. For an extra free complete ATI TEAS practice exam, please email us at hut8testprep@gmail.com. Please include "ATI TEAS Free Practice Exam" in the subject line and the following information in the email:

1. Your rating of the book from 1 - 5 (5 being the best).
2. Your feedback about the book. What did you like about the book? What do you think can be improved?

This offer expires 12/31/2020.

Biology

*The ATI TEAS Science section contains 53 questions, around 32 questions are about human anatomy and physiology, so focus on this.

Human Anatomy and Physiology

Anatomy is the study of the structure of body parts; **physiology** is the study of the functions and relationships of body parts.

Anatomical Planes

Left and right are always in reference to the person's left and right. References to the human body always assumes an anatomical position. In the **anatomical position**, the body is standing face forward, with arms at the side, and palms facing forward (thumbs on outside.)

The body can be divided into anatomical planes. The **sagittal plane or midline** is a vertical line that divides the body into left and right sections. Objects closer to the midline are called **medial** and objects further away are called **lateral**. The **transverse plane** is a horizontal line, parallel to the ground, at the level of the navel and divides the body into **superior** (top) and **inferior** (bottom) sections. Objects closer to the navel or trunk are **proximal** (next to); objects away from naval or trunk are **distal**. The **coronal plane** is a vertical line that divides the body into **anterior** (front) and **posterior** (back) sections.

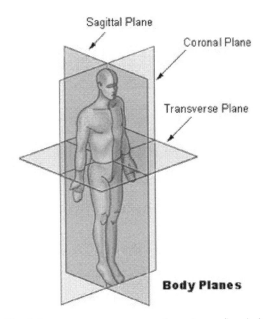

Image By https://training.seer.cancer.gov/anatomy/body/terminology.html

Musculoskeletal System

The **musculoskeletal system** includes **bones, tendons, ligaments, and cartilage** that form the body's framework and protects internal organs. The **axial skeleton** combined with the

appendicular skeleton form the complete skeleton. There are 206 bones in the human skeletal system.

Bones

There are two main types of bone tissue: **spongy (a.k.a cancellous) and compact**. Spongy bone contains red bone marrow and is located at the end of bones. **Red bone marrow** is where red and white blood cells are produced. **Yellow bone marrow** is found in long bones and consists of fat. Compact bone is very dense, supports the body, and stores calcium.

Bone tissue is made of many types of cells including: **osteoblasts, osteoclasts, and osteocytes**. **Osteoblasts** build bones in a process called **ossification**. **Osteoclasts** break down bones; they help regulate the body's calcium levels by breaking down bone to release calcium. **Osteocytes** regulate osteoblasts and osteoclasts in response to mechanical stress.

There are 5 types of bones: **long, short, flat, irregular, and sesamoid**.
- **Long** bones are longer than they are wide and make up the bones of the limbs (femur, tibia, ulna, humerus, etc.). They provide strength, structure, and mobility.
- **Short** bones are wider than they are long. They are found in the carpal bones (wrist) and tarsal bones (foot).
- **Flat** bones are thin bones that protect internal organs and provide a surface for muscles to attach to. The sternum, ribs, and pelvis are made of flat bones.
- **Sesamoid** bones are bones embedded within a tendon or muscle. The kneecap is a sesamoid bone.
- **Irregular** bones are bones that do not fit into the other categories. The vertebral column, skull, and elbow are examples of irregular bones.

Ligaments are fibrous connective tissue that connect bone to bone. **Tendons** connect muscles to bones. **Cartilage** is connective tissue that acts as a cushion between bones. A **joint** is where two bones meet.

There are 3 types of joints: **synovial, fibrous, and cartilaginous**.
- **Synovial** joints are the most common joints in the body. The joint contains synovial fluid which lubricates the joints. Two common types of synovial joints are: **ball and socket and hinge**. Examples of ball and socket joints include the hip and shoulder. Examples of hinge joints include the elbow and knee.
- In **fibrous** joints, bones are connected to each other by ligaments and are not movable. Skull bones are connected by fibrous joints.
- **Cartilaginous** joints hold bones together by cartilage; they can move more than fibrous joints, but less than synovial joints. Joints in the spine are cartilaginous.

Axial Skeleton

The **axial skeleton** consists of the bones of the head and trunk. The axial skeleton consists of 6 parts: the skull, rib cage, spinal column, ossicles of the middle ear, hyoid bone, and sternum.

The skull consists of the cranium and facial bones. Facial bones include the orbit (eye socket), nasal bone, maxilla (upper jaw) and mandible (lower jaw), and zygomatic bones (cheekbones).

The rib cage or thoracic cavity consists of 12 pairs of bones and the sternum (for a total of 25 bones.) It protects the heart, lungs, trachea, esophagus, and great vessels. The space between 2 rib bones is called the intercostal space. The sternum is divided into 3 parts: the manubrium (upper portion), middle body, and xiphoid process (lower tip of sternum).

The spinal column is composed of bones called vertebrae and protects the spinal cord. It consists of 5 parts: cervical (7 vertebrae), thoracic (12 vertebrae), lumbar/lower back (5 vertebrae), sacral/pelvic (5 vertebrae), coccyx/tailbone (4 vertebrae).

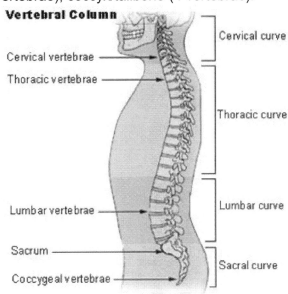

Image By: https://training.seer.cancer.gov/anatomy/skeletal/divisions/axial.html

Appendicular Skeleton

The **appendicular skeleton** consists of bones of the shoulder girdle, pelvis, and upper and lower limbs. The shoulder girdle includes the clavicle (collarbone), scapula (shoulder blade), and humerus (upper arm).

Bones of the arms include humerus, radius (lateral bone of forearm), ulna (medial bone of forearm), carpal bones(wrist), metacarpals (base of fingers), phalanges (fingers).

Bones of the leg include femur (thigh bone), patella (kneecap), tibia (medial bone of the lower leg), fibula (lateral bone of the lower leg), tarsal bone (ankle), metatarsal (base of toes), phalanges (toes).

The pelvis protects the internal reproductive organs, intestines, bladder, and rectum. It is composed of 3 bones: pubis (anterior portion of the pelvis), ischium (inferior portion of the pelvis), and iliac crests (wings of the pelvis).

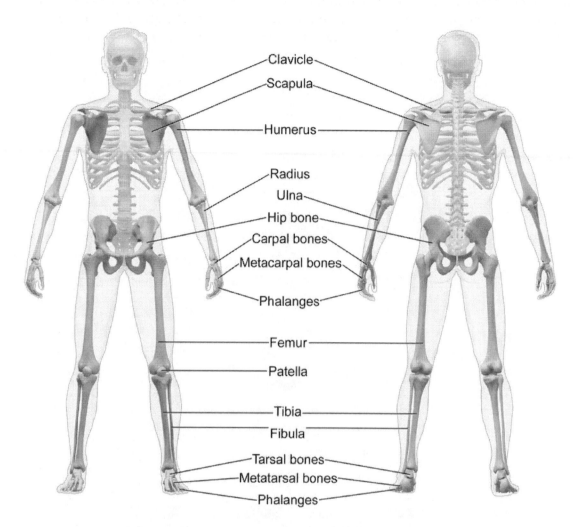

Clavicle
Scapula
Humerus
Radius
Ulna
Hip bone
Carpal bones
Metacarpal bones
Phalanges
Femur
Patella
Tibia
Fibula
Tarsal bones
Metatarsal bones
Phalanges

The Appendicular Skeleton

Image By: Blausen.com staff (2014)

Muscles

There are 3 types of muscle: **smooth, skeletal, cardiac**.

- **Cardiac** muscles are muscles of the heart and are not under voluntary control.
- **Smooth** muscles are not under voluntary control and are typically found in the digestive tract, blood vessels, and other internal organs.
- **Skeletal** muscles are striated muscles that are under voluntary control; they are the only muscles under voluntary control. Striated muscle fibers are composed of **myofibrils** which are responsible for contracting. Muscle fiber cells also have a lot of **mitochondria** that provide the cells with energy.

Muscles work by contracting, they do not extend. Muscles work in groups; one muscle (called the **agonist**) will contract, while the other muscle will relax (called the **antagonist**). For example, biceps and triceps work together. When the bicep contracts, the tricep relaxes, bending the arm. When the tricep contracts, the bicep relaxes, extending the arm.

When muscles are overworked, the following can happen:
- Depletion of **acetylcholine,** a neurotransmitter that triggers muscle contraction, so muscles can no longer contract
- Buildup of lactic acid, impairing the muscle's ability to contract

Nervous System

Neurons

Neurons are nerve cells that transmit information to other nerve, muscle, or gland cells of the body. Neurons rarely reproduce or regenerate. Each neuron has a **soma**, **dendrites**, and an **axon**.

- The **soma** is the neuron's body.
- **Dendrites** branch from the soma, receive information from other neurons, and carry that information to the soma. When dendrites receive information or an impulse, it generates an **action potential** (electrical signal) that travels to the soma and then, through the axon. Action potentials are like switches, they are either triggered on or off; there is no in between.
- The **axon** is a long and thin structure extending from the soma. It is mainly responsible for sending messages from the soma to other cells in the body. The axon is covered with a layer of **myelin sheath** (made from glial cells); the myelin sheath increases the speed at which electrical impulses travel through the axon. **Demyelinating disorders**, such as multiple sclerosis, reduce the speed at which signals travel through the axon.

Most neurons receive signals through the dendrites and send out signals through the axon. Neurons communicate with other neurons or cells through junctions or spaces called **synapses**. Communication in synapses can occur chemically (most of the time) or electrically.

- In **electrical synapses**, ions flow directly between cells through a channel called a **gap junction**. The main advantage of electrical synapses is that they transmit signals faster than chemical synapses.
- In **chemical synapses**, the electrical signal from the axon is converted into the release of a **neurotransmitter**. Neurotransmitters are chemical messengers that bind to receptors on the postsynaptic (receiving) neuron or cell to trigger an action.

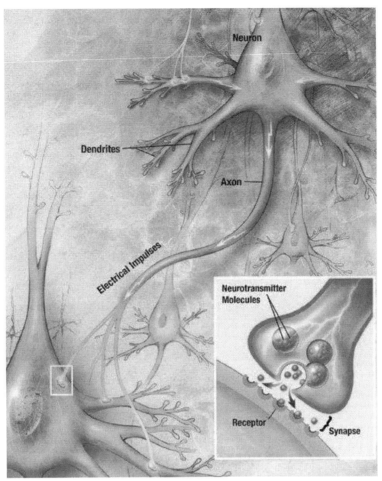

Source:
https://en.wikipedia.org/wiki/Neuron#/media/File:Chemical_synapse_schema_cropped.jpg

The Brain

The brain consists of gray matter and white matter. **Grey matter** is where all the nerve synapses are located and where the actual processing of signals happen. **White matter** mainly consists of neuron axons and is mainly responsible for transmitting signals between gray matter regions and between the brain and spinal cord.

The brain consists of 3 main parts: the **cerebrum, cerebellum, and brainstem**.

Cerebrum

The **cerebrum** is the largest part of the brain. The surface of the cerebrum is called the cerebral cortex. The **cerebral cortex**, made of gray matter, is where most of the brain's processing happens; it is responsible for higher brain functions such as thought and language.

The cerebrum is divided into two halves (right and left). The two halves are connected by and communicate with each other through the **corpus callosum**. Each half of the cerebrum is further divided into four lobes: **frontal, parietal, temporal, and occipital**.

- The **frontal** lobe is responsible for key functions such as decision making, problem solving, emotional expression, voluntary movement, memory, and personality.
- The **parietal** lobe is mainly responsible for processing sensory information such as taste, temperature, touch, spatial awareness, etc.
- The **occipital** lobe is mainly responsible for processing visual input.
- The **temporal** lobe is mainly responsible for processing auditory input.

Brainstem

The **brainstem** connects the cerebrum and spinal cord. The brainstem consists of the **medulla** and **pons**. The **medulla** is responsible for controlling critical involuntary body functions such as breathing, swallowing, blood pressure, beating of the heart, etc. The **pons** is responsible for transmitting signals between the cerebellum, spinal cord, medulla, and upper regions of the brain.

Cerebellum

The **cerebellum**, which is located behind the brain stem, is responsible for controlling and coordinating physical movement and maintaining posture and balance.

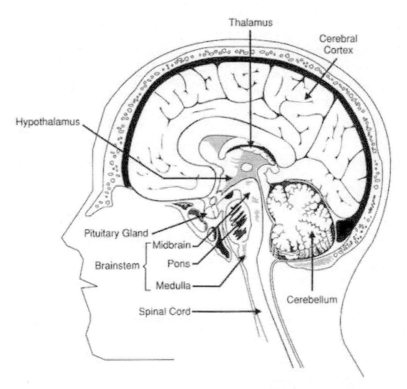

Source: https://www.ncbi.nlm.nih.gov/books/NBK234157/

Central and Peripheral Nervous System

The nervous system consists of the **central nervous system (CNS)** and the **peripheral nervous system (PNS).** The CNS consists of the brain and the spinal cord; the PNS is the nervous system outside of the brain and spinal cord.

The brain receives information from the PNS and sends commands to the PNS system. Communication between the brain and the PNS occurs through the spinal cord.

The PNS consists of **sensory neurons** and **motor neurons**. The sensory neurons send sensory information from the body to the CNS. The motor neurons relay commands from the CNS to the muscles of the body.

The PNS motor system is divided into **somatic** (voluntary) and **autonomic** (involuntary) portions. The **autonomic system** is further divided into the **sympathetic** and **parasympathetic** systems. The sympathetic division controls the "fight or flight" response and prepares the body for emergencies. The parasympathetic portion returns the body functions back to normal after a sympathetic "fight or flight" response.

Motor Neurons and Movement

Movement begins when an electrical signal is sent from the brain to a motor neuron in the spinal cord. Motor neurons control muscle cells. A **motor unit** consists of motor neurons and the muscle cells the neuron controls. Groups of motor units work together to contract a single muscle.

The motor neuron transmits a signal to the muscle fiber at the **neuromuscular junction**. A neuromuscular junction is a synapse between a motor neuron and muscle fiber cell. At the neuromuscular junction, **acetylcholine** (a neurotransmitter) is released. Acetylcholine triggers muscles to contract. The force of a muscular contraction depends on the number of motor units contracting at the same time.

Respiratory System

The respiratory system is a group of body organs that work together to take in oxygen and expel waste products such as carbon dioxide. The respiratory tract is lined with cells that secrete mucus/liquids or have **cilia** to keep the lungs moist and trap pathogens. Cilia are microscopic hairlike structures that have a wavelike motion that can help clear airways of mucus and dirt.

The **upper airway** consists of the **nose, mouth, nasopharynx, oropharynx, larynx (voice box), epiglottis** (valve that closes over the trachea during swallowing to prevent choking).

The **lower away** includes the **trachea** (tube that connects the pharynx to the bronchi), **bronchi** (tubes that lead to the lungs), and **alveoli**. The alveoli are tiny air sacs of the lungs where oxygen and carbon dioxide are exchanged. Alveoli diffuse oxygen to the red blood cells and **pulmonary capillaries** diffuse carbon dioxide from the body to the alveoli.

The **diaphragm** is a muscle at the bottom of the thoracic cavity and is the primary muscle used in ventilation. **Ventilation** (breathing) is the process of inhaling/exhaling air. Humans use negative pressure breathing; as the diaphragm is pulled downward and intercostal muscles contract, negative pressure is created in the thoracic cavity and the lungs expand, allowing air to flow in. As the diaphragm relaxes, pressure increases in the thoracic cavity and the lungs contract, forcing carbon dioxide to flow out.

Residual volume is the amount of air that is in the lungs at all times and helps prevent lung collapse. **Tidal volume** is the amount of air inhaled and exhaled in one normal breath. **Vital capacity** is the maximum amount of air a person can expel from the lungs after a maximum inhalation.

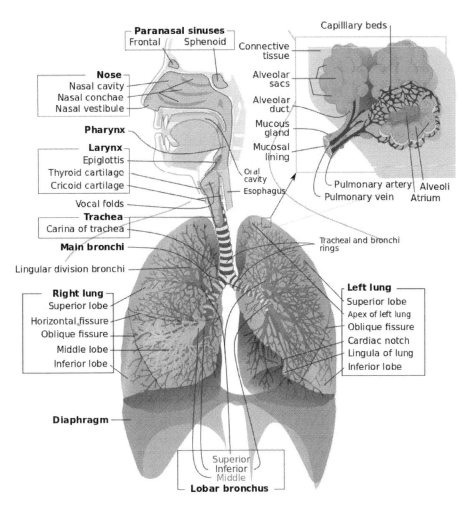

Paranasal sinuses
Frontal   Sphenoid

Connective tissue

Capilllary beds

Nose
Nasal cavity
Nasal conchae
Nasal vestibule

Alveolar sacs

Alveolar duct

Mucous gland

Mucosal lining

Pharynx

Larynx
Epiglottis
Thyroid cartilage
Cricoid cartilage

Oral cavity
Esophagus

Vocal folds

Trachea
Carina of trachea

Pulmonary artery
Pulmonary vein

Alveoli
Atrium

Main bronchi

Tracheal and bronchi rings

Lingular division bronchi

Right lung
Superior lobe
Horizontal fissure
Oblique fissure
Middle lobe
Inferior lobe

Left lung
Superior lobe
Apex of left lung
Oblique fissure
Cardiac notch
Lingula of lung
Inferior lobe

Diaphragm

Superior
Inferior
Middle
Lobar bronchus

Image By: https://commons.wikimedia.org/w/index.php?curid=3945169

Circulatory System

The circulatory or cardiovascular system is responsible for the flow of blood, nutrients, hormones, oxygen and other gases to the cells of the body. It is composed of the heart, blood, and blood vessels.

Arteries, Capillaries, and Veins

There are 3 types of blood vessels: **arteries, capillaries, and veins**.
- **Arteries** carry blood away from the heart and have thick, muscular, and elastic walls to withstand the high pressure of blood leaving the heart.
- **Veins** carry blood back to the heart and have one way valves to prevent backflow. They have thinner and less elastic walls than arteries because they do not have to withstand as high of a blood pressure.
- **Capillaries** are the smallest and most populous blood vessels. They have thin walls to allow substances and gases to be exchanged or diffused between the blood and cell tissues.

Blood

Blood is composed of **red blood cells or erythrocytes** (carries oxygen, nutrients, and waste products), **white blood cells or leukocytes** (fights infections), **plasma** (fluid component of blood), and **platelets or thrombocytes** (enables blood to clot). Red blood cells are produced in red bone marrow and contain **hemoglobin**. Hemoglobin is a protein that is rich in iron and helps with transporting oxygen.

The Heart

The heart is divided into 4 chambers: **left atrium, right atrium, left ventricle, and right ventricle**. The **atria** are the two upper chambers and the **ventricles** are the two lower chambers. The heart contains one-way valves that ensures blood flows in the correct direction. **Arteries** carry oxygen-rich blood away from the heart to body tissues, and **veins** carry oxygen-poor blood back to the heart. The only exceptions are the **pulmonary artery** (which carries oxygen-poor blood) and the **pulmonary vein** (which carries oxygen-rich blood). Blood returning to the heart always enter through the atria. The atria pump blood into the ventricles and the ventricle pumps blood out of the heart and into the blood vessels of the body.

Pulmonary and Systemic Loop

Blood flows through the body in a **closed circulatory system** of two loops: the **pulmonary and systemic loop**. Blood actually flows through the heart twice: once when oxygen-rich blood flows through the heart to the body and once more when oxygen-poor blood flows through the heart to the lungs.

In the **pulmonary loop**, when oxygen-poor blood enters the heart's right atrium, the atria contracts and pumps blood to the right ventricle. When the ventricles contract, blood is pumped from the right ventricle, through the pulmonary arteries, to the lungs where the blood becomes oxygenated (carbon dioxide is exchanged for oxygen). The now oxygen-rich blood is pumped through the pulmonary veins and into the heart's left atrium and then to the left ventricle.

In the **systemic loop**, oxygen-rich blood is pumped from the heart's left ventricle to the aorta (the largest artery in the body) and the blood vessels of the body. Oxygen-poor blood is then transported back to the heart's right atrium by veins.

Contractions

Contractions in the heart are caused by electrical impulses. There are 3 areas in the heart where electrical impulses are generated: **sinoatrial node (pacemaker of the heart), atrioventricular junction, and bundle of His**. Electrical signals from the brain enter the sinoatrial node and pass through the atria, causing the atria to contract. The signal than enters the atrioventricular junction and the bundle of His, causing the ventricles to contract. The inability to generate an electrical impulse or for heart muscles to respond to electrical impulse will result in cardiac arrest.

A **heart or cardiac cycle** is the period between the start of one heartbeat and the start of the next heartbeat. During **systole**, the heart muscles contract. During **diastole**, the heart muscles relax. **Blood pressure** is a measure of the pressure during systole (systolic pressure) and diastole (diastolic pressure).

The Lymphatic System

The **lymphatic system** plays an important role in the immune system and is our body's "sewage system". It is similar to the blood circulatory system except it's an open circulatory system and instead of blood vessels, the lymphatic system consists of **lymphatic vessels, lymphatic organs (tonsils, thymus, spleen, liver), lymph nodes**, and **lymph. Lymphatic vessels** are like blood vessels, except they carry lymph instead of blood. Waste products, foreign microorganisms (bacteria, etc.), and damaged cells from body tissues gets absorbed by lymph.

Lymph flows through the lymphatic vessels to and through lymph nodes. **Lymph nodes**, which have a high concentration of **lymphocytes** (a type of white blood cell), filter the lymph and trap and destroy foreign microorganisms. Waste products and the destroyed microorganisms are then carried in the lymph fluid back into the bloodstream and removed from the body with other body waste.

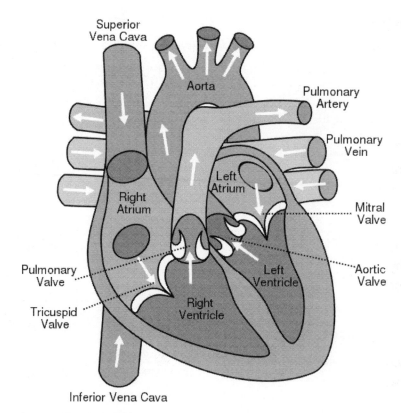

Image By: https://en.wikipedia.org/wiki/Circulatory_system

Endocrine System

The endocrine system produces **hormones** (chemical messengers) that maintain homeostasis, regulate metabolism, growth and development, sexual function, and sleep; essentially all bodily functions. The main glands of the endocrine system are the **thyroids, parathyroids, adrenal glands, gonads (testes and ovaries), islets of Langerhans, and pituitary gland.**

Maintaining Homeostasis

Homeostasis is maintained through **positive feedback** and **negative feedback** loops. Most endocrine glands operate under a negative feedback loop.

- In **negative feedback loops**, when conditions deviate from normal or ideal values, a response is triggered to bring conditions back to normal. An example of a negative feedback loop is the regulation of blood calcium levels. If blood calcium levels are low, the parathyroid glands sense the decrease and secrete more parathyroid hormone to increase calcium release from the bones and increase calcium uptake into the bloodstream.
- In **positive feedback loops**, deviation from normal values are increased. For example, during childbirth, oxytocin increases labor contractions. As the uterus contracts and the baby moves lower, pressure receptors in the cervix tell the brain to release even more oxytocin, which further increase contractions.

Hypothalamus and Pituitary

The hypothalamus and pituitary gland can be considered the "master" or "command center" of the endocrine system.

- The **hypothalamus** is the link between the nervous system and the endocrine system. Located at the base of the brain near the pituitary gland, it secretes hormones that control the pituitary gland.
- The **pituitary gland**, when triggered by the hypothalamus, secretes hormones that control multiple body functions. Below is a list of some of the hormones released (Source: Kaplan ATI TEAS, pg. 241). Oxytocin and Vasopressin are released by the posterior pituitary. Use the mnemonic **"FLAT PEG"** to remember the hormones released by the anterior pituitary.
    - **Oxytocin** stimulates the uterus to contract during labor.
    - **Vasopressin** causes kidneys to reabsorb water.
    - **Follicle-stimulating hormone (FSH)** stimulates ovarian follicle maturation and sperm maturation.
    - **Luteinizing hormone (LH)** induces ovulation and testosterone production.
    - **Adrenocorticotropic hormone (ACTH)** tells the adrenal glands to release hormones.
    - **Thyroid stimulating hormone (TSH)** tells the thyroid gland to release hormones.
    - **Prolactin** stimulates milk production.
    - **Endorphins** help relieve pain and stress and boost feelings of pleasure.

Pancreas

The **pancreas** secretes hormones that control blood glucose levels. It releases **insulin** when blood glucose levels are high; insulin increases cell uptake of glucose, reducing the levels of glucose in blood. The pancreas releases **glucagon** when blood glucose levels are low; glucagon causes cells to release glucose into the blood.

Pineal Gland

The **pineal gland** releases **melatonin** to regulate sleep cycles.

Parathyroid Glands

The **parathyroid glands** release parathyroid hormones to control calcium and phosphorus levels in the body.

Thyroid Gland

The **thyroid** gland controls metabolism and growth and development. The thyroid gland is stimulated by thyroid-stimulating hormone (TSH), which is released by the pituitary gland, to release **thyroid hormones** (T3 and T4). Thyroid hormones control the metabolic rate.

Adrenal Glands

The **adrenal glands** are divided into two parts: the **cortex** (outer part) and **medulla** (inner part). The medulla regulates hormones associated with the "fight or flight" or stress response such as **epinephrine (adrenaline), noradrenaline**, etc. The cortex regulates hormones such as **cortisol** (which helps regulate metabolism and helps your body respond to stress) and **aldosterone** (which helps control blood pressure).

Testes

The **testes** produce testosterone which is responsible for the development of male sex characteristics.

Ovaries

The **ovaries** release **estrogen** which is responsible for the development of female sex characteristics. It also releases **progesterone** which regulate the uterine lining.

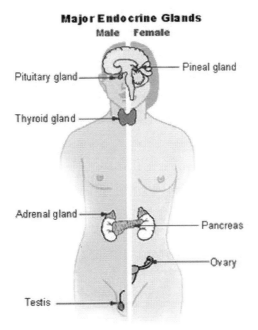

Major Endocrine Glands

Male   Female

Pituitary gland

Pineal gland

Thyroid gland

Adrenal gland

Pancreas

Ovary

Testis

Image By: http://training.seer.cancer.gov/module_anatomy/unit6_3_endo_glnds.html

Gastrointestinal System

The gastrointestinal system is responsible for digestion and nutrient absorption. **Digestion** is the process of breaking down food into components absorbable by the body. The gastrointestinal system is composed of the **gastrointestinal (GI) or digestive tract and the liver, pancreas, and gallbladder**. The GI tract consists of hollow organs such as the **mouth, esophagus, stomach, small intestine, large intestine, and anus**.

Digestion begins in the mouth and ends at the anus. Food is broken down mechanically by chewing and chemically by **digestive enzymes** in saliva. Once the food is swallowed, it travels through the **pharynx** (throat) to the esophagus to the stomach.

- The **epiglottis** is a flap of tissue in the throat that prevents food from entering the trachea.
- The **esophagus** is a muscular tube that pushes food down or up (during vomiting) using wave-like muscle contractions called **peristalsis**. It has sphincters at the top and bottom that close to prevent backflow of stomach contents.
- The **stomach** releases **gastric juice**, which consists of highly acidic hydrochloric acid, pepsin (an enzyme), and mucus.
  - The acid kills bacteria in food.
  - Pepsin is used to break down food proteins.
  - Mucus protects the stomach lining from the acid and enzymes.

Chyme, food mixed with water and gastric juices, exits the stomach and enters the small intestines. The small intestine is where digestion ends and absorption begins. It is lined with **villi** to help with absorption. The small intestine is divided into three parts: **the duodenum, jejunum, and ileum**.

- The **duodenum** is the first part of the small intestine. Chemical secretions from the pancreas and gallbladder mix with the chyme in the duodenum to break down the chyme even more. Proteins are broken down into amino acids; carbohydrates are broken down into simple sugars; fat is broken down into fatty acids and glycerol.
  - The **liver** filters the blood coming from the digestive tract, detoxifies chemicals, and metabolizes drugs. It also produces **bile** and stores it in the gallbladder. The gallbladder secretes bile into the duodenum to break down fats. The liver also helps control blood glucose level. When blood glucose rises, the liver removes extra glucose and stores it. The liver releases the stored glucose when glucose levels are low.
  - The pancreas secretes pancreatic amylase (breaks down carbohydrates), trypsin (breaks down proteins), and pancreatic lipase (breaks down fats).
- The **jejunum** is the second part of the small intestine; it is where most nutrients are absorbed.
- The **ileum** is the third part of the small intestine; it is where nutrients, not absorbed by the jejunum, are absorbed. Vitamin B12, bile salts, and bile acids are absorbed here.

Undigested or unabsorbed food gets passed onto the large intestine (also called the **colon**). Water, salt, and some vitamins are absorbed in the large intestine; what is leftover is solid waste (**feces or stool**). Stool is stored in the rectum and expelled through the anus.

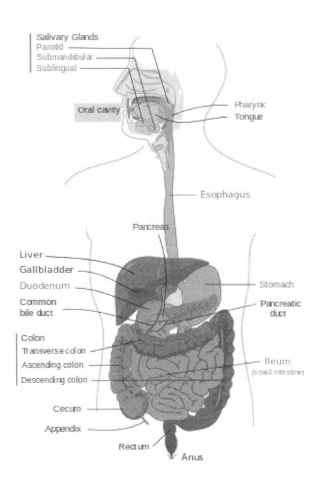

Urinary/Renal System

The urinary or renal system is responsible for filtering and excreting waste from the blood and maintaining the body's blood pressure and balance of water and chemicals (**homeostasis**). It consists of the **kidneys, ureters, bladder, and urethra**. The kidneys filter blood, produce urine, and help regulate blood pressure. The ureters carry waste from the kidneys to the bladder. The bladder stores urine and the urethra is where urine exits out of the body.

Kidney Function

Blood, containing cellular waste products, travels through the **renal arteries** to the kidneys, where filtering of waste occurs. **Nephrons**, which are tiny tubes in a kidney, are the functional units of the kidney; each kidney contains millions of nephrons. The nephron is responsible for filtering blood as well as reabsorbing valuable proteins, salts, water, and glucose.

Each nephron contains clusters of capillaries, called a **glomerulus'**, where the main filtering of blood occurs. From there, the blood travels to the **renal tubule**, where valuable substances are **reabsorbed**. Most of the water that was filtered out of the blood is reabsorbed in the **loop of Henle**. The loop of Henle is responsible for conserving water. Whatever is not reabsorbed goes to the **collecting duct**, where it is converted to urine. Urine goes through the ureters to the bladder, where it is stored.

The bladder contains two sphincters to control the release of urine; the internal sphincter is made of involuntary muscle and the external sphincter is made of voluntary muscle. In males, the external sphincter closes during sexual activity to prevent seminal fluid from entering the bladder. Urine exits the bladder through the urethra.

Reproductive System

Males

The reproductive system consists of sex organs that aid in sexual reproduction. The **penis** is the male external sexual organ. In males, **sperm** is produced in the **testes (specifically, in the seminiferous tubules)** and stored in the **scrotum (specifically, in the epididymis)**. The **prostate gland** produces seminal fluid; it is located below the bladder and surrounds the urethra. The **vas deferens** is a duct that carries ejaculated sperm from the epididymis to the urethra. The urethra is the duct through which semen exits the body.

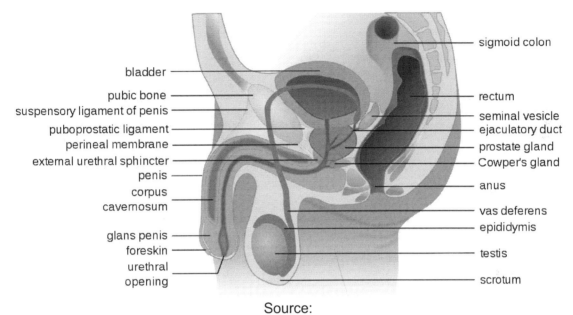

Source:
https://en.wikipedia.org/wiki/Male_reproductive_system#/media/File:Male_anatomy_en.svg

Females

The main components of the female reproductive system are the ovaries, uterus, and vagina. The **ovaries** are responsible for egg production and release. Eggs travel through the **fallopian tubes** to the uterus. The **uterus** is where developing fetuses are held. The **vagina** includes a vaginal opening that leads **cervix** which leads to the uterus.

Menstrual Cycle

A menstrual cycle is counted from the first day of 1 period to the first day of the next period. The female menstrual cycle is about 28 days, though this varies among individuals. The menstrual cycle consists of two phases: the follicular phase and the luteal phase.

During the **follicular phase**, the pituitary gland releases **follicle-stimulating hormone (FSH)**. FSH stimulates the ovaries to release estrogen. Estrogen causes an ovarian follicle to mature and the uterine wall/lining (also called **endometrium**) to thicken. As more estrogen is released, the pituitary gland is induced into releasing luteinizing hormone (LH). LH induces **ovulation** (when a follicle bursts and releases a mature egg from the ovary into a fallopian tube). The follicular phase ends with ovulation.

During the luteal phase, which begins after ovulation, the burst follicle (which stayed on the surface of the ovary) develops into the **corpus luteum**. The corpus luteum releases progesterone and oestrogen to maintain a thickened uterine lining, in preparation for a fertilized egg to implant. If a fertilized egg implants in the uterine lining, the corpus luteum continues to release progesterone to maintain the lining. If fertilization does not occur, the corpus luteum shrinks and stops releasing progesterone. The drop in progesterone levels causes the uterine lining (endometrium) to shed; the shedding of the uterine lining is called **menstruation**.

Fertilization

Fertilization occurs in the fallopian tubes. If an egg is fertilized, it will travel to the uterus and implant in the endometrium. The endometrium forms the placenta; the **placenta** is where nutrients and waste products are exchanged between the mother and the developing embryo.

If an egg is not fertilized, the endometrium is shed during menstruation.

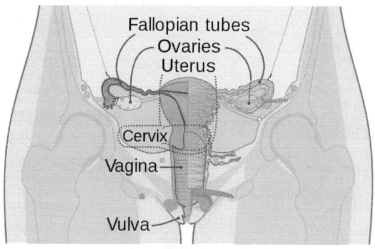

Source:
https://en.wikipedia.org/wiki/Female_reproductive_system#/media/File:Scheme_female_reproductive_system-en.svg

Integumentary (Skin) System

The skin is the largest organ of the body and protects the body from pathogens. The skin also helps regulate body temperature and serves our sense of heat, cold, pain, and pressure. It consists of the **epidermis** (outermost layer); **dermis** (contains blood vessels, nerve endings, hair follicles, sweat/oil glands); and **subcutaneous** layer (fatty tissue below the dermis and above the muscles). The epidermis also contains **melanocytes**; melanocytes are responsible for producing skin pigmentation and protecting the skin from ultraviolet rays.

Glands in the integumentary system include:
- **Sweat glands (sudoriferous glands)**: There are two types of sweat glands: eccrine and apocrine. **Eccrine** glands are the major sweat glands and located all over the body, with most of it located in the palms of hands, soles of feet, and head. **Apocrine** glands, located in the armpits, nipples, and groin, release pheromones and are not active until puberty.
- **Sebaceous glands** secrete sebum which lubricates the skin.

The integumentary plays several key roles:
- As a physical barrier, it's the first line of defense in the immune system.
- **Thermoregulation**: the integumentary system helps maintain body temperature.
  - When nerves in the skin detect that the body is overheated (**hyperthermia**), the integumentary system will trigger blood vessels to dilate and sweat glands to produce and release sweat. Sweat evaporating from the skin surface cools the body. Dilated blood vessels allow more blood to travel to the surface of the skin where excess heat is released to the environment through thermal radiation.
  - When nerves in the skin detect that the body is cold, it triggers blood vessels to constrict, reducing the amount of blood near the skin surface and thus reducing the heat that would be lost through thermal radiation. It also causes hair follicle muscles to contract, which appear as "goose bumps", to trap air between the hair and body for heat.
- Skin surface capillaries allow substances, such as medication, to enter the bloodstream.

Immune System

The immune system consists of 3 main parts: physical barriers, **innate immune system**, and **adaptive immune system**.

Physical Barriers (First Line Of Defense)

Our skin, mucus, tears, saliva, stomach acid, etc. act as a physical barrier to prevent pathogens from entering and infecting the body. If the physical barrier is breached, the innate immune system and adaptive immune system kicks in to kill the pathogens.

Innate Immune System (Second Line of Defense)

The innate immune system:
- Is quicker to respond than the adaptive immune system
- Does not target a specific pathogen
- Does not remember pathogens for future use

The innate immune system responds to pathogens by causing inflammation and/or fever. When body tissue is damaged or infected, **basophils** (a type of white blood cell) release **histamine**. Histamines raise the temperature and increase the blood flow to an area which draws more neutrophils to the area. **Neutrophils** are a type of white blood cell that **phagocytize** (eat) bacteria.

Infected cells also release **interferon** which causes nearby cells to increase their defense and helps prevent cell to cell infections.

Adaptive Immune System (Third Line of Defense)

The adaptive immune system:
- Is slow to respond
- Targets specific pathogens that display specific **antigens** (proteins on pathogens' surfaces that the body does not recognize)
- Forms memory cells which can quickly initiate an immune response the next time it encounters the same pathogen; memory cells are responsible for how and why vaccines work

The adaptive immune system triggers an **immune response** when it detects pathogens with specific antigens. The main cells involved in the immune response are: **B lymphocytes (B-cells) and T lymphocytes (T-cells)**. T-cells are responsible for detecting antigens. When T-cells detect an antigen, **helper T-cells** are triggered to find and bind to the antigens. The helper T-cells also activate **cytotoxic T-cells** (only kills host cells that display specific antigens) to destroy the infected cells; this is called a cell-mediated response. In **cell-mediated responses**, phagocytes and cytotoxic T-cells are activated to destroy infected cells.

B-cells are responsible for an **antibody mediated response or humoral response**. Antibody mediated response involves producing antibodies to destroy pathogens. Antibodies are proteins that bind to antigens and stimulate phagocytes to destroy the infected cell.

There are two types of B-cells: plasma cells and memory cells. **Plasma cells** produce antibodies and **memory cells** remember the antigen and stores information for creating the antibody. If antibodies are acquired through plasma production, then it is called **active immunity**. If the antibodies are acquired through an external source, then it is called **passive immunity.** An example of passive immunity is the transfer of antibodies through breastfeeding.

White Blood Cells

There are two classes of white blood cells: granular leukocytes (or granulocytes) and agranular leukocytes. **Granular leukocytes** include **basophils, eosinophils, and neutrophils**. Basophils release histamine; eosinophils kill viruses and parasites; neutrophils digest bacteria. **Agranular leukocyte**s include lymphocytes and monocytes. **Lymphocytes** include natural killer cells, T-cells, and B-cells. Lymphocytes are responsible for targeting and killing pathogens with specific antigens. **Monocytes** include macrophages and dendritic cells. **Macrophages** digest dead cells. **Dendritic cells** are antigen-presenting cells; they process antigen material and present it on the cell surface to the T cells. Dendritic cells initiate the adaptive immune response.

Pathophysiology

Cellular Metabolism

Cellular metabolism is the process in which the body breaks down glucose for energy. There are two types of cellular metabolism: aerobic and anaerobic. **Aerobic metabolism** occurs with oxygen. By-products of aerobic metabolism include heat, carbon dioxide and water. **Anaerobic metabolism** occurs without oxygen. By-products of anaerobic metabolism include **lactic acid**. High acid levels interrupt body functions by inactivating enzyme functions, disrupting cell membranes and interfering with the **Sodium/Potassium pump.** Sodium is moved out of cells and Potassium is moved into cells in the Sodium/Potassium pump. Without the Sodium/Potassium pump, muscle cells can't contract and nerve impulse can't transmit; this can lead to cell death.

Perfusion

Perfusion is the flow of blood through the body. Perfusion delivers oxygen, glucose, and other substances to the cells of the body. Any disturbance with respiration or the circulatory system can lead to poor perfusion. Inadequate perfusion means cells may not get enough energy and oxygen, leading to use of anaerobic metabolism and high acid levels. Disturbances with respiration can be improved by ventilation and oxygenation. Improving perfusion involves increasing blood flow, increasing availability of hemoglobin, and increasing delivery of oxygen to the cells.

Blood Pressure

The **systolic blood pressure** is a measure of cardiac output. It tells you the pressure in your arteries when your heart contracts. **Diastolic pressure** tells you the pressure when your heart is at rest, between beats. It is a measure of systemic vascular resistance. Systemic vascular resistance is the resistance blood faces when flowing through a vessel. When necessary to maintain perfusion, the body will compensate by increasing blood pressure. Blood needs to be pushed with enough force to provide adequate perfusion.

Macromolecules

Macromolecules are large organic molecules composed of thousands of atoms. **Organic molecules** are molecules that contain carbon atoms; **inorganic molecules** are those that do not contain carbon. There are 4 major types of macromolecules: **carbohydrates, lipids, proteins, and nucleic acids**. Together, the 4 major types of macromolecules, make up more than 95% of all living matter.

Carbohydrates, proteins, and nucleic acids are **polymers**; polymers consist of many repeated subunits called monomers. In a process called condensation, water molecules are removed to bond monomers together. In a process called hydrolysis, the opposite of condensation, water is added to break the bonds between monomers.

Carbohydrates

Carbohydrates, such as sugars and starches, are composed of carbon, hydrogen, and oxygen. Carbohydrates are grouped based upon how many saccharide (sugar) molecules they have:

Type	Description	Examples
monosaccharide	Consists of a single molecule of sugar. Its chemical formula is $C_6H_{12}O_6$.	Glucose, fructose, galactose
disaccharide	Consists of two sugar molecules. One water molecule is lost when the two sugar molecules are linked and that is why the formula is $C_{12}H_{22}O_{11}$ and not $C_{12}H_{24}O_{12}$	Sucrose, lactose
polysaccharide	Consists of multiple sugar molecules.	Starch, cellulose, glycogen

Carbohydrates can easily be converted to **glucose** which can be broken down into **adenosine triphosphate (ATP)**, the primary source of energy for a cell.

Lipids

Lipids or fats consist mainly of **hydrocarbon chains**. Lipids are **hydrophobic,** which means that they do not dissolve or mix with water. There are three main types of lipids: **triglycerides, phospholipids, and steroids**.

Triglycerides consist of 3 fatty acids linked to a glycerol molecule. Triglycerides can be saturated or unsaturated. Saturated fats are solid at room temperature. Unsaturated fats are liquid at room temperature. Triglycerides are important because they are the main form of long term energy storage, they insulate the body, and they are components in the myelin sheath.

Phospholipids consist of 2 fatty acids that are linked to a hydrophilic phosphate; because of this phospholipids are both hydrophilic (on the phosphate side) and hydrophobic (on the fatty acid side). The fact that phospholipids are both hydrophilic and hydrophobic is important to the function of the cell membrane; this is what allows a cell to be semi-permeable and create a barrier between its contents and its environment.

Steroids do not contain fatty acids and are also hydrophobic. Examples of steroids include cholesterol and hormones such as testosterone and estrogen.

Proteins

Proteins are composed of protein monomers called **amino acids**. Amino acids consist of an amine group ($-NH_2$), a carboxyl group (-COOH), and an R group that is unique to each type of amino acid. A protein's structure and function is determined by the sequence of its amino acid chain.

Proteins are extremely important; they take part in nearly all cellular processes and can be found in almost all cells and tissues (hair, muscle, bone, etc.). Some important protein functionality include:
- Acting as a catalyst in biological reactions
- Transporting molecules across membranes
- Helping with DNA replication
- Helping regulate the cell cycle

Enzymes

Enzymes are types of proteins that act as **catalysts**; they help accelerate reactions. Enzymes speed up reactions by lowering the activation energy (the energy required for a reaction to take place). Enzymes act on molecules called **substrates** and convert the substrates into different molecules called products. Different types of enzymes have different shapes that uniquely fit into specific substrates, in a **"lock and key"** manner. The site on the enzyme where the substrate binds to the enzyme is called the "**active site**".

Nucleic Acids

Nucleic acids consist of monomers called nucleotides. Nucleotides consist of a 5 carbon sugar, a phosphate group, and a nitrogenous base. The two main types of nucleic acids are deoxyribonucleic acid (**DNA**) and ribonucleic acid (**RNA**). DNA is found in chromosomes and stores genetic information. RNA translates instructions, found in DNA, to create proteins.

There are 5 bases: **adenine, guanine, cytosine, thymine, and uracil (A,G,C,T,U)**. Adenine and guanine are purine bases; the other 3 are pyrimidine bases. DNA contains the following bases: **adenine, guanine, cytosine, and thymine (A,G,C,T)**. RNA contains the following bases: adenine, guanine, cytosine, and uracil (A,G,C,U).

DNA

DNA has a double helix or twisted ladder shape where each rung of the ladder is formed by the pairing or hydrogen bonding of two bases. The "side rails" of the ladder consist of sugar and phosphate. In DNA, adenine (A) always pairs with thymine (T) and cytosine (C) always pairs with guanine (G). It is the ordering of these bases in DNA that is responsible for genetic diversity.

The ends of a DNA strand are called the 3' end and the 5' end. When describing or referring to DNA strands, you must specify the direction of replication because the direction matters. Below is an example of how to refer to a DNA strand:

5'-CATGTTAAGC-3'

RNA

RNA exists as a single strand. In RNA, adenine (A) always pairs with uracil (U) and cytosine (C) always pairs with guanine (G).

Differences Between DNA and RNA

- DNA has deoxyribose sugar whereas RNA has ribose sugar.
- Only DNA contains thymine; only RNA contains uracil.
- DNA consists of 2 strands; RNA consists of 1 strand.

Cells

Cells are the smallest unit or "building block" of life. According to **cell theory**:

- All living organisms are composed of one or more cells.
- The cell is the basic unit of structure and organization in organisms.
- Cells arise from pre-existing cells by division.

There are two main types of cells: **prokaryotes and eukaryotes**. A comparison of the two is below.

	Prokaryotes	Eukaryotes
Organization	Single celled	Single or multicellular
Typical Organisms	Bacteria, archaea	Protists, fungi, plants, animals
Nucleus	Does not have a nucleus	Has a nucleus
Size	Very small	Large (10 times larger than prokaryotes)
Organelles	Have organelles, but the organelles do not have membranes.	Have organelles
DNA / chromosomes	Single, usually circular chromosome	Multiple linear chromosomes
RNA / protein synthesis	RNA and protein synthesis occurs in the cytoplasm	RNA synthesis occurs in the nucleus; protein synthesis occurs in the cytoplasm
Mitochondria	None	Many
Chloroplast	None	In algae and plants
Cell division	Binary fission	Mitosis and meiosis

Cell Structure

Cell Wall

In plants, fungi, and certain prokaryotes, the **cell wall** surrounds the cell membrane, providing an additional layer of protection.

Cell Membrane

All cells have a **cell membrane**, also called a **plasma membrane**, which surrounds the cell. The cell membrane is a phospholipid bilayer consisting of lipids and proteins. Embedded within the cell membrane is a variety of protein molecules that help move different molecules into and out of the cell. Cell membranes also contain **receptor proteins that allow cells to communicate** with the external environment and other molecules (such as hormones).

The cell membrane controls what enters or leaves the cell. It is **semi-permeable and selectively permeable**; permeability is usually based on size, charge, and solubility. Molecules that are soluble in phospholipids can usually pass through the membrane. Small molecules, such as water and oxygen, can also pass through the membrane. **Ions** with opposite charges will be attracted to the membrane and those with like charges will be repelled. Molecules may also be transported across the membrane by active transport or vesicles.

Cytoplasm

Cytoplasm refers to all the fluid and substructures (organelles) inside the cell, excluding the nucleus.

Cytoskeleton

The **cytoskeleton** provides the cell with its shape and allows the cell to move. It also holds all the organelles in place.

Organelles

Organelles are substructures inside a cell. Each organelle has its own membrane and each organelle has a specialized function within the cell. As an analogy, **organelles are to the cell what organs are to the body.** Below is a table of organelles and their functions.

Organelle	Main Function	Organisms That Have It
Chloroplast	Traps energy from sunlight for photosynthesis	Eukaryotic plant cells
Nucleus	The cell's information and control center; it regulates all cell activity. It is where DNA storage/replication and RNA synthesis occurs.	All eukaryotes

Ribosomes	There are many, if not thousands, of ribosomes in a cell. They can be found floating freely in the cell or bound to the endoplasmic reticulum. Ribosomes link amino acids together to build or synthesize proteins.	Eukaryotes and prokaryotes
Mitochondria	The cell's powerhouse; it is where cell respiration and energy production occur. Oxygen is used to burn glucose to produce ATP.	Most single cell eukaryotes and all multicellular eukaryotes
Endoplasmic reticulum (ER)	Rough ER has ribosomes on the surface; smooth ER does not. Rough ER is involved in protein synthesis. Smooth ER is involved in lipid or fat synthesis.	All eukaryotes
Golgi complex (Golgi apparatus)	Processes and packages macromolecules, such as proteins and lipids, into vesicles for secretion outside of the cell.	All eukaryotes
Vesicle	Used to transport material.	Prokaryotes and eukaryotes
Vacuoles	Vesicles that usually contain water; used for storage, transportation, and waste removal. Animal cells have numerous small vacuoles. Plant cells have one large vacuole.	All eukaryotes
Flagellum	Used for cell locomotion and sensory.	Prokaryotes and some eukaryotes.
Centrosomes	Each centrosome consists of 2 centrioles. Centrosomes play a key role in cell division.	Animals
Centrioles	Occuring in pairs, these structures are near the nucleus and organize cell division by forming mitotic spindle fibers. They also act as an anchor for	Animals

	cytoskeleton.	
Lysosome	Digests proteins, lipids, and carbohydrates; transports undigested material to the cell membrane for removal.	Animals
Cilia	Hairlike structures on the surface of a cell; involved in movement of the cell itself, or of other substances and objects past the cell . Also helps remove contaminants such as mucus and bacteria from a cell.	Animals, protists, few plants

DNA and RNA

Deoxyribonucleic acid (DNA) is stored in chromosomes inside the cell nucleus; there is some DNA stored in the mitochondria, but mitochondrial DNA does not affect our genetic traits. Ribonucleic acid (RNA) is found in the cell cytoplasm, but it is synthesized or created in the cell nucleus.

The cell's genetic "blueprint" is stored and encoded in DNA. DNA contains all the information necessary to build or replicate the cell, which is important because it allows a cell to make an exact copy of itself during cell division. **RNA acts as a messenger**, translating instructions from DNA for synthesizing proteins. **The flow of genetic information in a cell goes from DNA to RNA to proteins**.

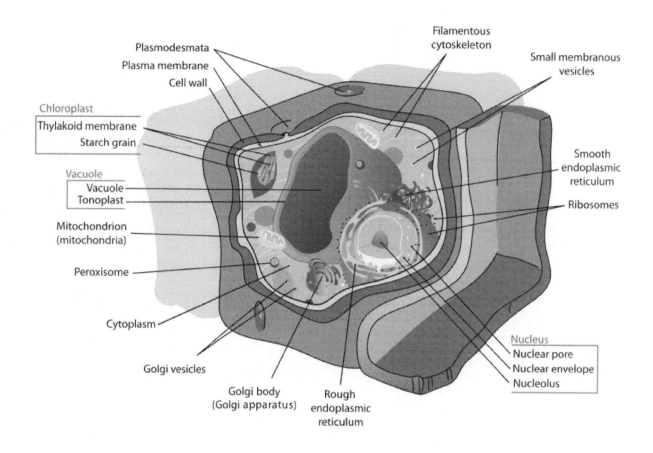

Plant Cell

https://en.wikipedia.org/wiki/Cell_(biology)#/media/File:Plant_cell_structure-en.svg

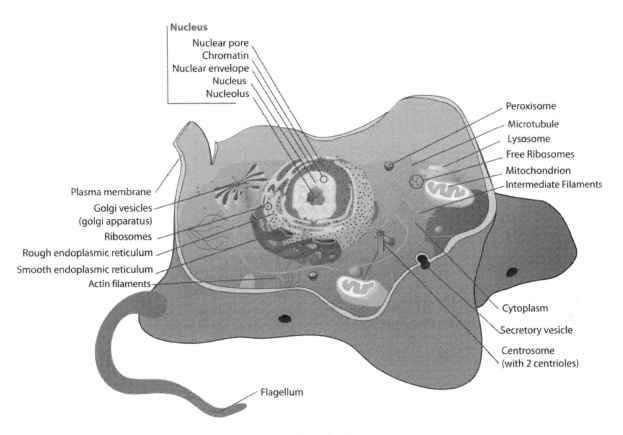

Animal Cell
https://en.wikipedia.org/wiki/Cell_(biology)#/media/File:Animal_cell_structure_en.svg

Cell Cycle

The **cell cycle** is the series of steps that occur from when a cell is first created to when the cell replicates or divides into two daughter cells. The length of time to complete a cell cycle varies. Some cells divide often, while some cells (like neuron cells) do not divide once they are mature. In eukaryotes, the cell cycle is divided into two main phases: interphase and mitotic (M) phase.

Interphase

During **interphase**, which takes up 80 to 90 percent of a cell cycle, the cell grows, perform normal cell functions, and makes a copy of its DNA. Interphase consists of 3 main stages:

1. G1 phase: The cell grows, makes copies of organelles, and increases its supply of proteins.
2. S phase: The cell makes a copy of its DNA. At the end of this stage, all the chromosomes have been replicated. Each chromosome consists of two identical sister chromatids. The centrosome is also duplicated at this stage.
3. G2 phase: The cell continues to grow larger in preparation for mitosis. The G2 phase ends when mitosis begins.

Mitotic (M) Phase

During the **mitotic phase**, the cell divides its DNA and cytoplasm to form two new daughter cells. The mitotic phase consists of two main steps: **mitosis and cytokinesis**. During mitosis, the nucleus (which contains the chromosomes which contain DNA) is divided in two. Cytokinesis occurs after mitosis. During cytokinesis, the two nuclei, organelles, cytoplasm, and cell membrane are divided in two, making two new cells.

DNA Replication

DNA replication is the process used to create an identical copy of DNA. The result of DNA replication is two DNA molecules that each have a new and an old DNA strand. The steps are below:

1. An enzyme called helicase is used to break the bonds between DNA base pairs, "unzipping" the double helix structure into 2 separate strands of DNA. The separation of the DNA strands results in a "Y" shape called a "replication fork". The two strands will be used as templates for making new complementary DNA strands.
2. One of the DNA strands is called the leading strand; it runs from the 3' to 5' direction and towards the replication fork. The other strand is called the lagging strand; it runs from the 5' to 3' direction and away from the replication fork. The leading and lagging strands are replicated differently.
3. The leading strand is replicated in a continuous manner. **DNA polymerase**, an enzyme, binds to the leading strand and creates a complementary strand. Since DNA polymerase can only read in the 3' to 5' direction, the replicated strand can only be synthesized in the 5' to 3' direction. For example, if the leading strand is 3'-TTAACCGG-5', then the complementary strand will be 5'-AATTGGCC-3'.
4. Since the lagging strand runs in the 5' to 3' direction and DNA polymerase can only read in the 3' to 5' direction, the lagging strand is replicated in fragments called Okazaki fragments. The Okazaki fragments are later joined together by DNA ligase.
5. Once the complementary strands have been created, DNA polymerase is used to check the strands for errors.
6. DNA ligase, an enzyme, is used to help join the DNA strands.

Mutations

Mutations are mistakes that occur when replicating DNA. Mutations may be benign, harmful, or helpful.

- Point mutations occur when a single DNA nucleotide base is erroneously substituted, inserted, or deleted.
- Frameshift mutations occur when the deletion or addition of DNA bases changes the read frame. Insertions, deletions, and duplications can all be frameshift mutations

Cell Division

Prokaryotic cells divide by **binary fission**, while eukaryotic cells can divide through **mitosis or meiosis**. In mitosis, the resulting daughter cell is an exact copy of the parent. In meiosis, which produces specialized reproductive cells called **gametes** (sperm and eggs), the resulting daughter cells have half the number of chromosomes of the parent cell and are genetically different from the parent cell. A **zygote** is a cell formed by a fertilization event between two gametes. Most human cells are produced through mitosis.

Mitosis

Mitosis consists of 5 stages:
1. Prophase: Chromatin in the nucleus is condensed into chromosomes. The sister chromatids (a **chromatid** is half of a replicated chromosome) are joined at the **centromere**. A mitotic spindle forms as the centrosomes move apart. The nucleolus disappears and the nuclear membrane breaks down.
2. Metaphase: During metaphase, the centrosomes are on opposite ends or "poles" of the cell and the chromosomes are lined up in the middle of the cell. Spindle fibers connect to each chromosome's centromere.
3. Anaphase: During anaphase, the replicated chromosomes or sister chromatids are separated. Once the sister chromatids are separated, they are each considered a chromosome. The cell structure begins to lengthen and pull apart.
4. Telophase: During telophase, the mitotic spindle breaks down and nuclear membranes form around each set of chromosomes. The nucleoli also reform. The chromosomes revert back to chromatin.
5. Cytokinesis: Cytokinesis involves the splitting of the cell membranes and cytoplasm into two daughter cells. In animals, the cell membranes are pinched to form two cells. In plants, a new cell wall is formed in the middle of a cell to form two cells.

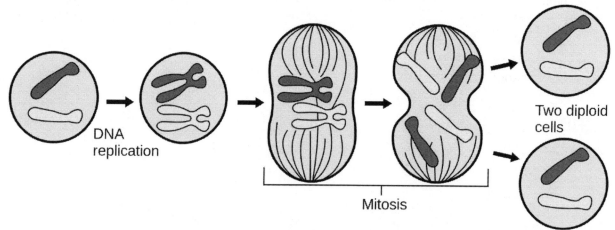

https://en.wikipedia.org/wiki/Mitosis#/media/File:Major_events_in_mitosis.svg

Meiosis

During **meiosis**, a **diploid** cell divides twice, resulting in four daughter cells. Each daughter cell is a **haploid**. Diploid cells contain a homologous pair of chromosomes; haploid cells contain one chromosome. Homologous chromosomes consists of one chromosome from the father and one chromosome from the mother. Homologous chromosomes are similar but not identical. Humans have 23 sets of homologous chromosomes. Meiosis increases genetic diversity.

Meiosis consists of 2 stages: Meiosis I and Meiosis II. During Meiosis 1, the homologous chromosomes are separated. During Meiosis II, the sister chromatids are separated.

Meiosis I

1. Prophase I: During prophase I, chromosomes condense and pair up. The homologous pair of chromosomes "**cross over**" or "recombine" to form chromosomes with unique combinations of alleles. After crossing over, the spindle microtubules attach to the chromosomes and move them toward the center of the cell. At the end of prophase I, the nuclear membrane dissolves.
2. Metaphase I: During metaphase I, the homologous chromosomes (not the individual chromosomes) are aligned at the center of the cell and begin to be pulled apart.
3. Anaphase I: During anaphase I, the homologous chromosomes are pulled apart and move to opposite sides of the cell.
4. Telophase I and Cytokinesis I: During telophase I and cytokinesis I, the cells separate, forming two haploid daughter cells. Each cell has one chromosome from each homologue pair.

Meiosis II

1. Prophase II: During prophase II, chromosomes condense and the spindle microtubules attach to the chromosomes and begin to move the chromosomes to the center of the cell.
2. Metaphase II: During metaphase II, the chromosomes are aligned in the middle of the cell.
3. Anaphase II: During anaphase II, the sister chromatids are pulled apart to opposite ends of the cell.
4. Telophase II and Cytokinesis II, the cell splits, resulting in 4 unique haploid cells. Each chromosome has only one chromatid.

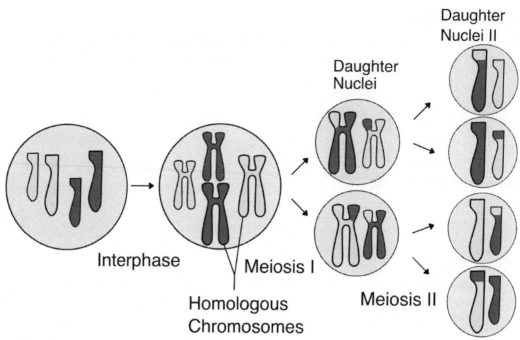

Daughter
Nuclei II

Daughter
Nuclei

Interphase

Meiosis I

Homologous
Chromosomes

Meiosis II

https://en.wikipedia.org/wiki/Meiosis#/media/File:Meiosis_Overview_new.svg

Membrane Transport

Cells can move substances across (in or out) the cell membrane through **active or passive transport**. Active transport requires energy, passive transport does not. The energy used is in the form of adenosine triphosphate (ATP).

Passive Transport

Diffusion is the movement of particles from an area of high concentration to an area of low concentration and does not require energy. **Facilitated diffusion** is a form of passive transport. In facilitated diffusion, molecules are passively moved across the membrane with the help of a membrane transport protein. The **transport protein** contains a "channel" that allows a specific type of molecule to flow through.

Active Transport

Active transport is the movement of particles against the concentration gradient, going from an area of low concentration to an area of high concentration, and requires energy. In active transport, ATP binds to the proteins in the cell membrane and is hydrolyzed. The hydrolysis of ATP produces the energy needed to change the structure of the cell membrane protein and allows the protein to move molecules across the membrane.

Cell Tonicity

Tonicity is the concentration of solutes in a cell and determines whether osmosis pushes water into or out of a cell. **Osmosis** is the movement of a solvent (such as water) across a membrane from a less concentrated solution (less solutes) to a higher concentrated (more solutes) solution to equalize the solute concentration.

Isotonic

In an **isotonic** environment, the concentration of solutes inside and outside of the cell is the same, so there is no movement of water.

Hypertonic

When a cell is in a **hypertonic** environment, the concentration of solutes outside the cell is higher than inside the cell; this causes water to flow out of the cell.

Hypotonic

When a cell is in a **hypotonic** environment, the concentration of solutes inside the cell is higher than outside the cell; this causes water to flow into the cell.

Cell Growth and Metabolism

Outside of cell division, cells grow (increase cytoplasm and organelles) by processing nutrient molecules. **Cell metabolism** is the process of processing nutrient molecules. There are two types of cell metabolism: **catabolism and anabolism**. In catabolism, complex molecules (polysaccharides, lipids, nucleic acids and proteins) are broken down into smaller units (monosaccharides, fatty acids, nucleotides, and amino acids) to produce energy. In anabolism, the cell uses energy to build molecules and perform other functions.

Cellular Respiration

Cellular respiration is the process that takes place in cells to convert nutrients into ATP and release waste products. Cellular respiration is a part of cellular metabolism. Cellular metabolism involves both anabolic and catabolic reactions, while cellular respiration is only catabolic.

During cellular respiration, glucose is broken down and carbon dioxide, water, and 38 ATPs are produced. There are two types of cellular respiration: aerobic (with oxygen) and anaerobic (without oxygen).

Aerobic Respiration

Aerobic respiration involves 3 steps:
1. **Glycolysis**: Glucose is broken down into pyruvic acid and 2 ATPs are produced.
2. **Kreb's Cycle (Citric Acid Cycle)**: Pyruvic acid moves into the mitochondrial matrix where it is broken down; carbon dioxide, 2 ATPs, NADH, and FADH2 are produced.
3. **Electron Transport Chain**: This process produces 34 ATPs and only occurs when oxygen is available. NADH and FADH2 deposit electrons onto the electronic transport chain. As electrons move down the chain (from high energy to low energy), energy is released and used to pump protons out of the mitochondrial matrix, forming a proton gradient. It is the proton gradient that powers ATP production, NOT the flow of electrons. Protons flow back into the matrix through an enzyme called ATP synthase, making ATP. At the end of the chain, oxygen accepts electrons and protons to form water.

Anaerobic Respiration

Anaerobic respiration involves 2 steps. It only produces 2 ATPs so is very inefficient compared to aerobic respiration.
1. **Glycolysis**: Glucose is broken down into pyruvic acid and 2 ATPs are produced.
2. **Fermentation**: Pyruvic acid is converted into ethanol or lactic acid.

Cell Communication

Cells can communicate by sending or receiving signals.

Cell Signaling

In local or direct signaling, cells can communicate with other cells it is in direct contact with or cells that are nearby. It does this by forming **gap junctions** that connect their cell cytoplasm to the cytoplasm of adjacent cells; the gap junction allows signaling molecules to enter the cells. Cells can also have direct cell-to-cell communication through protein receptors located in the cell membrane.

In **long range or endocrine signaling**, hormones are used to communicate between cells. **Hormones** are produced by endocrine cells and travel through the circulatory system (blood) to reach other cells in the body. The hormones bind to cells that have the appropriate receptor; the target cells respond to the hormones and produce a result.

Cell Differentiation/Specialization

In multicellular organisms, different cell types have different specialization or functions. Cellular differentiation is the process where a cell changes into a cell with a specialized function.

Tissues

Tissues are groups of cells that are joined together to perform a specific function. There are four main types of tissues:

- muscle tissue (there are 3 types of muscle tissue: smooth, cardiac, and skeletal)
- nerve tissue (brain, spinal cord, and nerves)
- epithelial tissue (organ surfaces, mouth lining, and skin)
- connective tissue (bone and cartilage)

Organs

Organs are groups of tissues that are joined together to perform a specific function. Organ systems are groups of organs that work together to perform a specific function.

Protein Synthesis

Proteins are composed of amino acids. Cells synthesize or create proteins based on the information stored in DNA. There are two major steps in protein synthesis: **transcription and translation**.

Transcription

In transcription, information in DNA is used to produce a complementary messenger RNA (mRNA). In mRNA, each amino acid is represented by a codon. A **codon** is a sequence of 3 nucleotide bases. For example, AAG (adenine-adenine-guanine) is a codon for the amino acid lysine.

Transcription has 3 stages: initiation, elongation, and termination.
1. During initiation, RNA polymerase separates the DNA strands into 2 strands. A DNA strand, called the template strand, will be used as a **template** to create mRNA; the other DNA strand is called the **coding** or "mRNA-like" strand.
2. During elongation, as RNA polymerase reads the DNA template strand, it creates mRNA out of complementary nucleotides. Remember that in RNA, uracil is used instead of thymine. The mRNA strand is basically equivalent to the DNA "coding" strand, except it contains uracil instead of thymine. See the example below.

DNA "coding" strand	TGCA
DNA "template" strand	ACGT
mRNA strand	UGCA

3. During termination, RNA polymerase releases the mRNA when it reads a termination sequence.

Translation

In translation, messenger RNA (mRNA) is decoded in a ribosome to produce a protein (an amino acid chain). There are stop and start codons that tell the ribosome where to start or stop processing the mRNA.

Translation has 3 stages: initiation, elongation, and termination.
1. During initiation, mRNA, transfer RNA(tRNA), and the first amino acid gather in the ribosome. tRNAs connect mRNA codons to amino acids. On one end of a tRNA is an anticodon which can bind to a complementary mRNA codon; on the other end of a tRNA is the amino acid specified by the codon. Amino acids can be represented by multiple codons.
2. During elongation, the amino acid chain grows. Each time a mRNA codon is read, a matching tRNA is bound to the codon, and the amino acid of the tRNA is linked to the growing/existing amino acid chain by peptide bonds.

3. During termination, when a stop codon is read, the amino acid chain is released from its tRNA and moved out of the ribosome.

Genetics

Genotype is a set of genes for an organism; **phenotype** is a physical expression of a gene.

DNA molecules are tightly packed to make structures called **chromosomes**. A single chromosome can contain thousands of genes. A **gene** is a section on the chromosome that codes for proteins, which affect how a cell functions. Genes also determine how a trait will be expressed or passed onto offspring.

Alleles are variations of a gene. For example, the gene for eye color has several variations (alleles) such as an allele for blue eyes (b) or an allele for brown eyes (B). There are two alleles for each gene, one allele from each parent for each gene. If a person has the same two alleles for a gene (for example, BB or bb), that person is said to be **homozygous** for that gene. If a person has different alleles for a gene (for example, Bb), that person is said to be **heterozygous** for that gene.

According to Mendel's laws, alleles can be **dominant or recessive**. Dominant traits will be expressed even if a person only has 1 copy of the dominant allele; recessive traits will only be expressed if a person has 2 copies of the recessive allele. Not all genes will behave according to Mendel's laws, as explained in the section, "Non-Mendelian Genetics".

A person can have the same **phenotype**, but different **genotype**. For example, two people can have brown eyes, but different genotypes (BB or Bb).

Mendel's Laws

Mendel's laws describe the laws of genetic inheritance. There are 3 laws:
- The **Law of Segregation** states that there are two alleles for each gene and that each parent can only pass 1 allele each to the offspring.
- The **Law of Independent Assortment** states genes are passed on independently and are not influenced by other genes. For example, a person that has the gene for brown eyes has no bearing on whether or not they will have the gene for detached earlobes. Linked traits are an exception to this law.
- The **Law of Dominance** states that some alleles are dominant and some are recessive.

Punnett Squares

Punnett squares are used to determine the probability that an offspring will inherit a specific genotype. To fill out a punnett square, write the genotype of 1 parent across the top of the grid and the genotype of the other parent down the left side of the grid. Fill the boxes of the grid with 1 allele from each row and column. Below is an example of a cross between two heterozygous brown eyed (Bb) parents.

B	BB	Bb
b	Bb	bb

In the above example, the offspring has a ¼ or 25% chance of having blue eyes (bb). The offspring has a ¾ or 75% chance of having brown eyes (BB, Bb).

Since the punnett square above has one BB, two Bb, and one bb, the genotypic ratio is 1:2:1. Since there are two phenotypes (brown eyes or blue eyes) and there 3 combinations that result in brown eyes (BB, two Bb) and 1 combination that results in blue eyes, the phenotypic ratio is 3:1.

Monohybrid and Dihybrid Crosses

A **monohybrid** cross refers to a cross involving a single trait with two alleles. Below is an example of a monohybrid cross between two heterozygous brown eyed (Bb) parents.

	B	b
B	BB	Bb
b	Bb	bb

A **dihybrid** cross refers to a cross involving two traits, each with two alleles. Below is an example dihybrid cross between two parents who are both heterozygous for brown eyes (Bb) and heterozygous for free earlobes (Ee); brown eyes (B) are dominant to blue eyes (b) and free earlobes (E) are dominant to attached earlobes (e).

BbEe X BbEe

	BE	Be	bE	be
BE	BBEE	BBEe	BbEE	BbEe
Be	BBEe	BBee	BbEe	Bbee
bE	BbEE	BbEe	bbEE	bbEe
be	BbEe	Bbee	bbEe	bbee

The above results in a 9:3:3:1 phenotypic ratio:
- 9/16 will have brown eyes and free earlobes (two dominant traits).
- 3/16 will have brown eyes and attached earlobes (1 dominant trait, 1 recessive trait).
- 3/16 will have blue eyes and free earlobes (1 dominant trait, 1 recessive trait).
- 1/16 will have blue eyes and attached earlobes (two recessive traits).

Non-Mendelian Genetics

Non-Mendelian genetics refers to gene inheritance patterns that do not fit the typical dominant and recessive allele relationship. Some common non-mendelian genetic inheritance patterns include incomplete dominance, codominance, sex-linked, pleiotropy, lethal allele, polygenic inheritance, and multiple alleles.

Incomplete Dominance

Incomplete dominance is when both heterozygous alleles are expressed, resulting in a phenotype that is different from either parent. For example, a flower with a red allele and a white allele results in a pink flower when the alleles are incompletely dominant.

Codominance

Codominance is when both alleles are independently expressed. For example, a flower with a red allele and a white allele results in a flower with both red and white patches.

Multiple Alleles

Although genes will only contain two alleles, **multiple alleles** describes genes that have 3 or more possible alleles. An example of multiple alleles is the gene for blood type. The gene for blood type has three possible alleles: A, B, and O. A person's blood type can be any combination of 2 of the 3 possible alleles (AA, AB, AO, BB, BO, OO).

Pleiotropy

Pleiotropy is when one gene affects multiple traits. For example, Marfan syndrome is linked to a single gene, but those with Marfan syndrome are unusually tall, have lens dislocation, and have heart problems.

Lethal Alleles

Lethal alleles are alleles that cause death of organisms that have those alleles. Lethal alleles may be dominant, recessive, or conditional.

Polygenic Inheritance

Polygenic Inheritance refers to traits that are influenced by multiple genes and/or environmental factors. Human skin color is an example of a trait that is influenced by multiple genes. An example of environmental factors influencing traits is the color of hydrangea flowers. Two hydrangea flowers may have the same genotype, but vary in color from blue to pink depending on the pH of the soil.

Sex-Linked

Sex-Linked traits refer to genes that are located on the X or Y chromosome. Since females have 2 X chromosomes, X-linked traits, such as color blindness, are only expressed if there is a dominant allele. Since males only have 1 X chromosome, X-linked traits are expressed regardless of whether the allele is dominant or recessive. Below is an example of a cross between a non-color-blind female who carries the recessive color-blind allele and a color-blind male:

	X^c	Y
X^c	X^cX^c	X^cY
X	X^cX	XY

The above cross results in 1 color-blind female, 1 color-blind male, 1 non-color-blind female, and 1 non-color blind male.

Chemistry

Atoms, Elements, and Molecules

Atoms

Matter is anything that has mass and takes up space. An **atom** is the smallest unit of all elements and matter. Atoms consist of a nucleus and electrons. The **nucleus** consists of protons and neutrons. Electrons are much smaller than protons and neutrons; protons and neutrons have a mass of approximately 1.00 atomic mass units (amu) whereas electrons have a mass of approximately 0.00055 amu. **Neutrons** have no electric charge. **Protons** are positively charged. **Electrons** are negatively charged and orbit the nucleus; it is the opposite charge attraction between protons and electrons that makes the electrons orbit the nucleus.

Atoms that have an equal number of protons and electrons are neutral. Atoms with more protons than electrons are positively charged and called **cations**. Atoms with more electrons than protons are negatively charged and called **anions**. Cations and anions are **ions** (atoms with a positive or negative charge).

Elements

Elements are essentially the kinds of atoms that exist. An element is identified by its atomic number and atomic mass. The atomic number indicates the number of protons in the atom's nucleus. **Isotopes** are elements that have the same number of protons, but different number of neutrons. Isotopes are named using their mass number.

The atomic mass (A) is equal to Z (the number of protons) plus N (the number of neutrons). Based on the equation $A = Z + N$, if you know any two of the following values: atomic mass, number of protons, or number of neutrons, you can solve for the missing value. For example, the atomic number of oxygen is 8 which means it has 8 protons and its atomic mass is 16, so oxygen has 8 neutrons ($16 = 8 + N$).

Elements are arranged by their atomic number, in ascending order, in the periodic table.

Molecules and Compounds

Molecules consist of two or more atoms/elements. **Compounds** are molecules that consist of at least two different types of atoms/elements. For example, hydrogen (H) is an element; H_2 is a molecule; H_2O is a compound.

Electron Configuration

The **electron configuration** tells us the locations of all of the electrons in an atom. Electrons can be found around the nucleus in **orbital clouds**. Each orbital can hold two electrons that orbit the nucleus in opposite directions. Orbitals are grouped into **subshells**; each subshell has a specific maximum number of electrons it can hold.

Subshell Name	Number of Orbitals	Maximum Number of Electrons
s	1	2
p	3	6
d	5	10
f	7	14

Subshells are grouped into **shells**. Shells are numbered, in ascending order, starting at 1 near the nucleus. Shells with a lower number have a lower energy level. Shells that have a high number are further away from the nucleus and have a higher energy level. All electrons in a shell have the same energy level.

Electrons completely fill low energy shells before filling higher energy shells. Most elements follow the below order when filling in electrons:

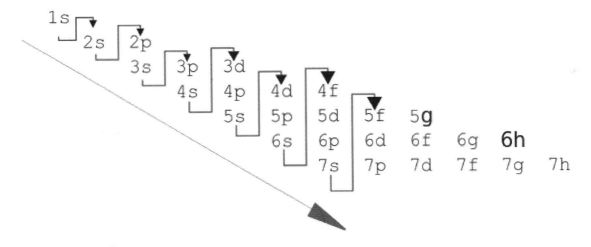

https://commons.wikimedia.org/wiki/File:Klechkowski_rule_2.svg

For example, Sodium (Na) has 11 protons and so will have 11 electrons in its neutral state.
- 2 electrons will be in shell 1, subshell s ($1s^2$)
- 2 electrons will be in shell 2, subshell s ($2s^2$)
- 6 electrons will be in shell 2, subshell p ($2p^6$)
- 1 electron will be in shell 3, subshells ($3s^1$)

The electron configuration for Na would be: $1s^2 2s^2 2p^6 3s^1$.

Valence electrons are electrons in the outermost shell. The number of electrons in the outermost shell (valence shell) affect how reactive an element is. Most atoms seek or want to have 8 electrons in the valence shell. Noble gases, which have a full valence shell (8 valence electrons), are non-reactive. Elements that have a single valence electron or only need one more valence electron to have a full valence shell are the most reactive.

Periodic Table

The **periodic table** is a table of elements. Each cell in the table includes the element's symbol, **atomic number** (appears above the symbol), and **atomic mass** (appears below the symbol). In the example below, the symbol for Lithium is Li, its atomic number is 3, and its atomic mass is 6.9.

The elements are arranged by their atomic number, in increasing order. The rows of the periodic table are called periods; the columns are called groups.

- All elements in a row or period have the same highest shell number. For example, Na has an electron configuration of $1s^2 2s^2 2p^6 3s^1$, so its highest shell number is 3, which corresponds to row or period 3.
- All elements in a column or group have the same number of valence electrons and share similar properties.

Below is a listing of important groups: (group numbers correspond to column numbers in the periodic table):

- **Group 1 (Alkali Metals)**: Alkali metals are soft and silvery metals that have only 1 valence electron and therefore are very reactive; they form acids when mixed with water.
- **Group 2 (Alkali Earth Metals)**: Alkali earth metals are similar to alkali metals, except they are not as reactive, though alkali earth metals are still highly reactive.
- **Group 3 through 12 (Transition Metals)**: Transition metals are interesting because they have partially filled d orbitals. They are malleable, moderately reactive, and can conduct electricity.
- **Group 17 (Halogens)**: Halogens are non-metals that have 7 valence electrons and therefore are highly reactive. It is the only group that includes elements that can, at room temperature, exist as solids, liquids, or gases. In its gaseous form, halogens are often hazardous to humans. Halogens often bond with metals to form salts such as NaCl (Sodium Chloride).
- **Group 18 (Noble Gases)**: Noble gases have a full valence shell and therefore are rarely reactive.

Periodic Table Trends

Atomic Radius

The **atomic radius** is the distance between the nucleus and the outermost electron shell. The atomic radius decreases from left to right, this is because as you move right, the elements have more protons to attract/pull the electrons toward the center of the atom. The atomic radius increases as you move down because of the addition of a new energy level.

Electronegativity

Electronegativity is a measure of an atom's ability to attract electrons. Electronegativity increases as you move right because there are more protons to attract electrons. It decreases as you move down due to the longer distance between the nucleus and the outermost electrons, decreasing the attraction. Fluorine has the greatest electronegativity since noble gases have full valence shells and so do not attract electrons.

Ionization Energy

Ionization is the process by which an atom or a molecule acquires a negative or positive charge by gaining or losing electrons. **Ionization energy**, measured in joules, is the amount of energy needed to remove an electron from an atom. The lower the attraction (electronegativity) between an atom and electron, the easier it is to remove the electron. Ionization energy increases as you move right and as you move up the periodic table.

Metallic Character

Metallic character refers to an atom's tendency to lose an electron; a key element of metals is that they lose electrons to form cations. Metallic character increases as you move left, because there are fewer protons to pull/hold on to the electrons. Metallic character increases as you move down because the atomic radius increases; greater distances between the nucleus and the outermost electron shells means less attraction, increasing the ability to lose an electron.

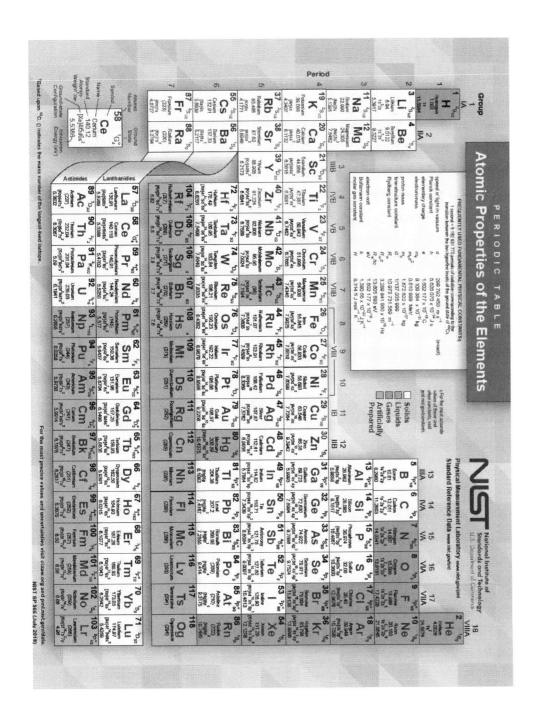

The Periodic Table of the Elements (NIST — Atomic Properties of the Elements)

Physical and Chemical Properties

Substances are matter with the same or uniform physical and chemical properties. **Mixtures** are matters made of multiple substances.

Physical Properties

Physical properties are attributes that can be observed, touched, or measured without a chemical reaction. Examples of physical properties include:

- Color, shape, texture.
- **Melting point**: the temperature at which a substance changes from a solid to a liquid.
- **Boiling point:** the temperature at which a substance changes from a liquid to a gas.
- **Freezing point**: the temperature at which a substance changes from a liquid to a solid.
- **Density**: the mass divided by volume.

Chemical Properties

Chemical properties are attributes that can be observed or measured when a substance undergoes a chemical reaction. Examples of chemical properties include:

- Flammability, toxicity, stability, solubility
- **pH level:** measures how acidic or basic/alkaline a solution is; a pH of 7 is neutral, a pH > 7 is basic, a pH < 7 is acidic.
- **Heat of combustion**: the amount of heat produced when 1 mole of a substance is burned.

Important Properties Of Water

Water (H_2O) molecules are **polar molecules**. Polar molecules have an uneven distribution of electrons (one side of the molecule has a slight positive charge, the other side a slight negative charge). In the case of water molecules, oxygen is more electronegative (better able to attract electrons), causing the oxygen end of the water molecule to have a slight negative charge and the hydrogen end to have a slight positive charge. It is this polarity that gives water most of its important qualities.

- **Cohesion** is the attraction between molecules of the same substance. Water molecules are very attracted to other water molecules and stick together through hydrogen bonds; this makes water **cohesive.** Cohesion is the reason why water has a high surface tension. Water's high surface tension allows insects to walk on water and water to flow through capillaries without much energy. Water's cohesiveness is also responsible for water's high melting point, high boiling point, and high specific heat capacity. It is also why water is a liquid, instead of a gas, at moderate temperatures.
- **Adhesion** is the attraction between molecules of different substances. Water is attracted to other substances it can form hydrogen bonds with. It is the combination of water's cohesion and adhesion that accounts for capillary action. **Capillary action** is the ability of a liquid to flow through narrow spaces against gravity or without help. Capillary action helps move water from the roots of a plant to the leaves of a plant.

- Water's **polarity** allows it become attracted to many other different types of molecules and disrupt the attractive forces that hold other molecules together, and, thus, dissolve it. This is why water is considered a "universal solvent".
- Water has a very **high specific heat capacity** and **high heat of vaporization**. Specific heat capacity is the amount of energy required to raise the temperature of 1 gram of a substance by 1 degree Celsius. Heat of vaporization is the amount of energy required to change 1 gram of liquid into gas. Water's high specific heat capacity and high heat of vaporization allow water to moderate climate temperatures and body temperatures (through sweating).
- Ice is less dense than water, allowing ice to float on top of water. Ice's lower density is due to more stable and spaced out hydrogen bonds.

Osmosis vs. Diffusion

Diffusion is the movement of particles from an area of high concentration to an area of low concentration to reach a state of equilibrium. **Osmosis** is the movement of solvent (water) from a low solute concentration across a semipermeable membrane to a high solute concentration to reach a state of equilibrium. It can also be said that osmosis is a type of diffusion that occurs across a semipermeable membrane where only the water or other solvent crosses the membrane. Both diffusion and osmosis are spontaneous and passive transport processes.

Diffusion can occur with or without a membrane; osmosis only occurs across a semipermeable membrane. Diffusion can occur in any medium, whether it is liquid, solid, or gas; osmosis only occurs in a liquid medium. During diffusion, any particle (solvent or solute) can move, but in osmosis only the solvent or water moves.

In organisms, osmosis is important for maintaining cellular water levels, transporting nutrients, and cell to cell diffusion. Diffusion helps in the exchange of gases during respiration.

In plants, osmosis helps absorb water from the soil and maintain plant turgidity. Diffusion helps with transpiration and photosynthesis.

States of Matter

Matter can exist in four different states (or phases): **solid, liquid, gas, and plasma**. Particles, such as atoms and molecules, are held together by intramolecular forces. The TEAS exam will focus mainly on solids, liquids, and gases.

- Solids have tightly packed and strong bonds between particles. Solids have fixed shapes and volumes. Solids cannot be easily compressed.
- Liquids have bonds that are strong enough to hold the particles together, but weak enough to allow them to move around. Liquids have an undefined shape and fixed volume. Liquids cannot be easily compressed.
- Gases have very weak bonds, or no bonds, so gas particles move around freely. Gas does not have a fixed shape, nor a fixed volume. The volume of gas depends on the amount of pressure used to compress the gas particles together in a space.

Phase Transitions

The state of matter is most affected by **temperature and pressure**. Temperature and pressure influence the state of matter by affecting **intramolecular forces** between particles.

- As temperature increases, substances will transition from a solid state to a liquid state to a gaseous state. This is because as temperature increases, **kinetic energy** increases. Kinetic energy is the energy an object has due to its motion. When particles have high kinetic energy, bonds are less able to hold them together, so the particles spread apart.
- As pressure increases, substances will transition from a gaseous state to a liquid state to a solid state. This is because increased pressure presses particles closer together.

In order for substances to change states, it must acquire energy or release energy. Processes that require energy are **endothermic**; processes that release energy are **exothermic**. Changes in state from solid to liquid to gas are usually endothermic; changes in state from gas to liquid to solid are usually exothermic.

Types of Phase Changes

Process	Phase Change	Energy
Melting	Solid to liquid	Endothermic
Vaporization	Liquid to gas	Endothermic
Sublimation	Solid to gas	Endothermic
Condensation	Gas to liquid	Exothermic
Freezing	Liquid to solid	Exothermic
Deposition	Gas to solid	Exothermic

Phase Diagrams

Phase diagrams show the relationship between phases, temperature, and pressure; specifically, how temperature and pressure affects the phases of matter. The **triple point** is the temperature and pressure at which a substance can exist in all 3 states. The **critical point** is the temperature and pressure at which the liquids and gases have the same density and are identical.

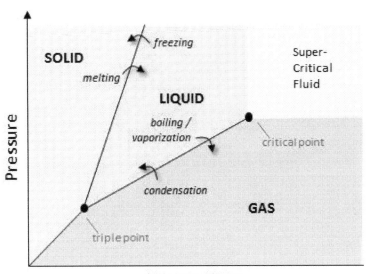

Temperature

https://blogs.nasa.gov/J2X/

Each substance has their own phase diagram and goes through phase transitions at different temperatures (i.e. each substance may have a different boiling points, freezing points, etc.). Changes in pressure can affect the melting point, boiling point, etc. Decreases in pressure allow particles to spread out more, allowing for liquids to change to gas at lower temperatures. This is why water has a lower boiling point at higher altitudes.

Chemical Bonds and Reactions

Chemical Bonds

A **chemical bond** is a force that holds or binds atoms together to form molecules. Bonds occur because atoms want to fill their valence shells, by losing or gaining electrons, to become more stable. There are 3 main types of bonds: **ionic, covalent, and hydrogen**. Ionic and covalent bonds are considered strong bonds; hydrogen is considered a weak bond.

Ionic Bonds

Ionic bonds are bonds between ions with opposite charges. An ionic bond occurs when an atom gives up one or more electrons (becoming positively charged) and another atom accepts one or more electrons (becoming negatively charged); the positively charged atom and negatively charged atom bond because opposite charges attract. An example of an ionic bond is sodium chloride (table salt).

Covalent Bonds

Covalent bonds occur when atoms share electrons instead of gaining or losing electrons. Covalent bonds can be single (1 pair of electrons shared), double (2 pairs of electrons shared), or triple (3 pairs of electrons shared) bonds. An example of covalent bonds is water. Water consists of 2 hydrogen atoms bonded to 1 oxygen; each hydrogen atom shares an electron with the oxygen atom.

There are two main types of covalent bonds: **polar and nonpolar**.

Polar Covalent Bonds

In **polar covalent bonds**, electrons are not shared equally between atoms so one part of the molecule is more positive or negative than the other part. One example of polar covalent bonds is the bond between hydrogen and oxygen in water molecules; the oxygen side of the water molecule is more negative. This charge imbalance is called a **polarity** and the small charge is called a **dipole**. It is this polarity that gives water most of its unique properties.

Nonpolar Covalent Bonds

In **nonpolar covalent bonds**, electrons are shared equally between atoms.

Hydrogen Bonds

Hydrogen bonds are bonds between hydrogen and strongly electronegative atoms such as oxygen, nitrogen, fluorine, etc. Hydrogen bonds are critical for life. Hydrogen bonds are responsible for many important properties of water and are also important components in proteins, nucleic acids, and DNA.

Chemical Reactions

A **chemical reaction**, which can be **endothermic or exothermic**, occurs when atoms interact, by breaking or forming chemical bonds, to form new substances. The inputs of a chemical reaction are called **reactants**, the outputs are called **products**. If a reactant is all used up before the completion of a chemical reaction, thus, limiting the use of other reactants, it is called the **limiting reactant**. The limiting reactant determines the **theoretical yield** (the maximum number of products that can be produced).

Chemical reaction rates are affected by factors such as **temperature, pressure, particle surface area, and reactant concentrations**. According to **collision theory**, a chemical reaction cannot occur until molecules collide in the proper orientation, and must have enough energy to react. The amount of energy required to react is called the **activation energy**. Since molecules need to collide before reacting, chemical reactions usually occur in liquids and gases since particles in solids do not move much. Reaction rates increase when opportunities for particles to collide increase.

- Increasing reactant concentrations increase the number of particles, which means more particles are likely to collide, and increases the reaction rate.
- Particles with larger surface area are more likely touch or collide with other particles, increasing the reaction rate.
- Increasing the temperature increases the speed of particles, which means more particles are likely to collide, and increases the reaction rate.

For some reactions, **catalysts** can be added to lower the amount of energy required for reactions to occur and speed up the chemical reaction rate. Catalysts are not consumed in the chemical reaction and do not appear as reactants or products. Examples of chemical catalysts include platinum, nickel, and cobalt. An example of a biological catalyst are enzymes.

How To Balance Chemical Equations

Chemical reactions can be written as chemical equations. When writing chemical equations, an arrow is drawn between the reactants and products to indicate the direction of the reaction. **Chemical equations must be balanced**; the number of atoms of each element on the left side of the equation must equal the number of atoms of each element on the right side. The reason why chemical equations must be balanced is because the **law of conservation** states that matter is never created nor destroyed.

Below is an example of a balanced chemical equation. Methane (CH_4) reacts with oxygen (O_2) to produce carbon dioxide (CO_2) and water (H_2O). Notice the 2 in front of O_2 and H_2O, those are referred to as coefficients. **Coefficients** tell you how many molecules of that reactant or product are part of the reaction.

$$CH_4 + 2O_2 \rightarrow CO_2 + 2H_2O$$

Below is an example of an unbalanced chemical equation.

$$C_3H_8 + O_2 \rightarrow H_2O + CO_2$$

To balance the above equation:

1. Create a table listing the number of atoms for each element for reactants and products.
   a.

Reactants	Products
C = 3	C = 1
H = 8	H = 2
O = 2	O = 3

2. Balance elements with single atoms first. Balance hydrogen and oxygen atoms last because they are common in reactions and often appear on both sides of the reaction.
   a. Since there is only 1 carbon atom in the product side, we'll balance that first. There is 1 carbon atom in the product side and 3 carbon atoms in the reactants side. To balance the carbon atoms, we need to multiply the CO_2 molecule in the product side by 3. **In a chemical equation, you can change coefficients, but you must never change the subscripts.** Below is the result.

$$C_3H_8 + O_2 \rightarrow H_2O + 3CO_2$$

Reactants	Products
C = 3	C = 3
H = 8	H = 2
O = 2	O = 7

3. Since all non-hydrogen and non-oxygen atoms are now balanced, balance the hydrogen atoms next. There are 2 hydrogen atoms in the product side and 8 hydrogen atoms in the reactants side. To balance the hydrogen atoms, we need to multiply the H_2O molecule in the product side by 4. Below is the result.

$$C_3H_8 + O_2 \rightarrow 4H_2O + 3CO_2$$

Reactants	Products
C = 3	C = 3
H = 8	H = 8
O = 2	O = 10

4. Balance the oxygen atoms. There are 2 oxygen atoms in the reactant side and 10 oxygen atoms in the product side. To balance the oxygen atoms, we need to multiply the O_2 molecule on the reactant side by 5. Below is the result.

$$C_3H_8 + 5O_2 \rightarrow 4H_2O + 3CO_2$$

Reactants	Products
C = 3	C = 3
H = 8	H = 8
O = 10	O = 10

5 Types Of Chemical Reactions

There are 5 main types of chemical reactions: **synthesis, decomposition, single replacement or displacement, double replacement or displacement, and combustion.**

- Synthesis reaction: two or more reactants interact to form a single product
- Decomposition reaction: a single reactant breaks down into multiple products
- Single replacement or displacement: a single element switches places with another element in the product. For example, in the equation $Zn + 2\,HCl \rightarrow ZnCl_2 + H_2$, Zn replaced the H that was originally paired with Cl.
- Double replacement or displacement: two elements switch places in the product.
- Combustion reaction: a reactant combines with oxygen to produce carbon dioxide and water

Type of Reaction	General Pattern	Example
Synthesis	A + B → C	$C + O_2 \rightarrow CO_2$
Decomposition	A → B + C	$2H_2O \rightarrow 2H_2 + O_2$
Single Replacement	AB + C → A + BC	$Zn + 2\,HCl \rightarrow ZnCl_2 + H_2$, Zn
Double Replacement	AB + CD → AD + CB	$AgNO_3 + NaCl \rightarrow AgCl + NaNO_3$
Combustion	$C_xH_yO_z + O_2 \rightarrow CO_2 + H_2O$	$CH_4 + 2O_2 \rightarrow CO_2 + 2H_2O$

Oxidation-Reduction Reactions

Oxidation-reduction reactions, also known as **redox reactions**, are a type of chemical reaction where electrons are exchanged. The particle that loses electrons is a reducing agent and is said to be oxidized; the particle that gains electrons is an oxidizing agent and is said to be reduced.

Redox reactions play an important role in photosynthesis, respiration, combustion, and many other critical processes.

Acids and Bases

The **potential of hydrogen (pH)** tells us the concentration of hydrogen ions in a substance. The pH scale goes from 0 to 14. Substances with a pH of 7 are neutral; those with a pH < 7 are **acidic**; those with a pH > 7 are **basic**. Common acids include hydrochloric acid (HCL), nitric acid (HNO_3), sulfuric acid (H_2SO_4), vinegar, orange juice, etc.. Common bases include sodium hydroxide (NaOH), sodium bicarbonate ($NaHCO_3$), calcium hydroxide ($Ca(OH)_2$), bleach, detergent, etc.

Acids share the following properties:
- Ionize in water
- Produce **hydrogen (H^+) ions** when dissolved in solution
- Accept electrons
- Taste sour
- React strongly with metals and bases

Bases share the following properties:
- Ionize in water
- Produce **hydroxide (OH^-) ions** when dissolved in solution
- Donate electrons
- Taste bitter and have a soapy or slippery texture
- Reacts strongly with acids

Strong or Weak

The strength of an acid or base depends on the number of atoms that have ionized; **the more ionized atoms, the stronger the acid or base**. Strong acids have a low pH, strong bases have a high pH, weak acids and bases have a pH near neutral (7). Strong bases and acids are highly reactive and dissolve completely in water; weak acids and bases only partially dissolve.

Salts

When acids and bases are combined, they become **neutralized** and produce a salt and water.

Buffers

Buffers are weak acids or weak bases that react with strong acids or strong bases to prevent a sharp change in pH levels. Buffers play an important role in maintaining homeostasis; for example, buffers are used to stop sudden changes in blood pH levels.

Mixtures and Solutions

Mixtures can be any combination of solids, liquids, and gases. The components of a mixture are not chemically altered and can be separated by physical means such as filtering, etc.. A **solution** is a homogeneous mixture that cannot be separated by physical means; however, solutions can be separated by other processes, such as evaporation. In solutions, one of the substances dissolves in the other. A **solute** is what is dissolved; A **solvent** is what does the dissolving. The solution's **concentration** is the ratio of solute to solvent. Concentrations can be in the following units:

- Moles of solute per volume of solution (e.g., moles per liter) - also called **molarity**
- Moles of solute per mass of **solvent** (e.g., moles per kilogram) - also called **molality**
- Mass of solute per volume of solution (e.g., grams per milliliter)
- Volume of solute per volume of solution (e.g., milliliter per liter)
- Mass of solute per mass of solution (e.g., milligrams per gram)

Solubility is the ability of a substance to dissolve in a solvent. Solubility is affected by factors such as temperature, pressure, etc. When temperature is increased, solubility of liquids and gas generally increases, but solubility of gases decreases. Increased pressure increases solubility for gases, but does not affect liquids and solids. When a solution has dissolved the maximum number of solutes possible, the solution is considered **saturated**. If you add more solute to a saturated solution, the solute will not dissolve; the saturated solution will instead create a **precipitate**.

Scientific Reasoning

Metric System

In the field of science, the metric system is used to take measurements. The metric system is a decimal based system, which means it is based on powers of 10. Below are common prefixes you should know:

Prefix	Meaning	Symbol
micro-	One millionth (10^{-6})	μ
milli-	One thousandth (10^{-3})	m
centi-	One hundredth (10^{-2})	c
deci-	One tenth (10^{-1})	d
deca- or deka-	Ten	da
hecto-	One hundred (10^{2})	h
kilo-	One thousand(10^{3})	k
mega-	One million (10^{6})	M

Length is usually measured in meters; mass is usually measured in kilograms; liquid volume is usually measured in liters; and solid volume is usually measured in cubic meters (m^3). It's important to take into account the size of something before choosing what units will be used. For example, when measuring the length of a pencil, you may choose to express the measure in centimeters, but if you're measuring the distance between cities, you may want to choose kilometers instead.

Length	Mass	Liquid Volume
1000 millimeters = 1 m	1000 milligrams = 1 g	1000 milliliters = 1 L
100 centimeters = 1 m	100 milligrams = 1 g	100 milliliters = 1 L
10 decimeters = 1 m	10 decigrams = 1 g	10 deciliters = 1 L
1 meter = 1 m	1 gram = 1 g	1 liter = 1 L
1 dekameter = 10 m	1 dekagram = 10 g	1 dekaliter = 10 L
1 hectometer = 100 m	1 hectogram = 100 g	1 hectoliter = 100 L
1 kilometer = 1000 m	1 kilogram = 1000 g	1 kiloliter = 1000 L

Source: ATI TEAS Crash Course, pg. 193.

Lab Equipment

To minimize errors in measurement, always use the smallest tool necessary for the task. For example, when measuring a small volume of liquid, use a pipette instead of a graduated cylinder.

Weighing Equipment

A balance is used to weigh powder, liquid, and other substances. There are two common types of balances: **electronic balance** and **triple beam balance**.

- An electronic balance is used to measure very small masses. It displays the measurements digitally. Electronic balances are more accurate than beam balances but are more sensitive to environmental factors that can cause an inaccurate reading.
- A triple beam balance consists of 3 scales and a balance mark. The middle scale measures in 100 gram increments; the top scale measures in 10 gram increments; and the bottom scale measures grams to the tenth. Ensure that the beam balance is at the zero mark before taking measurements.

Balances should always be placed on a level surface. A clean weighing paper or boat should always be used for each new substance to prevent cross contamination. Use a spatula to add or remove substances from the balance instead of pouring it directly from the bottle.

Volumetric Equipment

Volumetric equipment is typically used to measure and transfer liquid. Some common volumetric equipment are: **pipettes, graduated cylinders, flasks, and burets**. To minimize errors in measurement, always use the smallest equipment capable of holding the desired amount of liquid.

Liquids have a **meniscus** (surface of the liquid curves downward toward the center) when they are poured into containers. When measuring liquids, hold the container so that the meniscus is at eye level and read the graduation mark at the bottom of the meniscus.

Beakers and Flasks

Beakers and flasks are used for mixing and transporting liquids; they are not good for making accurate measurements.

Graduated Cylinders

Graduated cylinders are used to measure liquids. They are more accurate than flasks or beakers. If measuring volumes less than 20 mL, it's better to use a syringe or pipette.

Pipettes

Pipettes are thin tubes made of glass or plastic typically used to measure volumes less than 25 mL and are required for volumes less than 1 mL.

Buret

Burets, or burettes, are graduated glass tubes used to accurately dispense a known amount of liquid.

Scientific Method

The scientific method is the process used by scientists to test ideas and acquire knowledge. It consists of the following steps.

1. **Observation**: A scientist has a question about something they've observed or has identified a problem that needs to be solved. The question usually involves how, what, when, who, why, or where?
2. **Gather Information**: Gather information from the library, internet, other scientists, or past experiments to ensure you learn from past mistakes; this will also help you formulate hypothesis'.
3. **Hypothesis**: Formulate a hypothesis based on observation and research. A **hypothesis** is an "educated guess" and needs to be testable.
4. **Experiment**: Design an experiment to test the hypothesis; measurements and observations are gathered. See the following segment, "Experimental Design", for information on how to design an experiment.
5. **Data Analysis and Conclusion**: Analyze the data and determine whether or not the data supports the hypothesis. Note that you can never actually prove a hypothesis is correct; you can only disprove a hypothesis or provide evidence that supports a hypothesis.

Experimental Design

All experiments must have one or more **experimental groups and a control group**. The control group is a group in the experiment that does not receive any treatment or changes; the control group is the standard or benchmark to which comparisons are made. The e**xperimental groups** are the groups that receive treatment. Ideally, the experimental groups and control group are identical or very similar. A **control group** is essential to determining whether or not a treatment or change was the cause of the effect/result or a **placebo** effect. A placebo is a "fake" pill that is assumed to have no effect and is usually given to the control group.

In an experiment, it is important to control **variables** by changing only factor at a time and keeping all other conditions the same; otherwise, you would not be able to determine if a change caused the effect or something else in the environment caused the effect. All experiments must have an **independent variable (it should only have 1 independent variable), dependent variable(s), and control variable(s)**. The factor that is changed is called the independent variable. Independent variables are changed in the experimental group, but not changed in the control group. As the independent variable is changed, the responding or dependent variable(s) are observed, measured, and recorded. The control variable(s) are variables that may affect the dependent variable and need to be kept constant/unchanged.

Part	Definition	Example
Hypothesis	An educated guess	Solubility increases as temperature increases

Independent variable	Variable being changed and tested	Temperature
Responding/Dependent variable	Variable being measured	Solubility
Control variables	Variables that may affect the dependent variable and must be kept constant	Pressure, amount of stirring, type of solvent, type of solute

Experiments must also have the following:
- A large sample size to reduce the chance of random errors affecting the conclusions drawn
- **Validity**: valid conclusions can only be drawn if the experiment was properly controlled and it is measuring what it is supposed to measure
- **Reliability**: results of the experiment must be reproducible
- Must not be bias

Critiquing Experimental Design

In the TEAS exam, you may be asked to identify weaknesses or flaws in the design of an experiment. To do this, check that the experiment has the following:
- It has experimental groups and a control group
- Control group and experimental groups are very similar, if not identical
- It has only 1 independent variable
- Only 1 variable is changed at a time
- There is a large sample size
- It is valid
- It is reliable
- It is not bias

Reading

Key Ideas and Details

For the TEAS exam, you should be able to: identify the topic, main idea, and supporting details of a text; infer logical conclusions; and read graphs and directions.

The **topic** is the overall subject of the text. The **main idea (or theme)** is the point or argument the author is trying to make about the topic. **Supporting details** are information that support the author's main idea or argument.

Making Inferences

An **inference** is a conclusion drawn based on analysis of evidence or supporting details. For example, if a person is standing, you can infer that their heart is beating; otherwise, they would be dead and unable to stand.

Inferences are always unstated; if a statement is stated explicitly in the passage, it is not inferred. When you are asked to make an inference based on a passage, pay attention to the overall mood of the text, key terms and transition words, and distinguish between facts and opinions. Also, try eliminating answer choices that contradict the main idea of a passage.

Sometimes writers will provide hints or clues in the text about what will happen in the future; this technique is called **foreshadowing**.

Understanding Directions

The TEAS exam will test your ability to follow directions and understand the sequence of events. Always read through the entire set of instructions before performing a step or answering any questions because the steps may not be listed in sequential order. For example:
1. Before mixing the cake batter, preheat the oven.

Even though mixing the cake batter is mentioned before preheating the oven, the first step is to preheat the oven.

Pay attention to words like the following to help you determine the sequence of events: first, second, next, now, then, before, until, while, finally, after, once, when, etc.

Understanding Graphs

The TEAS exam will test your ability to understand visual information sources like graphs. When reading graphs, pay attention to general trends of the graph.
- **Bar graphs** use horizontal or vertical bars to represent numerical data.
- **Line graphs** have data points plotted on a grid with a line connecting the data points. Line graphs are used to show trends.

- **Pie charts** are circular graphs divided into "slices". Pie charts are used to show percentages of a whole.
- A **flow chart** depicts a sequence of events.
- A **map** depicts an area. It will usually include a **map legend** that tells you what the symbols on the map mean and the distance scale.

Craft and Structure

The TEAS exam will test your ability to identify an author's potential biases, point of view, and/or purpose for writing. It will also test your ability to understand how a writer uses style, word choice, and different kinds of text structure to convey ideas.

Author's Purpose and Point of View

There are four main purposes for an author's writing: **to entertain, to persuade, to describe, or to explain**. Understanding an author's purpose can help you answer questions like: "Which of the following statements would the author most likely disagree with?" or "Which idea would the author most sympathize with?" (Source: Kaplan ATI TEAS, pg. 81).

To help you determine the purpose of an author's writing, pay attention to the mood or tone of the text and word choices the author makes. An author who is trying to describe or explain a process is likely to use more detailed and precise wording. An author who is trying to persuade a reader is likely to use more opinionated words like *misguided, ingenious, I believe, most importantly,* etc.; they are also more likely to provide supporting evidence for their argument.

Modes of Writing

There are three main modes of writing: **persuasive, expository, and narrative**. Persuasive writing tries to persuade a reader. Expository writing is informational; the author tries to explain or describe a topic with facts and examples, not opinions. Narrative writing, such as plays and novels, tell a story.

Text Structure

Text structure refers to how sentences and paragraphs are ordered to help an author communicate his or her idea. There are four main text structures: sequence, problem/solution, cause/effect, and compare/contrast.

Sequence

A sequence is used to show an order of events. Sequence as text structures usually take the form of an ordered list, numbered steps, etc.

Problem/Solution

In a problem/solution text structure, the author presents a problem and then provides a solution. Look for keywords like: solve, hopeful, concern, challenge, resolve, etc. (Source: https://betterlesson.com/lesson/resource/2600115/text-structure-explained)

Cause/Effect

A cause is why something happened; an effect is what happened.

In a cause/effect text structure, the writer presents an event or action (the cause) and the results or effects of that action or event. The author may write about the causes and effects in any order; they may tell you about the effects before telling you about the cause, etc.

The cause/effect text structure is usually used in expository and persuasive writing. Look for keywords like: as a result, because, one reason, if..then, as a consequence, etc.

Though the cause/effect text structure and the problem/solution text structure may seem similar, the key difference is that a problem/solution text structure always presents a solution where as a cause/effect text structure does not.

Compare/Contrast

In a compare/contrast text structure, the writer presents the similarities and differences of two items or ideas. Look for keywords like: similarly, compared to, in spite of, on the contrary, etc.

Text Features

Text features are things like: titles, table of contents, headers, bold prints, map legends, captions, footnotes, indexes, etc. Text features are provided to help readers find and understand the information better.

Context and Word Meaning

Words have two different types of meaning: **denotative and connotative**. Denotative meaning is the dictionary meaning. Connotative meaning or connotations is the dictionary meaning plus the emotions associated with that word. For example, the word "smell" has a neutral connotation, "fragrance" has a positive connotation, and "stench" has a negative connotation.

Words can deviate from their dictionary meaning when used in **figurative language** or as a **figure of speech**. Examples of figurative language include:
- **Similes**: compare two things using the word "like" or "as".
  - Her smile was **like** sunshine.
- **Metaphors**: compare two things without using the word "like" or "as".
  - Her smile was sunshine.
- **Personification**: is when human characteristics are given to non-humans.
  - The wind howled.

Words can also have different meanings depending on the context. For example, "crying" at a funeral means something different from "crying" at a wedding or "crying" while chopping onions.

Integration of Knowledge and Ideas

Primary and Secondary Sources

A **primary source** is written by someone who was directly involved in the event or witnessed the event. Examples of primary sources include: autobiographies, diaries, photographs, letters, speeches, legal documents, etc. A **secondary source** is written by someone who was not directly involved. Examples of secondary sources include: biographies, history books, etc.

Evaluating an Argument

Writers will often present an **argument or claim** (what the writer wants you to agree with) and provide evidence to support their claim. To identify the writer's claim, look for keywords like: "I believe", "in my opinion", "it is clear that", etc. Be aware that writers may also sometimes make claims without stating that the claims are their opinions.

Evidence can be explicit or implicit. **Explicit evidence** is information that is directly stated in the text. **Implicit evidence** is evidence that is not directly stated. You may also be asked to identify assumptions that an author makes. **Assumptions** are things that the author accepts to be true, without having or providing any proof. For example, if the author states, "I can see that Sarah is sad because her eyes are watery." the author is assuming that watery eyes means Sarah has been crying and therefore is sad. This assumption may not necessarily be true because there are many reasons why Sarah may have watery eyes, such as: Sarah suffers from allergies, Sarah has been cutting onions, etc.

While paying attention to the evidence, explicit or implicit, that the author presents is important, it is also important to consider the source of the evidence. Primary sources that are up to date, unbiased, peer reviewed, etc. carry more weight than less reliable secondary sources. There is more risk of miscommunication and/or misunderstanding with secondary sources.

Integrating Data From Different Sources and Formats

On the TEAS exam, you will be asked to draw conclusions by combining or connecting data found in multiple sources, such as a text passage and its associated graphs and diagrams. Always read both the text and diagrams completely before answering any questions.

English and Language Usage

Conventions of Standard English

Standard Spelling

The ATI TEAS exam will test your ability to spell correctly, identify words that don't follow standard spelling rules, and differentiate between homonyms.

Homonyms

Homonyms are words that sound alike, but have different meanings and spellings. Below is a table of common homonyms.

Word	Word Used In A Sentence
accept	I will accept the award on his behalf.
except	All the ladies wore black dresses except the bride, who wore a white dress.
advise	I would advise you to seek a second opinion.
advice	You should listen to your mother's advice.
affect	Listening to loud music can affect your hearing.
effect	The effects of caffeine include insomnia and hyperactivity.
already	I already finished mopping the floor.
all ready	We are all ready to take the test.
complement	Milk is the perfect complement to cookies.
compliment	You should compliment employees for working hard.
conscious	After suffering a blow to the head, the patient was barely conscious.
conscience	It's hard to sleep with a guilty conscience.
content	I am content with life.
content	The film was rated R for its content.
device	We should learn how to use the new device.
devise	The prisoners devised an escape plan.
die	No one wants to die.
dye	She dyed her hair black.
fair	She had light hair, light eyes, and fair skin.
fair	It would be fair to split our winnings equally.
fare	He did not have enough money to pay for the bus fare.
eminent	He is one of the world's most eminent piano players.
imminent	He warned that an attack was imminent.
ensure	Please ensure your seat belts are buckled.

insure	Her legs are insured for $1000 dollars.
heal	Put antibiotic ointment over the cut to help it heal faster.
heel	The shoe dug into his heels.
hear	It's hard to hear over the loud music.
here	Please come over here.
hole	There is a hole in the bag.
whole	I ate the whole pizza by myself.
its (possessive)	The bird flew back to its nest.
it's ("it is")	It's hot in here.
lessen	Take Tylenol to lessen the pain.
lesson	The teacher spent two hours preparing for tomorrow's lessons.
principal	The principal is in charge of the school.
principle	She is a person of good moral principle.
plural	The word "books" is a plural noun.
pleural	The pleural cavity is the thin fluid-filled space between two lungs.
than	He is taller than me.
then	Put on your socks, then put on your shoes.
their (possessive)	That is their house.
they're ("they are")	They're moving into a new house.
there	He is not here, he is over there.
to	I am going to the store.
too	The soup is too hot to eat right now.
two	I have two dogs.
weak	I have not ate and feel weak.
week	There are 7 days in a week.
your (possessive)	Is she your sister?
you're ("you are")	You're cute.
who's ("who is")	Who's talking?
whose	Whose pants are these?

Spelling Rules

- The letter i goes before e except after c or when the word sounds like "a" as in "weigh", but "weird" is weird. Examples: friend, receive, neighbor. Exceptions: caffeine, neither, protein, science, weird.
- Rules for adding suffixes:

Word Criteria	Rule	Examples	Exceptions
Ends in a consonant that is preceded by a vowel, is only one syllable, and suffix begins with a vowel	Double the final consonant and add the suffix	Hit + ing = hitting Tag + ed = tagged	Do not double the consonant if it is a "w". Plow + ing = plowing Snow + ed = snowed
Ends in a consonant that is preceded by a vowel, is more than one syllable, and suffix begins with a vowel	Double the final consonant and add the suffix	Travel + ing = travelling Prefer + ed = preferred	Do not double the consonant if it is a "w". Eschew + ing = eschewing
Ends with a vowel and suffix begins with a vowel	Drop the final vowel and add the suffix	Preserve + ing = preserving Sue + ing = suing	Like+able = likeable
Ends with a vowel and suffix begins with a consonant	Keep the final vowel and add the suffix	Discourage + ment = discouragement Taste + ful = tasteful	Judge + ment = judgment
Ends with a y	Change the y to i and add the suffix	Crazy + est = craziest Pity + ful = pitiful	Keep the y if the suffix is "ing" Cry + ing = crying Pity + ing = pitying

Source: Kaplan ATI TEAS, pg. 317

- Rules for making words plural:

Word Criteria	Rule	Examples	Exceptions
Ends with a consonant or vowel	Add s	Bird -> birds Hat -> hats Llama -> llamas	Words that meet criteria for other rules. Tomato -> tomatoes Potato -> potatoes Veto -> vetoes
Ends with s, x, ch, or sh	Add es	Bench -> benches Brush -> brushes Bus -> buses	Ox -> oxen
Ends with a y and a consonant precedes the y	Replace y with ies	Party -> parties Patty -> patties	
Ends with a y and a vowel precedes the y	Add s	Key -> keys Holiday -> holidays	Money -> monies
Ends with a f or fe	Replace f or fe with ves	Leaf -> leaves Knife -> knives	Hankerchief -> hankerchiefs

Words that have the same singular and plural spelling (Source: ATI TEAS Test Study Guide, pg. 169):

- Sheep
- Deer
- Moose
- Pants
- Binoculars
- Scissors

- Words that don't follow the rules (Source: ATI TEAS Test Study Guide, pg. 169)
  - Man -> men
  - Woman -> women
  - Child -> children
  - Person -> people
  - Tooth -> teeth
  - Mouse -> mice
  - Ox -> oxen
  - Axis -> axes

Standard Punctuation

Periods

Periods are used for abbreviations and to end sentences. Examples:
- This sentence ends with a period.
- Dr., Mrs., etc.

Question Marks

Questions marks end questions.
- What's your name?

Exclamation Points

Exclamation points express an extreme emotion.
- I hate cilantro!

Commas

Commas are used in the following ways:
- To list items or phrases.
  - My favorite colors are red, white, and blue.
  - I have to clean my house, go to the grocery store, and make dinner.
- After phrases that come before a subject
  - In addition to her beauty, Maria was also intelligent.
- When joining clauses with a coordinating conjunction (and, so, but, for, or, nor, yet)
  - Mark was poor, but he was generous.
  - I didn't want to burn my mouth, so I waited for the soup to cool before eating the soup.
- To set apart phrases that are not critical to a sentence; basically, if you remove the phrase between the commas, the sentence is still complete.
  - Jason, who attends Grossmont High, loves to play football.
  - Aspirin, when taken daily, can reduce the risk of heart attacks.
- Put commas between coordinate adjectives. To determine if the adjectives are coordinate adjectives, put an "and" between the adjectives and reverse the order; if the resulting phrase still makes sense, then they are coordinate adjectives.
  - I am wearing a red cotton shirt. (It doesn't sound right to say "a cotton and red shirt", so the adjectives are not coordinate adjectives and do not need a comma between them.)
  - I hate lifting bulky, heavy boxes. (It still makes sense if you say "heavy and bulky boxes", so the adjectives are coordinate adjectives and need a comma between them.)

Apostrophes

Apostrophes are used to form contractions, show possession, and to pluralize letters or numbers that have no plural form.

To show possession:
- Mike's bike
- Anna and Maria's house (belongs to both)
- Marcus' hat (do not add an 's' after the apostrophe if the word already ends in a 's')

Example of pluralizing letters and numbers:
- Dot your i's and cross your t's

Examples of contractions include:

do + not = don't	you + are = you're	I + am = I'm	is + not = isn't
it + is = it's	they + are = they're	you + have = you've	will + not = won't

Quotation Marks

Use quotations when identifying a direct quote. The first word in a quotation that is a complete sentence is capitalized, but the first word in a partial quotation is not. You should use a comma to introduce quoted material or dialogue.
- Jason said, "We live in a crazy world."

Use quotations when identifying titles of songs, poems, and small works. Do not use quotations when identifying titles of books or titles of larger works.
- My favorite song is "Somewhere Over the Rainbow."

Colons

Colons are used at the start of a list, an explanation, a long quotation, a definition, or an example.
- You will need the following items to make bread: yeast, flour, eggs, and water.
- Tylenol has one major advantage over Aspirin: it can be used in children with fevers.

Semicolons

Semicolons are used to join two independent clauses.
- My favorite color is orange; it reminds me of sunsets.

Semicolons are used to separate list items that have commas.
- I have travelled to: San Diego, CA; Miami, FL; and Austin, TX.

Parentheses

Parentheses are used to surround additional information that would interrupt the flow of a sentence.
- Roses (my favorite type of flower) are perennials.

Capitalization

- The first word of a sentence is always capitalized.
- **Proper nouns** are always capitalized. A proper noun is the specific name of a person, place, organization, or thing.
  - Jason, Canada, Disneyland, Lamborghini
- Titles are capitalized if they immediately precede the name.
  - My favorite president is President Obama.
  - My favorite uncle is Uncle Jason.
- Months, day of the week, and holidays are capitalized. The word day in a holiday's name is only capitalized if it is part of the holiday's name.
  - Monday, January, Memorial Day (Day is capitalized), Christmas day (*day* is **not** capitalized)

Parts of Speech

There are eight parts of speech.

Nouns

A noun is a person, place, or thing.

Pronouns

A pronoun is used in place of a noun.
- I, me, she, her, he, him, you, they, them, it, etc.

Adjectives

Adjectives describe nouns or pronouns.
- Red car (*red* is the adjective)
- Long hair (*long* is the adjective)

Verbs

Verbs show actions or states of being.
- The baby cried. (*Cried* is the verb.)
- I am hungry. (*Am* is the verb.)

Adverbs

Adverbs modify verbs, adjectives, or other adverbs.
- Anna very quickly smothered the fire with a large white blanket. (*Quickly* is the adverb that modifies the verb *smothered*; *very* is the adverb that modifies the adverb *quickly*; and *large* is the adverb that modifies the adjective *white*.)

Prepositions

A preposition is a word that links nouns, pronouns, or other words to other words in the sentence.
- The woman in the car. (*In* is the preposition that links the woman to the car.)
- Michael arrived after lunch. (*After* is the preposition that links when Michael arrived and lunch.)

Conjunctions

Conjunctions are words that connect words, phrases, and clauses.
- and, but, if, etc.
- Ethan and Charlize like eating fruits, but they like eating ice cream more. (*And* and *but* are conjunctions.)

Interjections

Interjections are words or phrases that express strong emotions.
- Wow! Your house is beautiful. (*Wow* is an interjection.)

Sentence Structure

Note: On the test, you will have to identify and create different types of sentences.

Parts of Sentences

- The **subject** of a sentence is the person, place, or thing that is doing something or being described.
- The **object** of a sentence is the person, place, or thing that is acted upon by the subject.
- A **predicate** is the part of the sentence that contains the verb and tells us what the subject does or is.
- A **modifier** is a word or phrase that describes another word. Adjectives and adverbs are modifiers.

Phrases and Clauses

A **clause** is a group of words that has both a subject and a verb. A **phrase** is a group of words that is missing either a subject or verb or both.

Clauses can be independent or dependent. **Independent clauses** must be able to stand alone as sentences. **Dependent clauses** do not express a complete thought and cannot stand alone as a sentence.

Below is an example of an independent clause:
- I rode my bike to work. (This sentence has both a subject and verb and expresses a complete thought.)
  - Subject: I
  - Verb: rode
  - Predicate: rode my bike to work

Below is an example of a dependent clause:
- Because I ate salad for lunch (This sentence has both a subject and verb, but does not express a complete thought.)
  - Subject: I
  - Verb: ate
  - Predicate: ate salad for lunch

4 Types of Sentence Structure

There are 4 types of sentence structure: simple, compound, complex, and compound-complex.

Simple sentences contain one independent clause.
- She went to the grocery store.

Compound sentences contain two or more independent clauses. The two clauses are usually joined using a coordinating conjunction (for, and, nor, but, or, yet, and so). Use the acronym "FANBOYS" to help you remember the coordinating conjunctions.
- I bought eggs and milk, but I forgot to buy bread.

Complex sentences contain an independent clause and at least one dependent clause.

- I planned to go to Ava's birthday party, but I can no longer attend. ("But I can no longer attend" is the dependent clause.)

Compound-Complex sentences contain two or more independent clauses and one or more dependent clauses.

- I bought peanut butter cupcakes, but Ethan did not eat any cupcakes because he is allergic to peanuts. ("Because he is allergic to peanuts" is the dependent clause.)

Knowledge of Language

Grammar

Past, Present, and Future Tense

Past, present, and future tense should be used consistently.

- Incorrect: He *gave* her a rose that *will brighten* her day. (This is incorrect because the past tense verb 'gave' is used with the future tense phrase 'will brighten'.)
- Correct: He gave her a rose that brightened her day. (This is correct because the past tense verb 'gave' is used with the past tense word 'brightened'.)
- Incorrect: I think the movie was good. (This is incorrect because 'was' is a past tense word, but 'think' is a present tense word.)
- Correct: I thought the movie was good. (This is correct because both 'thought' and 'was' are past tense words.)

Sentence Fragments

Sentence fragments are incomplete sentences (they are missing a subject or verb or both) and should be avoided.

- Incorrect: *Gone with the Wind* is my favorite book. Best book ever! ('Best book ever' is a sentence fragment because it is missing a verb.)
- Correct: *Gone with the Wind* is my favorite book. It is the best book ever.

Run-on Sentences

A run-on sentence is a sentence where two or more independent clauses are joined without a word or punctuation mark to connect them. Run-on sentences should be avoided.

- Run-on sentence: It was so cold outside even the dog was shivering.
- Correct version: It was so cold outside; even the dog was shivering.
- Another correct version: It was so cold outside that even the dog was shivering.

Subject and Verb Agreement

Subject and verb plurality should be in agreement. If you are using the singular form of a subject, you should use the singular form of a verb. If you are using the plural form of a subject, you should use the plural form of a verb.

- Incorrect: Anna speak English. (*Anna* is a singular subject, but *speak* is a plural verb.)
- Correct: Anna speaks English.
- Incorrect: The clothes is too big for me. (*Clothes* is a plural subject, but *is* is a singular verb.
- Correct: The clothes are too big for me.

When two subjects are joined by "and", a plural verb form is required.

- Incorrect: Anna and Jason is at home.
- Correct: Anna and Jason are at home.

When two subjects are joined by "and" and they both refer to the same thing, a singular verb form is required.

- Incorrect: Rice and beans are the national dish of Puerto Rico. (*Rice and beans* refer to a singular national dish, but *are* is a plural verb.)
- Correct: Rice and beans is the national dish of Puerto Rico.

If "each", "every" or "no" precedes a subject, a singular verb is required.

- Incorrect: Every perfume smell good. (Smell is a plural verb, but a singular verb should be used.)
- Correct: Every perfume smells good.

Antecedent and Pronoun Agreement

Antecedents and pronouns must be in agreement. An **antecedent** is the noun that the pronoun refers to.

- When you see Jonathan, please tell him to clean his room. (*Jonathan* is the antecedent; it is the word that the pronoun *him* refers to.)

When replacing a subjective noun, use a subjective pronoun. Examples of subjective pronouns include: I, you, he, she, we, and they.

- Correct: Ethan is riding his bike.
- Incorrect: Him is riding his bike. (Since Ethan is the subject in this sentence, a subjective pronoun should be used.)
- Correct: He is riding his bike.

When replacing an objective noun, use an objective pronoun. Examples of objective pronouns include: me, you, him, us, her, and them.

- Correct: Please give the ball to Ethan.
- Incorrect: Please give the ball to he. (Since Ethan is the object in this sentence, an objective pronoun should be used.)
- Correct: Please give the ball to him.

Ambiguous Language

Ambiguous language is language that is unclear and should be avoided.

- Ambiguous sentence: I saw Ethan on the hill. (Is Ethan on the hill or did you see Ethan while you were on the hill?)
- Unambiguous sentence: I saw Ethan while I was on the hill.

Transition Words

Transition words help connect sentences and ideas. Examples of transition words include: moreover, since, therefore, however, then, for example, etc.

Formal and Informal Writing

You should be able to tell the difference between formal and informal writing. Formal writing is used when writing academic papers, business letters, etc. When writing formal works, avoid using the following: first person narrative, slang, cliches, or colloquialisms. **Colloquialisms** are expressions that are associated with a specific region and/or time period. Formal papers may include jargon; **jargon** is the set of words that are common or specific to an industry or profession.

The Writing Process

There are 3 main stages in the writing process: planning, writing, and editing.

Planning Stage

During the planning stage, you should **brainstorm** ideas or topics, research, come up with a thesis, and create an outline. A **thesis** is the main idea or argument for a paper.

Writing Stage

During the writing stage, you should use your research notes and outline to write your first draft.

Paragraphs

Thoughts should be organized into logical paragraphs. Each paragraph should have:
- a **topic sentence** that tells you the main idea of the paragraph
- additional sentences that support the main idea of the paragraph
- a concluding or transitional sentence that wraps up the main idea or connects the current paragraph to the next paragraph

Citations

You must provide citations when:
- Using direct quotes
- Using ideas from another author or source
- Using information that is not well known

You do not have to provide citations when:
- Using information that is common knowledge
- Using information that cannot be attributed to a specific person or group

Vocabulary Acquisition

Context Clues

When you encounter an unfamiliar word, look for context clues. Context clues provide hints about the meaning of a word or phrase. Examples of context clues include: synonyms, antonyms or contrast words, mood or tone words, etc.

Synonyms

Synonyms are words that have the same or very similar meanings.

- Julia's animosity, or hatred, of child molesters is understandable. (*Hatred* is a synonym for *animosity*.)

Antonyms or Contrast Words

An antonym is a word that has the opposite meaning of another word.

- I expected the crowd to be rowdy, but they were surprisingly quiet. (The words 'but' and 'surprisingly' should clue you into thinking that 'rowdy' means the opposite of 'quiet'.)

Mood or Tone Words

The overall mood or tone of a sentence or paragraph can clue us into the meaning of word.

- Maria was ecstatic when she received her acceptance letter from Harvard; she was jumping up and down and screaming with glee. (From the mood and tone of the sentence, you can guess that ecstatic means very happy.)

Parts of a Word

You can sometimes figure out the meaning of a word by looking at a word's root, prefix, and/or suffix. For example:

- Hyperthermia = hyper (over) + therm (heat) + ia = overheated

Common Root Words

Root	Meaning	Example
acu	sharp	acute, accurate
amor	love	amorous
anni, annu, enni	year	annual, anniversary
anthrop	man	anthropology
audi	hear	audible
auto	self	autobiography
bene	good	benefit, benefactor
bio	life	biology
cardi	heart	cardiac
carn	flesh	carnivore, carnal
chrono	time	chronological
corp	body	corpse

cosm	world	microcosm
crat, cracy	rule	autocrat
demo	people	democracy
dent	tooth	dental
dict	say	dictate
endo	within	endoskeleton
gen	race, kind, family, or birth	genocide, generate
geo	earth	geology
fila, fili	thread	filament
fin	end	final, finish
fort	strong	fortify
gastr(o)	stomach	gastric
helio	sun	heliograph
hema, hemo	blood	hemoglobin
hetero	different	heterogenous
homo	same	homosexual
hydr	water	hydrate
loc, loco	place	locality
mania	madness	pyromaniac
medi	middle	mediocre
micro	small	microscopic
mort	death	mortal
nym	name	pseudonym
ped	foot	pedal, pedestrian
phil	love	bibliophil
pneuma	lungs	pneumonia
port	carry	transport
psych	mind	psychology
sacr	sacred	sacrosanct
sent,sens	feel	sentiment, sense

tele	far away	teleport, telegraph, television
therm	heat	hyperthermia
vac	empty	vacuous
vita	life	vitality

Common Prefixes

Prefix	Meaning	Example
a, an	without	apathy
ante	before	anteroom
anti	against	antibiotics
belli	combative	belligerent
bi	two	bisexual
de	opposite, down	decelerate
di	double	dimorphism
dis	not, remove	disengage
ego	self	egotistical
hypo	under	hypothermia
in, im	not	infertile, impossible
inter	between	international
intra	inside, within	intrastate
micro	small	microscopic
mis	wrongly	misspoke
pre	before	prelude
re	again	redo
semi	half	semicircle
sub	under	subsurface
trans	across	transatlantic
un	not	undress

Common Suffixes

Suffix	Meaning	Example
algia	pain	neuralgia
cian	person with a skill	magician
ectomy	removal	appendectomy
emia	blood condition	anemia
ist	a person who	pianist
itis	inflammation	colonitis
less	without	childless
ology	study of	biology

Mathematics

Note: There are 32 scored Math questions on the exam; 23 of them will be on "Numbers and Algebra" so focus your studying on that.

Numbers and Algebra

Positive and Negative Numbers

A positive number is a number that is greater than or equal to 0. A negative number is a number less than 0. Remember that values get smaller as you move **left** on the number line; so negative 8 (-8) is less than negative 5 (-5). A **signed number** is a number preceded by a plus (+) sign to indicate a positive value and a minus (-) sign to indicate a negative value.

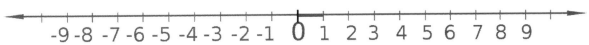

Source: https://en.wikipedia.org/wiki/Negative_number#/media/File:Number-line.svg

Another way to think of positive and negative numbers is to think of it in terms of money. 0 means you have no money, positive means you have money, and negative means you are in debt. The more debt you have, the greater the negative number, meaning you have less money.

Operations With Negative and Positive Numbers

- When adding numbers with the same signs, add the numbers and keep the same sign.
  - $1 + 2 = 3$
  - $-3 + -4 = -7$
- When adding numbers with different signs, find the difference between the two numbers and use the sign of the larger number. Adding a negative value is the same thing as subtracting a positive value.
  - $2 + (-7) = 2 - 7 = -5$ (The difference between 2 and 7 is 5 and since the larger number 7 has a minus sign, put a minus sign in front of the 5.)
  - $3 + (-1) = 3 - 1 = 2$ (The difference between 1 and 3 is 2 and since the larger number 3 is positive, the result is positive as well.)
- Subtracting a negative number is the same as adding a positive number.
  - $5 - (-2) = 5 + 2 = 7$
  - $-5 - (-2) = -5 + 2 = -3$
- When multiplying or dividing signed numbers, count the number of negative numbers. If the number of negative numbers is odd, the result will also be negative; otherwise, the result will be positive.
  - $-3 * -3 = 9$ (There are 2 negative numbers and since 2 is even, the result is positive.)
  - $-4 * -4 * -4 = -64$ (There are 3 negative numbers and since 3 is odd, the result is negative.)

Order of Operations

Order of operations tell you the order in which to evaluate operations in an expression. Use the mnemonic **PEMDAS** to remember the order of operations. Another mnemonic is **P**lease **E**xcuse **M**y **D**ear **A**unt **S**ally.

- Parentheses
- Exponents
- Multiplication and Division (from left to right)
- Addition and Subtraction (from left to right)

Example:

- 6 % 2(1 + 2) = ?
  - First, we evaluate what is inside the parentheses, so the equation becomes:
    - 6 % 2(3) = ?
    - 6 % 2 * 3 = ? ('2(3)' is the same thing as '2 * 3')
  - Since the only operations left in the equation are multiplication and division and multiplication and division have the same precedence, we evaluate the equation from left to right.
    - 6 % 2 * 3 = 3 * 3 = 9

Fractions, Decimals, and Percentages

Fractions

A fraction represents a part of a whole. It has 2 parts, the numerator and the denominator. The **numerator** is the number above the bar and the **denominator** is the number below the bar. The denominator can never be 0. If the denominator is greater than the numerator, it is called a **proper fraction**. If the numerator is equal to or greater than the denominator, it is called an **improper fraction**. A **mixed number** consists of a whole number and a proper fraction.

Converting Between Improper Fractions and Mixed Numbers

To convert a mixed number into an improper fraction:
1. Multiply the whole number by the denominator and then add the numerator. The resulting value will be the new numerator.
2. Place the new numerator over the original denominator.

Example of converting $2\frac{5}{8}$ into an improper fraction:
1. (2 * 8) + 5 = 16 + 5 = 21 (21 will be the new numerator.)
2. 21/8 (Place the new numerator over the old denominator to get the resulting improper fraction.)

To convert an improper fraction into a mixed number:
1. Divide the numerator by the denominator. The whole number result of the division will be placed to the left of the fraction. The remainder of the division will become the new numerator for the fraction; the old denominator will be used as the denominator for the fraction.

Example of converting 22/7 into a mixed number:
1. 22 % 7 = 3 with a remainder of 1 (7*3 = 21 and 21 +1 = 22)
2. 1/7 (To get the fraction part of the mixed number, place the remainder of the division over the old denominator.)
3. $3\frac{1}{7}$ is the resulting mixed number.

Adding and Subtracting Fractions

In order to add or subtract fractions, the fractions must have the same denominator. To find a common denominator, find the smallest multiple of both denominators or multiply the two denominators. Once you have the common denominator, you'll need to convert the fractions to their equivalent fractions. Once the fractions have the same or common denominator, add or subtract the numerators and write the result over the common denominator. Reduce the fraction result if needed. See examples below.

Example 1:

1. $\dfrac{1}{4} + \dfrac{1}{6} = ?$

2. To find the common denominator, multiply the two denominators: 4 * 6 = 24

3. To convert the fractions to their equivalents:

   a. $\dfrac{1}{4} = \dfrac{(1 * 6)}{(4 * 6)} = \dfrac{6}{24}$

   b. $\dfrac{1}{6} = \dfrac{(1 * 4)}{(6 * 4)} = \dfrac{4}{24}$

4. Now that the fractions have the same denominator, we can add them.

   a. $\dfrac{(4 + 6)}{24} = \dfrac{10}{24}$

5. Reduce the fraction. To reduce a fraction, divide the numerator and denominator by the largest common multiple.

   a. $\dfrac{(10 \% 2)}{(24 \% 2)} = \dfrac{5}{12}$

Example 2:

1. $\dfrac{1}{3} + \dfrac{3}{4} = ?$

2. Common denominator = 3 * 4 = 12

3. Equivalent fractions:

   a. $\dfrac{1}{3} = \dfrac{(1 * 4)}{(3 * 4)} = \dfrac{4}{12}$

   b. $\dfrac{3}{4} = \dfrac{(3 * 3)}{(4 * 3)} = \dfrac{9}{12}$

4. Add the fractions:

   a. $\dfrac{(4 + 9)}{12} = \dfrac{13}{12}$

5. $\dfrac{13}{12}$ does not have a common multiple, so cannot be reduced further.

Multiplying and Dividing Fractions

When you see the word "of" in a problem, that usually means multiplication is needed. For example, $\frac{1}{4}$ of 20 means you should multiply 20 by $\frac{1}{4}$.

To multiply fractions, multiply the two numerators to get the new numerator and multiple the two denominators to get the new denominator. Reduce the new fraction as needed. See examples below.

Example 1:

1. $\dfrac{1}{4} * \dfrac{2}{5} = ?$

2. Multiply the two numerators and then multiply the two denominators:

   a. $\dfrac{(1 * 2)}{(4 * 5)} = \dfrac{2}{20}$

3. Reduce as necessary. $\dfrac{2}{20}$ reduces to $\dfrac{1}{10}$.

Example 2:

1. $\dfrac{1}{10} * 20 = ?$

2. Since 20 is a whole number, use 1 as the denominator.

   a. $\dfrac{1}{10} * \dfrac{20}{1} = ?$

3. Multiply the two numerators and the two denominators:

   a. $\dfrac{(1 * 20)}{(10 * 1)} = \dfrac{20}{10}$

4. Reduce as necessary. $\dfrac{20}{10}$ reduces to 2.

To divide fractions, multiply the first fraction by the **reciprocal** (switch the numerator and denominator) of the second fraction. See examples below.

Example 1:

1. $\dfrac{1}{2}$ % $\dfrac{3}{5}$ = ?

2. Multiply the first fraction by the reciprocal of the second fraction.

   a. $\dfrac{1}{2} * \dfrac{5}{3} = \dfrac{(1 * 5)}{(2 * 3)} = \dfrac{5}{6}$

3. Reduce as necessary. $\dfrac{5}{6}$ cannot be reduced any further.

Adding, Subtracting, Multiplying, and Dividing Mixed Numbers

When adding, subtracting, multiplying, or dividing mixed numbers:

1. Convert the mixed numbers into improper fractions.
2. Follow the rules for adding, subtracting, multiplying, or dividing fractions.

Comparing Fractions

To compare fractions:

1. Convert the fractions so that they have the same denominator.
2. Compare the numerator to determine which fraction is greater than, less than, etc.

Converting Fractions Into Decimals

Fractions can be converted into decimals by dividing the numerator by the denominator. For example:

1. $\frac{1}{2}$ = 1 % 2 = 0.5
2. $\frac{3}{4}$ = 3 % 4 = 0.75

Decimals

Decimals are numbers based on a system of 10s. A decimal represents a whole number plus a fraction of a whole number (tenths (1/10), hundredths (1/100), thousandths (1/1000), etc.). Numbers placed to the left of the decimal represent the whole number; numbers to the right of the decimal represent the fractional part of the number.

Example: 123.456 (Whole number: 123 Fraction: 456/1000)

- 1 is in the hundreds place
- 2 is in the tens place

- 3 is in the ones place
- 4 is in the tenths place
- 5 is in the hundredths place
- 6 is in the thousandths place

Adding and Subtracting Decimals

When adding or subtracting decimals, align the decimal points so that similar place values are aligned (i.e. the ones place in both numbers should line up, the tens place should line up, etc.) before adding or subtracting. You may add 0s to the beginning or end of a number to help line up the numbers.

Example 1:
Add 1.11 + 1.1

```
   1.11
 +1.10
 --------
   2.11
```

Example 2:
Add 1.11 + 2
```
   1.11
 +2.00
 --------
   3.11
```

Example 3:
Add 1. 11 + .5
```
   1.11
 +0.50
 --------
   1.61
```

Multiplying Decimals

To multiply decimals, multiply the numbers as if there were no decimals. Then place the decimal point, starting at the right, a number of places equal to the total number of decimal places in both numbers.

Example 1:
Multiply 2.45 * 3.4
1. 245 * 34 = 8330
2. 2.45 has 2 decimal places and 3.4 has 1 decimal place, so there is a total of 3 decimal places
3. Place decimal point, starting at right, equal to the total number of decimal places
   a. 8330 = 8.330

Converting Between Decimals and Percents

A **percentage** is a number divided by 100. For example, 50% can be written as 50/100, which reduces to ½.

To convert from decimals to percentages, move the decimal point two places to the right and add a % sign.
Example:

$$0.15 = 15\%$$

To convert from percents to decimals, move the decimal point two places to the left and remove the % sign.
Example:

$$45\% = 0.45$$

Converting a Decimal Into a Fraction

To convert a decimal into a fraction:
1. Figure out what denominator to use by looking at what place the leftmost digit of the decimal else. Use 10 as the denominator if the leftmost digit is in the tenths place; use 100 as the denominator if the leftmost digit is in the hundredths place; etc.
2. Write the original decimal number (without the decimal point) over the denominator.

Example for converting 2.45 to a fraction:
1. Since the leftmost digit (5) is in the hundredths place, the denominator should be 100.
2. The resulting fraction is 245/100

Example for converting 2.456 to a fraction:
1. Since the leftmost digit (6) is in the thousandths place, the denominator should be 1000.
2. The resulting fraction is 2456/1000

Ratios and Proportions

A **ratio** is a relationship between two numbers indicating how many of one thing exists in relation to another. For example, if you have 3 females for every 1 male, the female to male ratio is 3 to 1 or (3:1). You can write ratios as fractions expressed as a part to a whole. In the example above, you have 3 females to 1 male, so a total of 4 people; so ¾ are females and ¼ are males.

Proportions are equations stating that 2 ratios are equal. They are usually written as two fractions like below:

$$\frac{a}{b} = \frac{c}{d}$$

When solving problems using proportions, keep in mind the following rules:
1. Numerators must have the same units.
2. Denominators must have the same units.
3. 3 of the 4 values in the proportion must be known.

To solve proportion problems, you need to cross multiply and solve for the missing variable using algebra. Cross multiply means to multiply the numerator of each fraction with the denominator of the other fraction. See below:

$$\frac{a}{b} = \frac{c}{d} \rightarrow ad = cb$$

Example: A prescription reads amoxicillin, one tablet twice a day for 7 days. How many tablets are needed to fill the prescription?
1. The patient needs a total of 2 tablets per day. We need to figure out how many tablets in 7 days equals the same ratio as 2 tablets per day. Set up the proportion:

$$\frac{X \text{ tablets}}{7 \text{ days}} = \frac{2 \text{ tablets}}{1 \text{ day}}$$

2. Cross multiply and solve for X:

$$X \text{ tablet} = \frac{2 \text{ tablets} * 7 \text{ days}}{1 \text{ days}} = 14 \text{ tablets}$$

Example: A car travels 20 miles in 30 minutes. How long will it take the car to travel 50 miles?

1. The problem states that the car travels 20 miles in 30 minutes. We need to figure out how many minutes over 50 miles equals the same ratio as 30 minutes over 20 miles. Set up the proportion:

$$\frac{X \text{ minutes}}{50 \text{ miles}} = \frac{30 \text{ minutes}}{20 \text{ miles}}$$

2. Cross multiply and solve for X:

$$X \text{ minutes} = \frac{30 \text{ minutes} * 50 \text{ miles}}{20 \text{ miles}} = 75 \text{ minutes}$$

Estimating and Rounding

Rules For Rounding Whole Numbers

Look at the digit to the right of the place value to be rounded. If it is greater than or equal to 5, change it and all digits to the right to 0 and add 1 to the previous digit. If it is less than 5, change it and all digits to the right to 0.

Example: Round 745 to the nearest tens place.
- The place value to be rounded is the tens place. 4 is in the tens place.
- The digit to the right of 4 is 5. Since we round up if the value is greater than or equal to 5, we change 5 to a 0 and add 1 to 4.
- 750 is the result.

Example: Round 749 to the nearest hundreds place.
- The place value to be rounded is the hundreds place. 7 is in the hundreds place.
- The digit to the right of 7 is 4. Since 4 is less than 5, we change 4 and everything to the right of 4 to a 0.
- 700 is the result.

Rules For Rounding Fractions and Mixed Numbers

To round a mixed number to the nearest whole number, look at the numerator of the fraction. If the numerator is less than half of the denominator, round down. If the numerator is greater than or equal to half of the denominator, round up.

Example: Round $5\frac{1}{4}$ to the nearest whole number.
- The numerator is 1 and the denominator is 4. Half of the denominator is 2. Since 1 is less than 2, round down.
- 5 is the result.

Example: Round $5\frac{2}{4}$ to the nearest whole number.
- The numerator is 2 and the denominator is 4. Half of the denominator is 2. Since 2 is equal to or greater than 2, we round up.
- 6 is the result.

Rounding Time

When rounding time, if the minute is greater than or equal to 30, round up; if the minute is less than 30, round down.

Example: 2:30 rounded to the nearest hour is 3:00.
Example: 2:29 rounded to the nearest hour is 2:00.

Estimating

Estimating involves using methods like rounding to solve a problem. Estimating doesn't give you an exact value, but it does give you a good approximation.

Example: What is the approximate value of 17 * 19?
- Round 17 to 20, round 19 to 20, and then multiply to get the approximate value.
- 20 * 20 = 400

Inequality Symbols

Inequality symbols are used to show things are not equal.

Inequality Symbol	Meaning
>	The number or expression on the left is greater than the number or expression on the right. Example: 7 > 1
<	The number or expression on the left is less than the number or expression on the right. Example: 1 < 7
$\geq$	The number or expression on the left is greater than or equal to the number or expression on the right. Example 1: 7 $\geq$ 1 Example 2: 7 $\geq$ 7
$\leq$	The number or expression on the left is less than or equal to the number or expression on the right. Example 1: 1 $\leq$ 7 Example 2: 1 $\leq$ 1

Algebra

A **variable** is a letter, such as x, used to represent an unknown value.

A **constant** is a value that does not change. For example, in the expression x + 7, 7 is a constant.

A **term** is either a single number or variable, or numbers and variables multiplied together.

Terms are separated by + or – or % signs. For example, in the expression x + 7 + 2y, the terms are x, 7, and 2y.

Like terms are terms that are either constants or have the same variables and powers. You can simplify expressions by combining like terms; you cannot combine unlike terms. For example:
- 2a + 3a can be simplified into 5a
- 3a - 2a can be simplified into 1a
- 2a + 5 + 7 can be simplified into 2a + 12
- 2a + 5 - 7 can be simplified into 2a + (-2) = 2a - 2
- $2a^2 + 3a^2$ can be simplified into $5a^2$
- $2a^2 + 3a$ cannot be simplified because they are not like terms since the powers are different; one is a^2 and the other is a.
- 2a + 2b cannot be simplified because they are not like terms since the variables are different; one variable is a and the other is b.

Solving Equations

"Solving an equation means finding a value for the variable that makes the equation true." (Source: ATI TEAS Crash Course, pg. 91) To solve an equation, you have to move all the variables to one side of the equal sign and all the values to the other side. You can use **inverse operations** to isolate variables and move terms from one side of the equation to the other; you cannot just randomly move terms around. Inverse operations are opposite operations that cancel or undo each other. Addition and subtraction are inverses of each other. Multiplication and division are inverses of each other. Whatever operation you perform to one side of an equation, you must perform on the other side as well. So, if you add 5 to one side, you have to add 5 to the other side as well.

Example: y + 3 = 7
- In order to isolate the variable *y*, you have to subtract 3 from both sides of the equation.
   - y + 3 - 3 = 7 - 3
   - y = 4
- You can double check your work by substituting y with 4 in the original equation.
   - y + 3 = 7
   - 4 + 3 = 7
   - 7 = 7 (7 equals 7 is a true statement, so the answer is correct.)

Example: a - 6 = 5
- In order to isolate the variable *a*, you have to add 6 to both sides of the equation.

- ○ a - 6 + 6 = 5 + 6
- ○ a = 11

Example: 7b = 21
- In order to isolate the variable *b*, you have to divide both sides of the equation by 7.
  - ○ 7b % 7 = 21 % 7
  - ○ b = 3

Example: $\dfrac{Z}{9}$ = 3
- In order to isolate the variable z, you have to multiply both sides of the equation by 9.
  - ○ $\dfrac{Z}{9}$ * 9 = 3 * 9
  - ○ Z = 27

Example: 5 = 7 - x

There are two ways you can solve this problem.
- One way of solving the problem:
  - ○ You isolate the variable x by subtracting 7 from both sides of the equation (since 7 is a positive value here, you have to subtract 7).
    - ▪ 5 - 7 = 7 - x - 7
    - ▪ -2 = -x
  - ○ Since -x = -2, you can divide -x by -1 to to make x positive.
    - ▪ -x % -1 = -2 % -1
    - ▪ X = 2
  - ○ Double check your work by substituting 2 into the original equation.
    - ▪ 5 = 7 - x
    - ▪ 5 = 7 - 2
    - ▪ 5 = 5
- The second way of solving this problem:
  - ○ Make the variable x positive by adding x to both sides of the equation.
    - ▪ 5 + x = 7 - x + x
    - ▪ 5 + x = 7
  - ○ Then, isolate the variable x by subtracting 5 from both sides of the equation.
    - ▪ 5 + x - 5 = 7 - 5
    - ▪ X = 2

Example: $\dfrac{12}{b} = 3$

- First, multiply both sides of the equation by 'b'.
  - $\dfrac{12}{b} * b = 3 * b$
  - $12 = 3b$
- Isolate the variable b by dividing both sides of the equation by 3.
  - $12 / 3 = 3b / 3$
  - $4 = b$
- Check your work.
  - $12/4 = 3$
  - $3 = 3$

Example: $3x + 7 = 21 - \dfrac{X}{2}$

- First, move all the variables to one side of the equation by adding $\dfrac{X}{2}$ to both sides of the equation.
  - $3x + 7 + \dfrac{X}{2} = 21 - \dfrac{X}{2} + \dfrac{X}{2}$
  - $3x + 7 + \dfrac{X}{2} = 21$
- Then, move all the numbers to one side of the equation by subtracting 7 from both sides.
  - $3x + 7 + \dfrac{X}{2} - 7 = 21 - 7$
  - $3x + \dfrac{X}{2} = 14$
- To get rid of the fraction, multiply both sides of the equation by 2.

-
  - $2\left(3x + \dfrac{x}{2}\right) = 14 * 2$
  - $6x + x = 28$
  - $7x = 28$
  - $x = 4$
- Check your work.

-
  - $3x + 7 = 21 - \dfrac{x}{2}$

  - $3(4) + 7 = 21 - \dfrac{4}{2}$
  - $12 + 7 = 21 - 2$
  - $19 = 19$

Example: $(x - 2)^2 = 25$
- First, find the square root of both sides of the equation.
  - $\sqrt{(x - 2)^2} = \sqrt{25}$
  - $(x - 2) = \pm 5$ (Notice the plus/minus sign in front of the 5. When you take the square root of a number, the result can be positive or negative because when you square a negative number, it becomes positive.)
- Since $(x - 2)$ can equal 5 or negative 5, there are two possible values for x.
  - $x - 2 = 5$ or $x - 2 = -5$
  - $x - 2 = 5$
    - $x = 5 + 2 = 7$
  - $x - 2 = -5$
    - $x = -5 + 2 = -3$
  - x can be -3 or 7
- Check your work for $x = -3$
  - $(x - 2)^2 = 25$
  - $(-3 - 2)^2 = 25$
  - $(-5)^2 = 25$
  - $25 = 25$
- Check your work for $x = 7$
  - $(x - 2)^2 = 25$
  - $(7 - 2)^2 = 25$
  - $(5)^2 = 25$
  - $25 = 25$

Solving Inequalities

Equations that contain inequalities are solved the same way as equations with equal signs, except the inequality symbols are reversed when dividing or multiplying both sides with a negative number.

Inequality Symbol	Reversed Inequality
>	<
<	>
$\geq$	$\leq$
$\leq$	$\geq$

Example: -2x < - 6

- To isolate x, divide both sides of the equation by -2. Since there is an inequality sign and we're dividing by a negative number, we have to reverse the inequality sign.
- -2x % -2 > -6 % -2
- x > 3

Translating and Solving Word Problems

Most word problems can be translated into a mathematical equation. You should assign variables (x,y,etc.) to unknown numbers or values. Look for the following keywords that clue you into what type of operation is needed. Word problems may contain irrelevant information, so be sure to ignore the unnecessary information.

Keyword	Operation Needed
sum, increase, total, combined, more than, plus, added to	addition
difference, decrease, decreased/reduced by, fewer, less than, minus	subtraction
double, triple, times, of, product of, rate, multiplied, per	multiplication
half, out of, percent, quotient of, divided by, over, out of, into	division
is, equals, adds up to	equal (=) operator

Example: Anna has 8 more apples than Maria. Maria has double the number of apples Jason. Jason has 3 apples. How many apples does Anna have?

- How many apples Anna has is an unknown number, so assign a variable, 'a', to represent the number of apples Anna has.

- How many apples Maria has is an unknown number, so assign a variable, 'm', to represent the number of apples Maria has.
- Since Anna has 8 more (the 'more' keyword indicates that you should use addition) apples than Maria, the equation will look like the following:
  - $a = m + 8$
  - Now, we need to figure out what the value of 'm' is.
- Since Maria has double (the 'double' keyword indicates that you should use multiplication) the number of apples Jason has, the equation should look like the following:
  - $m = 2 * \text{(number of apples Jason has)} = 2 * 3 = 6$
- Now that you know the value of m, you can plug it into the equation for figuring out how many apples Anna has.
  - $a = m + 8$
  - $a = 6 + 8 = 14$ (Anna has 14 apples.)

Example: Thomas spent $125 on concert tickets for 5 people. How much did each concert ticket cost per person?
- The cost of a concert ticket is an unknown value, so assign the variable 'x' to represent the cost of a concert ticket.
- The 'per' keyword indicates the use of multiplication. Since Thomas bought 5 concert tickets and spent $125, the equation should look like the following:
  - $5x = 125$
  - $X = 125 \% 5 = 25$ (Each concert ticket cost $25.)

Example: In a class of 200 students, 12 percent are female. How many male students are there?
- How many male students are in the class is an unknown value, so assign a variable, 'y', to represent the number of male students.
- How many female students are in the class is an unknown value, so assign a variable, 'x', to represent the number of female students.
- The word problem states that 12 percent of the students are female. The 'percent' keyword tells you that the division operation will likely be needed. The equation should look like the following:
  - $$\frac{x}{200} = 12\%$$ (The number of female students out of 200 students is 12%)
  - $$\frac{x}{200} = \frac{12}{100}$$
  - To isolate x, multiple both sides by 200.

$$\blacksquare \quad \frac{x}{200}_{*\ 200} = \frac{12}{100}_{*\ 200}$$

$$\blacksquare \quad X = \frac{12\ *\ 200}{100} = \frac{2400}{100} = 24 \text{ (There are 24 female students in the class.)}$$

- The question asks how many male students are in the class. Since there are 200 students and students are either female or male, the equation to represent the male and female student population in the class should look like the following:
  - x + y = 200
  - 24 + y = 200 (We solved for x in the previous step, so replace x with the value 24.)
  - To isolate y, subtract 24 from both sides of the equation.
    - 24 + y - 24 = 200 - 24
    - y = 176 (There are 176 male students in the class.)

Example: There are 1000 jelly beans in a jar. The jar weighs 10 lbs. The jar consists of red, white, and blue jelly beans. 25% of the jelly beans are red. There are 300 blue jelly beans. How many jelly beans are white?

- Recognize that the jar weighing 10 lbs is irrelevant to solving the problem.
- How many jelly beans are white is an unknown value, so assign a variable, 'w', to represent the number of white jelly beans.
- The number of red jelly beans in the jar is an unknown value, so assign a variable, 'r', to represent the number of red jelly beans.
- Since the jar contains only red, white, and blue jelly beans, and there are 1000 jelly beans in the jar, the equation should look like the following:
  - r + w + 300 (There are 300 blue jelly beans.) = 1000
  - In order to solve for 'w', we need to figure out what 'r' is first.
- Since 25% of (the 'of' keyword indicates that you should use multiplication) the jelly beans are red, the equation should look like the following:
  - r = 25% * 1000
  - $r = \frac{25}{100}_{*\ 1000}$
  - r = 0.25 * 1000 = 250
- Now that you know the value of r, you can plug it into the original equation to figure out how many white jelly beans are in the jar:
  - r + w + 300 = 1000
  - 250 + w + 300 = 1000
  - w + 550 = 1000
  - w = 1000 - 550 = 450 (There are 450 white jelly beans in the jar.)

Example: This week, Jacob worked 3 times the number of hours he worked last week. If he works another 6 hours this week, he will have worked 30 hours this week. How many hours did Jacob work last week?

- The number of hours Jacob worked last week is an unknown value, so assign a variable, 'x', to represent the number of hours Jacob worked last week.
- The problem states that Jacob worked 3 times the number of hours he worked last week and that if he worked another 6 hours this week, the total number of hours worked this week would be 30 hours. Since the total number of hours worked this week is 30, we know that the sum of 6 and 3 times the number of hours worked last week should equal 30.
  - 30 = 6 + 3 times the number of hours worked last week
  - 30 = 6 + 3x (Replaced "number of hours worked last week" with the variable 'x' and used multiplication as indicated by the keyword "times".)
  - Move all constants to one side by subtracting 6 from both sides of the equation.
    - 30 - 6 = 6 + 3x - 6
    - 24 = 3x
  - Isolate x by dividing both sides of the equation by 3.
    - 24/3 = 3x/3
    - 8 = x (Jacob worked 8 hours last week.)

Example: Maria bought a purse for $125.50. It was on sale for 25% off. What was the original price of the purse?

- The original price of the purse is an unknown value, so assign a variable, 'x', to represent the original price of the purse.
- From the word problem, you know that the original price of the purse minus 25% off of the original price of the purse equals 125.50.
  - (original price of the purse) - (25% of the original price of purse) = 125.50
  - Replace the original price of the purse with the variable x
    - x - (25% of x) = 125.50
  - The 'of' keyword indicates that multiplication should be used.
    - x - (25% * x) = 125.50
    - x - (0.25 * x) = 125.50 (Simplified the equation by converting 25% to 0.25)
    - x - 0.25x = 125.50
    - 0.75x = 125.50 (You get 0.75x because 1 - 0.25 = 0.75)
    - Divide both sides of the equation by 0.75 to isolate x
      - x = 167.33 (The original price of the purse was $167.33.)

Solving Percent Increase/Decrease Problems

When solving percent increase or decrease problems, remember the following equation:

Percent Changed (decrease or increase) = $\dfrac{|\text{current value} - \text{original value}|}{\text{original value}}$ * 100

The two bars (|) surrounding "|current value - original value|" means absolute value. **Absolute value** means to make the value positive.

Example: Thomas weighed 250 lbs last year. This year he weighs 225 lbs. What was the percentage decrease in weight?

- Percent decreased = $\dfrac{|225 - 250|}{250}$ * 100

- Percent decreased = $\dfrac{|-25|}{250}$ * 100

- Percent decreased = $\dfrac{25}{250}$ * 100 (Negative 25 became positive because the equation says to use the absolute value.)
- Percent decreased = 10%

Example: Jason put $2500 into an investment fund. It is now worth $3500. What was the percentage increase?

- Percent increased = $\dfrac{|3500 - 2500|}{2500}$ * 100

- Percent increased = $\dfrac{|1000|}{2500}$ * 100

- Percent increased = $\dfrac{1000}{2500}$ * 100
- Percent increased = 40%

Solving Rate of Change Problems

Proportions are often used to solve rate of change problems. When setting up proportions, remember that the denominators must have the same units and the numerators must have the same units.

Example: A car is travelling 65 miles per hour. How many miles will it travel in 2 hours.

- $\dfrac{65 \text{ miles}}{1 \text{ hour}} = \dfrac{X}{2 \text{ hour}}$

- Cross multiply and solve for X.
  - 65 miles * 2 hour = X * 1 hour

  $$\frac{65 \text{ miles} * 2 \text{ hour}}{1 \text{ hour}} = X$$

  - 130 miles = X

Example: A car is travelling 65 miles per hour. How many miles will it travel in 30 minutes.

- $$\frac{65 \text{ miles}}{1 \text{ hour}} = \frac{X}{30 \text{ minutes}}$$

- Since denominators must have the same units and numerators must have the same units, we have to convert hours to minutes. There are 60 minutes in 1 hour.

  - $$\frac{65 \text{ miles}}{1 \text{ hour}} * \frac{1 \text{ hour}}{60 \text{ minutes}} = \frac{X}{30 \text{ minutes}}$$

  - $$\frac{65 \text{ miles}}{60 \text{ minutes}} = \frac{X}{30 \text{ minutes}}$$

- Cross multiply and solve for X.
  - 65 miles * 30 minutes = X * 60 minutes

  $$\frac{65 \text{ miles} * 30 \text{ minutes}}{60 \text{ minutes}} = X$$

  - 32.5 miles = X

Slope

The slope of a graph tells you the rate of change. To find the slope of a graph, compare two points on a graph using the following equation:

$$\text{Slope} = \frac{\text{rise}}{\text{run}} = \frac{y2 - y1}{x2 - x1}$$

y1 = y coordinate of point 1.
x1 = x coordinate of point 1.
y2 = y coordinate of point 2.
X2 = x coordinate of point 2.

Example: Find the slope between Point 1 and Point 2:
- Point 1 = (4, 5)
- Point 2 = (6, 10)

- $$\text{Slope} = \frac{y2 - y1}{x2 - x1} = \frac{10 - 5}{6 - 4} = \frac{5}{2}$$

Line 1

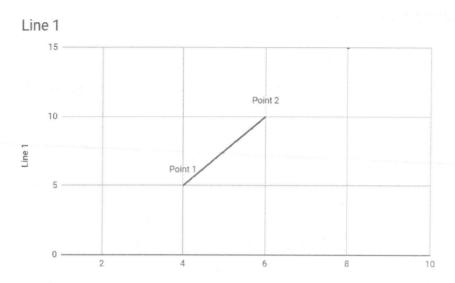

Measurement and Data

Converting Measurements

You do not have to remember conversion ratios, but you do have to know how to convert between different unit types.

The steps for converting between units are:

1. Find the conversion ratio. The conversion ratio will be given to you in the problem. An example of a conversion ratio is 1 foot = 12 inches. The conversion ratio can be written as $\dfrac{1 \text{ foot}}{12 \text{ inches}}$ or $\dfrac{12 \text{ inches}}{1 \text{ foot}}$.

2. Multiply the measurement you want to convert by the conversion ratio. Write the ratio so that the desired unit is in the numerator of the conversion ratio and undesired units cancel out. For example, if you want to convert to feet, use the ratio $\dfrac{1 \text{ foot}}{12 \text{ inches}}$; if you want to convert to inches, you the ratio $\dfrac{12 \text{ inches}}{1 \text{ foot}}$.

3. Cancel out common units.

Example: How many inches are in 3 feet?

1. Since our desired unit is inches, the conversion ratio to use is the ratio with inches in the numerator: $\dfrac{12 \text{ inches}}{1 \text{ foot}}$.

2. Multiply the measurement we want to convert (3 feet) by the conversion ratio ($\dfrac{12 \text{ inches}}{1 \text{ foot}}$) and then, cancel out common units.

   a. $3 \text{ feet} * \left(\dfrac{12 \text{ inches}}{1 \text{ foot}} \right)$

   b. $\dfrac{36 \text{ feet} * \text{ inches}}{1 \text{ foot}}$

   c. Cancel out the common unit (feet/foot)

   i. $\dfrac{36 \text{ feet} * \text{ inches}}{1 \text{ foot}}$ = 36 inches (There are 36 inches in 3 feet.)

Example: How many feet are in 48 inches?

1. Since our desired unit is feet, the conversion ratio to use is the ratio with feet in the numerator: $\dfrac{1 \text{ foot}}{12 \text{ inches}}$.

2. Multiply the measurement we want to convert (48 inches) by the conversion ratio ($\dfrac{1 \text{ foot}}{12 \text{ inches}}$) and then, cancel out common units.

   a. $48 \text{ inches} * (\dfrac{1 \text{ foot}}{12 \text{ inches}})$

   b. $\dfrac{48 \text{ inches } * \text{ foot}}{12 \text{ inches}}$

   c. Cancel out the common unit (inches)

      i. $\dfrac{48 \text{ inches } * \text{ foot}}{12 \text{ inches}}$ = 4 feet (48 inches is 4 feet.)

Example: How many inches are in 3 meters given that 1 meter equals 3.28 feet and 1 foot equals 12 inches?

1. There are two conversion ratios we need to use: 1 ft = 12 inches and 1 meter = 3.28 feet.

2. We first have to convert meters to feet. Since the desired unit is feet, we need to use the ratio with feet in the numerator: $\dfrac{3.28 \text{ feet}}{1 \text{ meter}}$.

   a. $3 \text{ meters} * \dfrac{3.28 \text{ feet}}{1 \text{ meter}}$ = 9.84 feet

3. Then we need to convert feet to inches. Since our desired unit is in inches, we need to use the ratio with inches in the numerator: $\dfrac{12 \text{ inches}}{1 \text{ foot}}$.

   a. $9.84 \text{ feet} * \dfrac{12 \text{ inches}}{1 \text{ foot}}$ = 118.1 inches (There are 118.1 inches in 3 meters.)

Note: Steps 2 and 3 above could have been combined into one equation:

- $3 \text{ meters} * \dfrac{3.28 \text{ feet}}{1 \text{ meter}} * \dfrac{12 \text{ inches}}{1 \text{ foot}}$
- Cancel the common units (meters and feet)
  - 3 * 3.28 * 12 inches = 118.1 inches

Graphs

On the TEAS exam, you will be tested on your ability to read and understand different types of graphs.

Line Graphs

A line graph is often used to show changes or trends over time.

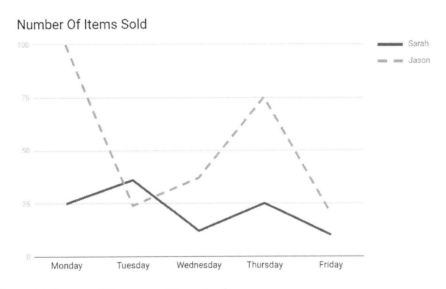

Question: Who sold the most items on Tuesday?
- From the graph, it looks like Jason sold 25 items on Tuesday and Sarah sold between 25 and 50 items; Sarah sold the most items on Tuesday.

Question: On what day of the week were most items sold?
- On Monday, Jason sold 100 items and Sarah sold 25 items, so 125 items were sold on Monday.
- On Thursday, Jason sold 75 items and Sarah sold 25 items, so 100 items were sold on Thursday.
- The most items were sold on Monday.

Bar Graphs

Bar graphs are typically used to show changes or trends over time, to categorize data, and/or to compare quantities.

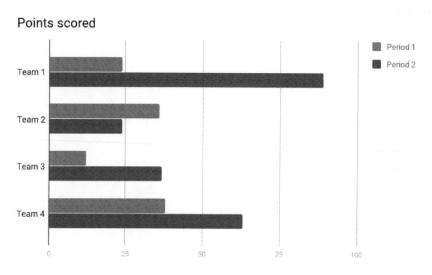

Points scored

Question: Which teams scored more during Period 2?
- Team 1, Team 3, and Team 4 all scored more during Period 2.

Pie Charts

A pie chart often presents data as a percentage of a whole.

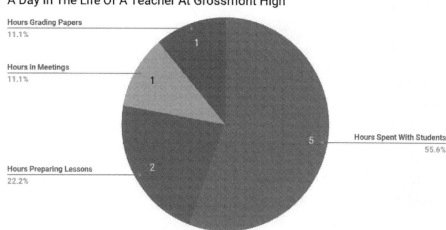

A Day In The Life Of A Teacher At Grossmont High

Question: Studies have shown that, in the best schools, teachers spend more than 50% of their time with students. What conclusion can be drawn from the above graph?

A. Grossmont is a bad school.
B. Grossmont is one of the best schools.
C. Teachers are spending too much time grading papers.
D. Teachers are not spending enough time preparing lessons.

- From the graph, teachers spend 5 out of 9 hours with students. 5/9 = 55.6%. Since, in the best schools, teachers spend more than 50% of their time with students and

Grossmont High School teachers spend 55.6% of their time with students, we can conclude that Grossmont High School is one of the best schools.

Measures of Central Tendency

Measures of central tendency include mean, mediang, and mode.

Mean

The mean is the average value of all data. To find the mean, add up all the numbers and then divide by how many numbers there are.

Example: Find the mean of {23, 45, 56}.
- (23 + 45 + 56) / 3 (We divide by 3 because there are 3 numbers.)
- 124/3 = 41.3

Median

The median is the middle number in a sorted list of numbers. If there are two middle numbers, as is the case when there is an even amount of numbers in a list, add the two middle numbers and divide by two.

Example: Find the median of {4, 2, 6, 18, 1}.
- Sort the list.
  - {1, 2, 4, 6, 18}.
- Find the middle number in the sorted list.
  - The median is 4.

Example: Find the median of {4, 6, 18, 1}.
- Sort the list.
  - {1, 4, 6, 18}
- Since there is an even amount of numbers in the list, there are two middle numbers. Add the two middle numbers and divide by 2.
  - (4+6) / 2
  - 10/2 = 5 (The median is 5.)

Mode

The mode is the number that appears most often in a list of numbers. There may be no modes if all numbers appear equally frequently. There may also be multiple modes.

Example: Find the mode of { 1, 2, 3, 3, 4, 5 }.
- The mode is 3.

Range

The range tells you the spread of the data. It is the difference between the highest and lowest value; a range is never negative.

Example: Find the range of { 1, 4, 9, 2, 12 }.
- Sort the list.
  - {1, 2, 4, 9, 12 }
- Find the difference between the highest and lowest value.
  - 12 - 1 = 11. (The range is 11.)

Example: Find the range of { -4, -10, 2, 6, 7 }.
- Sort the list.
  - {-10, -4, 2, 6, 7}
- Find the difference between the highest and lowest value.
  - 7 - (-10) = 7 + 10 = 17. (The range is 17.)

Independent vs Dependent Variables

An independent variable stands alone and is not affected by other variables. A dependent variable depends on or is affected by the independent variable. For example, time spent studying affects test scores. The "time spent studying" is an independent variable. The "test score" is the dependent variable.

The correlation in changes between two variables is called covariance. (Source: ATI TEAS Crash Course, pg. 121). A positive covariance or positive correlation is when both variables increase together or both variables decrease together. A negative covariance or negative correlation is when one variable increases and the other variable decreases and vice versa; they are inversely related.

Geometry

Lines and Angles

A **right angle** is an angle of 90 degrees.

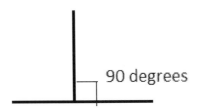

An **acute angle** is an angle less than 90 degrees.

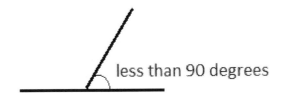

An **obtuse angle** is an angle greater than 90 degrees.

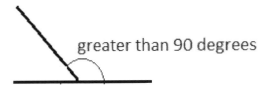

Parallel lines are lines that are always the same distance apart and never meet or intersect.

Parallel lines

Perpendicular lines are lines that intersect at 90 degree angles.

Perpendicular lines

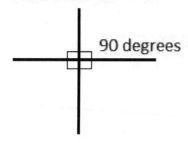

90 degrees

Vertical angles are the angles opposite each other when two lines cross. (Source: https://www.mathsisfun.com/geometry/vertical-angles.html). Vertical angles are always equal to each other. In the figure below, *a* and *c* are vertical angles and equal to each other; *b* and *d* are vertical angles and equal to each other.

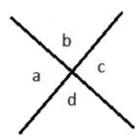

A **transversal line** is a line that cross two or more lines. If the transversal line crosses two or more parallel lines, all acute angles are equal to each other and all obtuse angles are equal to each other. (Souce: Kaplan ATI TEAS, pg. 176). In the figure below, all the acute angles (b,c,f,g) are equal to each other and all obtuse angles (a,d,e,h) are equal to each other.

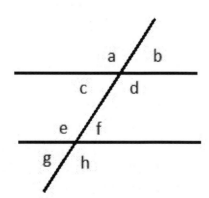

Pythagorean Theorem

A **right triangle** is a triangle with a right angle (90 degrees). All angles of a triangle add up to 180 degrees. The hypotenuse is the longest side of the triangle. In the figure below, *c* is the hypotenuse.

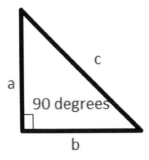

The **Pythagorean Theorem** is a formula used to find the value of one side of a triangle, when the other two sides of a triangle is known. The Pythagorean Theorem only works with right triangles. The formula is below:

$$a^2 + b^2 = c^2$$

Example: Given the figure below, what is the value of b?

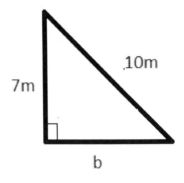

- Using the equation: $a^2 + b^2 = c^2$
  - $(7m)^2 + b^2 = (10m)^2$
- Solve for b
  - $49m^2 + b^2 = 100m^2$
  - $b^2 = 100m^2 - 49m^2$
  - $b^2 = 51m^2$
  - $b = \sqrt{51m^2}$
  - $b = \pm 7.14$ m (Since length is a positive value, the answer is +7.14m.)

Calculating Perimeter and Area

The perimeter is the sum of all sides of a 2D shape. The area is the amount of space enclosed in a 2D shape. The formulas for calculating perimeter and area for different shapes are below. Perimeter is calculated in units of inches, feet, meters, etc. Area is calculated in square inches (in.^{2}), square feet (ft.^{2}), etc.

Shape	Drawing	Perimeter	Area

Triangle		$P = a + b + c$	The area of a triangle is essentially half of the rectangle. **The base(b) and height(h) must be at right angles.** $A = \frac{1}{2}(b * h)$
Rectangle (A square is a rectangle that has the same length and width.)		$P = 2L + 2W$	$A = L * W$
Trapezoid		$P = a + b + c + l$	$A = \frac{1}{2}h(b + l)$
Circle		The perimeter of a circle is called the circumference. $P = 2\pi * r$ $\pi = 3.14$ r = radius (The radius is half of the circle's diameter.)	$A = \pi * r^2$

In the TEAS exam, you may be asked to calculate the perimeter and area of complex shapes. To calculate the perimeter and area of a complex shape, break the complex shape into simpler shapes.

Example: Find the perimeter and area of the following figure.

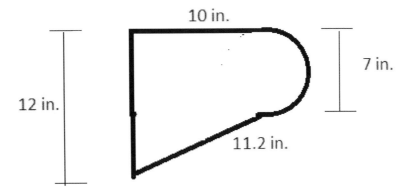

The above complex shape can be broken into a rectangle, a triangle, and half a circle.

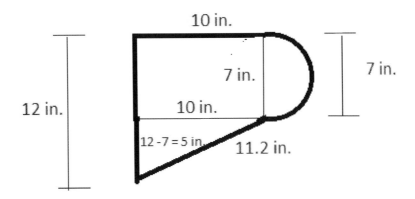

To calculate the perimeter:
- P = 12 in. + 11.2 in. + 10 in. + half the circumference of the circle
- The circle has a diameter of 7 inches, so the radius = 7/2 = 3.5 inches.
- The formula for calculating the circumference of a circle is P = 2π * r
  - P = 2π * 3.5 = 21.98 in.
  - Since the shape consists of only half a circle, divide the circumference by 2.
    - 21.98 in. / 2 = 10.99 in.
- P = 12 in. + 11.2 in + 10 in. + 10.99 in. = 44.19 in.

To calculate the area:
- A = area of rectangle + area of triangle + area of half circle
- The formula for calculating the area of a rectangle is A = length * width.
  - A = 7 in. * 10 in. = 70 in.²
- The formula for calculating the area of a triangle is A = ½ (base * height)
  - From the figure, we know that the height of the triangle is 10 in.
  - We have to find the value of the triangle base. From the figure, we know the total length of the complex shape is 12 in. and the length of the rectangle is 7 in.; we can find the value of the triangle base by subtracting the length of the rectangle from the total length of the complex shape.
    - Triangle base = 12 in. - 7 in. = 5 in.

- o   A = ½ (5 in. * 10 in.) = 25 in.²
- The formula for calculating the area of a circle is A = π * r²
  - o   The circle has a diameter of 7 inches, so the radius = 7/2 = 3.5 inches.
  - o   A = π * (3.5 in.)² = π * 12.25 in.² = 38.47 in.²
  - o   Since the shape consists of only half a circle, divide the area by 2.
    - ■   38.47 /2 = 19.24 in.²
- A = 70 in.² + 25 in.² + 19.24 in.² = 114.24 in.²

Arc Length

Arc length is the length of a fraction of a circle. The formula to calculate the arc length is:

$$\left(\frac{\text{arc angle}}{360}\right) * 2\pi r$$

Example: Find the arc length of the figure below.

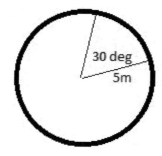

- Given that the arc angle is 30 degrees and the radius is 5m:
  - o $\left(\frac{30}{360}\right) * 2\pi(5)$
  - o   0.08 * 2 * 3.14 * 5 = 2.61m

Example: Find the arc length given that the circumference is 20m.

- Given that the arc angle is 20 degrees and the circumference (2πr) is 20m:
  - o $\left(\frac{20}{360}\right) * 20m$

- 0.06 * 20m = 1.2 m

Calculating Volume

Volume is the space occupied by a 3D object and is measured in cubic units. The formulas for calculating volume are:

Shape	Volume
Sphere	$V = (4/3)\pi r^3$
Cube or Rectangular Prism	V = length * width * height
Cylinder	$V = \pi r^2$ * height

Example: Calculate the volume of the cylinder:

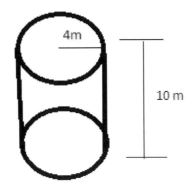

- From the figure, the height is 10m and the radius is 4m
  - $V = \pi r^2$ * height
  - $V = \pi(4m)^2$ * 10m
  - $V = \pi(16m^2)$ * 10m
  - $V = 502.4m^3$

About The Exam

The ATI Test of Essential Academic Skills (TEAS) is a nursing or health science school entrance exam. You can register for the exam at www.atitesting.com. The exam consists of 170 multiple choice questions, 20 of which are not scored. You will have 209 minutes to complete the exam. You are not penalized for wrong answers so answer every question.

The blueprint for the exam is below.

Content Area	Number of Questions	Time Limit

Reading
  a. Key Ideas and Details
  b. Craft and Structure
  c. Integration of Knowledge and Ideas
  d. Unscored Questions
	53
	  a. 22
	  b. 14
	  c. 11
	  d. 6
		64 minutes

Mathematics
  a. Number and Algebra
  b. Measurement and Data
  c. Unscored Questions
	36
	  a. 23
	  b. 9
	  c. 4
		54 minutes

Science
  a. Human Anatomy and Physiology
  b. Life and Physical Sciences
  c. Scientific Reasoning
  d. Unscored Questions
	53
	  a. 32
	  b. 8
	  c. 9
	  d. 6
		63 minutes

English and Language Usage
  a. Conventions of Standard English
  b. Knowledge of Language
  c. Vocabulary Acquisition
  d. Unscored Questions
	28
	  a. 9
	  b. 9
	  c. 6
	  d. 4
		28 minutes

Practice Exam 1

Science

1. The atomic number of oxygen is 8 and its atomic mass is 16. How many neutrons does oxygen have?
    a. 8
    b. 16
    c. 24
    d. Cannot be determined

2. Low blood pressure can be life-threatening. To help maintain a stable blood pressure, receptors in the heart detect changes in blood pressure. Information about blood pressure changes is then sent to the brain. If blood pressure is too low, the brain sends a message to the heart to beat faster.
    Based on this information, which of the following systems are directly involved in keeping blood pressure stable?
    a. circulatory, muscular, nervous
    b. circulatory, immune, skeletal
    c. excretory, immune, muscular
    d. excretory, nervous, skeletal

3. In Labrador retrievers, the allele for brown coat color (b) is recessive to the allele for black coat color (B). Information about two Labrador retrievers is given below.

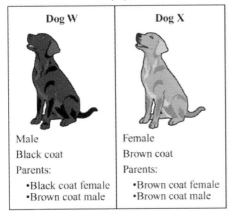

Dog W	Dog X
Male	Female
Black coat	Brown coat
Parents:	Parents:
•Black coat female	•Brown coat female
•Brown coat male	•Brown coat male

If dog W and dog X were crossed, what percentage of the offspring would be expected to be brown?
    a. 0%
    b. 25%
    c. 50%
    d. 100%

4. Which particle is a negatively charged ion?
    a. Hydrogen (H) with 1 proton, 0 neutrons, and 1 electron
    b. Sodium (Na) with 11 protons, 12 neutrons, and 10 electrons

   c.   Chlorine (Cl) with 17 protons, 18 neutrons, and 18 electrons

   d.   Magnesium (Mg) with 12 protons, 12 neutrons, and 12 electrons

5. A human CANNOT survive the loss of which of the following?
     a. The appendix
     b. The liver
     c. A lung
     d. A kidney

6. What information about organisms best helps scientists to determine the evolutionary relationships among them?
     a. DNA sequences
     b. Anatomical features
     c. Habitat types
     d. Reproductive strategies

7. Which pair of systems regulate and coordinate body functions?
     a. Excretory and digestive
     b. Nervous and endocrine
     c. Skeletal and muscular
     d. Immune and respiratory

8. What is the correct order for the levels of organization in living systems from the simplest to the most complex? (Note that not all levels of organization are included.)
     a. Elements to molecules to cells to tissues to organs
     b. Molecules to tissues to cells to organs to organisms
     c. Molecules to elements to tissues to organs to organisms
     d. Cells to organs to tissues to organisms to molecules

9. When you exercise strenuously, your body produces excess heat. What does your body do to help prevent your temperature from rising excessively?
     a. Dilate blood vessels
     b. Constrict blood vessels
     c. Hair follicle muscles contract
     d. None of the above.

10. In your body, what two organs work together to make sure that oxygen gets to all the other organs of your body?
     a. Lungs and kidneys
     b. Heart and lungs
     c. Brain and kidneys
     d. Heart and liver

11. Which statement about the offspring that result from sexual reproduction is generally true?

    a. The offspring show genetic variation from the parents.

    b. The offspring have genetic material identical to that of one another.

    c. The offspring have genetic material identical to that of one of the parents.

    d. The offspring have twice as much genetic material as each parent.

12. Scientists compared levels of a particular chemical found in the blood of two groups of male birds. The average concentration of the chemical was significantly higher in one group of males than in the other group of males. It was determined that the chemical caused different mating behaviors depending upon its concentration in the blood. Based on the information, this chemical is most likely which type of compound?

    a. an antibody

    b. a hormone

    c. a nucleic acid

    d. a sugar

13. Which is a function of a neuron?

    a. It carries oxygen to other cells.

    b. It secretes digestive enzymes.

    c. It removes foreign particles from the bloodstream.

    d. It receives signals from the internal and external environments.

14. Based on the information in the table below, which is a reasonable hypothesis regarding elements and their compounds?

	Charcoal	Carbon Dioxide
Formula	C	CO_2
State at Room Temperature	Solid	Gas
Soluble in Water	No	Yes
Combustible in Air	Yes	No

    a. An element retains its physical and chemical properties when it is combined into a compound.

    b. When an element reacts to form a compound, its chemical properties are changed but its physical properties are not.

    c. When an element reacts to form a compound, its physical properties are changed but its chemical properties are not.

    d. Both the chemical and physical properties of a compound are different from the properties of the elements of which it is composed.

15. Which statement best helps to explain how different structures could arise from a common precursor?

    a. Mutations in the genes regulating limb development led to gradual changes in structure, which provided a selective advantage to the organisms.

b. A single mutation in the genes regulating limb development resulted in a change in structure, which led to the modified limbs in offspring.

c. Changes in the environment caused mutations in the genes regulating limb development, which provided a means to thrive under the new conditions.

d. Limbs changed in response to the changing needs of the organisms, which led to the modified limbs in offspring.

16. Which of the following is the best evidence that two birds belong to the same species?
    a. The two birds eat the same food.
    b. The two birds have common behaviors.
    c. The two birds are the same size and color.
    d. The two birds mate and produce fertile offspring

17. Inhalation is the process that draws air into the lungs. How does the muscular system work with the respiratory system to make inhalation possible?
    a. The chest muscle relaxes to let air flow into the respiratory system.
    b. The smooth muscles of the esophagus relax to let air flow into the respiratory system.
    c. The diaphragm muscle contracts to expand the chest and draw air into the respiratory system.
    d. The skeletal muscles of the neck contract to pull on the pharynx and draw air into the respiratory system.

18. What is the main reason that water has the ability to dissolve many different substances?
    a. Water has a lower molecular mass than many substances.
    b. Water molecules attract ions and the charged parts of molecules.
    c. Water molecules are larger than the ions or molecules they dissolve.
    d. Water is more dense in the liquid phase than in the solid phase.

19. In the human body the digestion of proteins takes place primarily in which two organs?
    a. Mouth and stomach
    b. Stomach and small intestine
    c. Liver and gall bladder
    d. Pancreas and large intestine

20. Each diagram below shows the same front view of a human heart. Which diagram has arrows that correctly show the path of blood flow through the heart and the blood vessels leading to and from the heart?

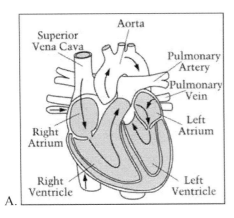

A.

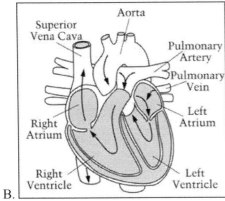

B.

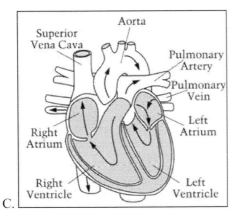

C.

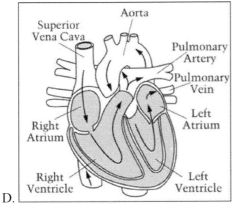

D.

21. Which of the following statements best explains why malaria causes fatigue in humans?
    a. Malaria destroys fat cells.
    b. Malaria slows the digestive system.
    c. Malaria reduces oxygen transport to cells.
    d. Malaria increases activity in the nervous system.

22. Which of the following is the best example of homeostasis?
    a. Heart rate increases when a person exercises.
    b. The chest cavity expands when the diaphragm contracts.
    c. The biceps muscle relaxes when the triceps muscle contracts.
    d. Digestive enzymes are secreted when food enters the stomach.

23. A body cell of a sand dollar has 52 chromosomes. How many chromosomes should a sand dollar gamete contain?
    a. 26
    b. 52
    c. 78
    d. 104

24. The axons of some vertebrate neurons are wrapped with special cells called Schwann cells. Which type of signal jumps from node to node between the Schwann cells to move down the axon?
    a. a digital pulse
    b. a magnetic pulse
    c. an electrical signal
    d. a glycoprotein signal

25. What is produced when the DNA sequence "TAGGAGCAT" is transcribed?
    a. a chain of three amino acids
    b. a set of three tRNA molecules
    c. a section of DNA with the base sequence ATCCTCGTA
    d. a section of mRNA with the base sequence AUCCUCGUA

26. Damage to neurons directly interferes with which of the following processes?
    a. delivery of glucose to cells
    b. filtering of wastes from blood
    c. transmission of nerve impulses
    d. exchange of oxygen and carbon dioxide

27. Most people with type 1 met-H have no symptoms except blue skin and mucous membranes. If the concentration of methemoglobin in the blood increases enough, the ability to carry oxygen decreases and other symptoms can develop.
    Which of the following symptoms would most likely result if there were large amounts of methemoglobin in the blood?

a. hyperactivity
b. lack of energy
c. increased appetite
d. inflammation of kidneys

28. The diagram below shows some food in a structure of the human digestive system.

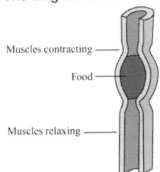

Muscles contracting

Food

Muscles relaxing

Which of the following describes the primary role of this structure?
a. to release enzymes that break down food
b. to make enzymes used in the digestion of food
c. to mechanically digest food into macromolecules
d. to push food toward an organ that breaks down macromolecules

29. The cartilage on the ends of long bones serves which of the following functions?
a. attaching the bones to muscles
b. connecting the bones to other bones
c. cushioning and resisting compression at joints
d. forming and storing red blood cells for the body

30. Valvular stenosis is a condition in which the heart valves are stiff and do not open completely. In people with this condition, blood flow to the body is decreased. How will valvular stenosis most likely affect body cells?
a. Body cells will produce less water than usual.
b. Body cells will receive less oxygen than usual.
c. Body cells will store more nutrients than usual.
d. Body cells will produce more waste products than usual.

31. Besides producing cholesterol and bile, which of the following is a function of the liver?
a. digesting fiber
b. making red blood cells
c. removing toxins from blood
d. storing stomach contents for digestion

32. Which of the following is the best example of homeostasis in the human body?
a. The secretions from oil glands in the skin decrease as a person ages.
b. Opposite muscles are used to bend and extend a person's arm at the elbow joint.

c. The villi of the small intestine increase the absorption of nutrients from the small intestine into the blood.

d. More growth hormone is released from the pituitary gland when the level of growth hormone in the blood falls too low.

33. Which of the following carries nerve impulses from pressure receptors in the skin to the central nervous system?
    a. capillary
    b. marrow
    c. motor neuron
    d. sensory neuron

34. Where does fertilization occur?
    a. Fallopian tubes
    b. Uterus
    c. Endometrium
    d. None of the above

35. What gland secretes hormones that control blood glucose level?
    a. Insulin
    b. Pancreas
    c. Liver
    d. Pineal gland

36. Which system responds to pathogens by causing inflammation and/or fever?
    a. Adaptive immune system
    b. Innate immune system
    c. Third line of defense system
    d. None of the above

37. A scientist is setting up an experiment to see how the concentration of sugar in water affects plant growth. The scientist will control the amount of sugar in the water fed to plants. What is the independent variable?
    a. Concentration of sugar water
    b. Plant growth
    c. Both the concentration of sugar water and plant growth, if no effect is seen

38. Water consists of 2 hydrogen atoms bonded to 1 oxygen; each hydrogen atom shares an electron with the oxygen atom. This is an example of what type of bond?
    a. Ionic
    b. carbon
    c. Covalent
    d. None of the above

39. Where does oxygen and carbon dioxide exchange occur in the lungs?
    a. Pharynx
    b. Bronchi
    c. Alveoli
    d. Pulmonary capillaries

40. What vertical line divides the body into left and right portions?
    a. Sagittal plane
    b. Transverse plane
    c. Coronal plane
    d. None of the above

41. Oxygen _____ blood flows from the heart to the lungs.
    a. Rich
    b. Poor

42. A _____ is essential to determining whether or not a treatment or change was the cause of the effect/result or a placebo effect.
    a. Control group
    b. Experimental group
    c. Dependent variable
    d. None of the above

43. How many decimeters are in 1 meter?
    a. 0.1
    b. 10
    c. 100
    d. None of the above

44. What happens during diastole?
    a. Heart muscles contract
    b. Heart muscles relax
    c. Diaphragm muscles contract
    d. Diaphragm muscles relax

45. In an experiment to study the effects of sugar on plant growth, one group of plants is given no sugar and the other group of plants is given 5mL of sugar. Which group is the control group?
    a. Group of plants given no sugar
    b. Group of plants given 5mL of sugar

46. The state of matter is most affected by
    a. Temperature and volume
    b. Temperature and pressure

c. Volume and pressure
d. Its previous state

47. Which of the following macromolecule consists mainly of hydrocarbon chains?
    a. Carbohydrates
    b. Lipids
    c. Proteins
    d. Nucleic acids

48. Which gland regulates hormones associated with the "fight or flight" response?
    a. Adrenal glands
    b. Pineal gland
    c. Parathyroid gland
    d. Thyroid glands

49. Damage to what lobe would affect your decision making abilities?
    a. Frontal lobe
    b. Parietal lobe
    c. Occipital lobe
    d. Temporal lobe

50. Urine is stored in
    a. The kidneys
    b. The urethra
    c. The bladder
    d. The ureter

51. Most neurons receive signals through _____ and send out signals through _____.
    a. axons, dendrites
    b. dendrites, axons

52. The heart contains
    a. One way valves
    b. Two way valves

53. Which of the following is an example of a demyelinating disorder?
    a. Diabetes
    b. Osteoporosis
    c. Multiple sclerosis
    d. Hypothyroidism

Mathematics

1. Solve the following equation.

$$\frac{((4 * 10) + (2 * 10))}{(3 * 10)}$$

   a. 2
   b. 4
   c. 10
   d. 14

2. A scatter plot is shown.

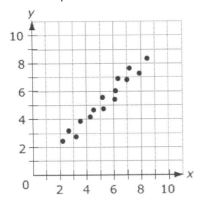

   Which statement is true for the scatter plot?
   a. The data shows no association.
   b. The data shows a positive correlation.
   c. The data shows a negative correlation.
   d. The data shows a nonlinear association.

3. A cylinder has a height of 6.4 inches and a diameter of 6 inches.
   What is the volume, in cubic inches, of the cylinder? Use 3.14 for π.
   a. 60.3 cubic inches
   b. 120.6 cubic inches
   c. 180.8 cubic inches
   d. 723.5 cubic inches

4. $2x + 2y = 3$ can have
   a. Zero solutions
   b. One solution
   c. Many solutions

5. Five hundred students were asked whether they prefer apple juice or orange juice. The table shown displays the results.

	Apple Juice	Orange Juice

Boys	30	100
Girls	210	160

How many more girls were surveyed than boys?
   a. 20
   b. 130
   c. 240
   d. 370

6. The next X questions are based on the following:

Mary and Kim each take 15 minutes to ride their bikes to school. The graphs of the functions that model their rides are shown, where x is the time, in minutes, and y is the distance, in miles.
The graphs are divided into time intervals A, B, and C.

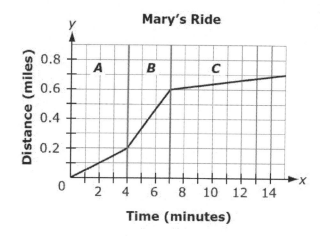

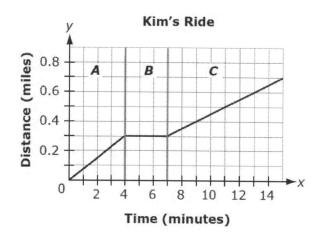

Who rode her bike fastest in interval A, as compared to the rest of her ride?
   a. Mary
   b. Kim

7. Who stopped for an interval of time?
    a. Mary
    b. Kim
    c. Both

8. Who rode slower in interval C than in interval B?
    a. Mary
    b. Kim
    c. Both

9. Who lives 0.7 miles from school?
    a. Mary
    b. Kim
    c. Both

10. A figure with parallel lines m and n is shown. What is the measure, in degrees, of angle b?

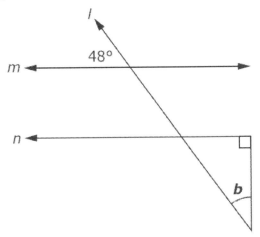

    a. 35
    b. 42
    c. 48
    d. 132

11. The manager of an ice cream shop is considering which ice cream flavor to offer as the special flavor next month. She asks 175 people whether they like mint or strawberry ice cream. The two-way table shows the results.

	Like Mint	Do Not Like Mint	Total
Like Strawberry	30	75	105
Do Not Like Strawberry	56	14	70
Total	86	89	175

What percentage of the customers surveyed liked mint?
- a. 40%
- b. 49%
- c. 51%
- d. 60%

12. What percentage of the customers surveyed like strawberry?
- a. 40%
- b. 49%
- c. 51%
- d. 60%

13. A company has three sales departments (local, regional, and national) at each of several locations across the United States. Each local sales department has 120 employees. The company wants to survey its employees to determine the most effective sales method. Which sample should the company use to arrive at the most reliable conclusion?
- a. 24 employees from one sales department at one location
- b. 24 employees from one sales department at each location
- c. 24 employees from each sales department at one location
- d. 24 employees from each sales department at each location

14. A recipe calls for ⅔ cup of sugar for every ½ teaspoon of vanilla. What is the unit rate of cups per teaspoon?
- a. $\dfrac{1}{3}$
- b. $\dfrac{4}{3}$
- c. $\dfrac{2}{5}$
- d. $\dfrac{5}{3}$

15. Which of the following containers has the greatest liquid capacity?
(1 gallon = 4 quarts = 8 pints = 128 ounces)

a. A 64-ounce orange juice container
b. A 16-pint water jug
c. A 5-quart punch bowl
d. A 2-quart cola bottle
e. A 1-gallon milk bottle

16. The manager of a company has to order new engines for its delivery trucks after the trucks have been driven 150,000 miles. One of the delivery trucks currently has 119,866 miles on it. This truck has the same delivery route each week and is driven an average of 40,000 miles each year. At this rate, the manager should expect this truck to reach 150,000 miles in approximately how many months?
    a. Less than 4 months
    b. Between 4 and 6 months
    c. Between 6 and 8 months
    d. Between 8 and 10 months
    e. More than 10 months

17. Angie has a bag containing n apples. She gives 4 to her brother and keeps 5 for herself. She then divides the remaining apples equally among 3 friends. Which of the following expressions represents the number of apples each friend receives?

    a. $\dfrac{n}{3} - 4 - 5$

    b. $\dfrac{n - 4 - 5}{3}$

    c. $\dfrac{4 + 5 - n}{3}$

    d. $\dfrac{n - 4}{3} - 5$

18. The cost to mail a first-class letter is 33 cents for the first ounce. Each additional ounce costs 22 cents. (Fractions of an ounce are rounded up to the next whole ounce.) How much would it cost to mail a letter that weighs 2.7 ounces?
    a. 55 cents
    b. 66 cents
    c. 77 cents
    d. 88 cents

19. If a 2 by 18 rectangle has the same area as a square, what is the length of a side of the square?
    a. 4
    b. 6

c. 8

d. 10

20. In a certain restaurant a whole pie has been sliced into 8 equal wedges. Only 2 slices of the pie remain. Three people would each like an equal portion from the remaining slices of pie. What fraction of the original pie should each person receive?

    a. 1/11

    b. 1/12

    c. 1/13

    d. 1/14

21. If $f(x) = x^2 + x$ and $g(x) = 2x + 7$, what is an expression for $f(g(x))$?

    a. $4x^2 + 30x + 56$

    b. $x^2 + 3x + 7$

    c. $4x^2 + 2x + 56$

    d. None of the above

22. What is the length, in feet, of the side whose dimension is not shown?

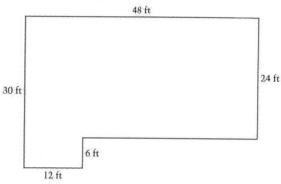

    a. 12

    b. 24

    c. 30

    d. 36

23. If you were to redraw a diagram using a scale of 3/4 inch equals 10 feet, what would be the length of a side that is 48 feet?

    a. 3.0 in

    b. 3.6 in

    c. 5.6 in

    d. 7.5 in

24. Easy Ride Van Company finds that about 40 percent of the time a person who makes an advance reservation for transportation does not keep the reservation. Therefore, for each of their 10-passenger vans, the Easy Ride Van Company schedules 13 persons on the basis of advance reservations. Based on the information above, about how many riders out of the 13 scheduled would not keep their reservations?

a. 1
b. 3
c. 5
d. 7

25. If the digit in the tens place of 37,241 is increased by one and the digit in the thousands place is decreased by one, how has the number been changed?
   a. The number has been decreased by 990.
   b. The number has been decreased by 1,000.
   c. The number has been decreased by 1,010.
   d. The number has been increased by 10.
   e. The number has been increased by 1,010.

26. x + 2y = 1 and 2x -y = 7, what is x?
   a. -1
   b. 2
   c. 3
   d. 4

27. The pulse rate per minute of a group of 100 adults is displayed in the histogram above. For example, 5 adults have a pulse rate from 40-49 inclusive. Based on these data, how many individuals from a comparable group of 40 adults would be expected to have a pulse rate of 80 or above?

RESULTS OF PULSE RATE SURVEY

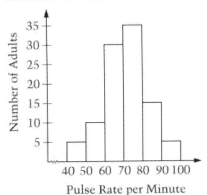

Pulse Rate per Minute

   a. 8
   b. 10
   c. 20
   d. None of the above

28. The table below shows the gender and color of 7 puppies. If a puppy selected at random from the group is brown, what is the probability it is a male?

GENDER AND COLOR OF PUPPIES

	Male	Female
Black	1	2
Brown	1	3

a. 1 / 4
b. 2 / 7
c. 1 / 3
d. 1 / 2

29. The first term in a sequence of numbers is 1/2 . Each term after the first term is 1 more than twice its previous term. What is the 4th term?
a. 2
b. 4
c. 5
d. 11

30. Rosa is twice as old as Byron.
Fred is one year older than Byron.
If Fred's age is represented by F, which of the following represents the ages of Rosa and Byron, respectively?

a. $\frac{1}{2}$(F - 1) and F - 1

b. $\frac{1}{2}$(F + 1) and F + 1

c. 2(F - 1) and F - 1

d. 2(F + 1) and F + 1

31. The town of Mayville taxes property at a rate of $42 for each $1,000 of estimated value. What is the estimated value of a property on which the owner owes $5,250 in property tax?
a. $42,000
b. $47,250
c. $125,000
d. $220,500

32. Yvonne has studied the cost of tickets over time for her favorite sports team. She has created a model to predict the cost of a ticket in the future. Let C represent the cost of a ticket in dollars and y represent the number of years in the future. Her model is as follows.

C = 2.50y + 13

Based on this model, how much will the cost of a ticket increase in two years?

    a. $5

    b. $8

    c. $13

    d. $18

33. A rectangle is twice as long as it is wide. If x represents the width of the rectangle, what represents the length?

    a. y

    b. 2

    c. 2x

    d. 2y

34. A rectangle is twice as long as it is wide. What is the area of the rectangle in terms of x ?

    a. xy

    b. 2xy

    c. 2x

    d. $2x^2$

35. Of the following, which is the best unit to use when measuring the growth of a plant every other day during a 2-week period?

    a. Centimeter

    b. Meter

    c. Kilometer

    d. Foot

36. Luis mixed 6 ounces of cherry syrup with 53 ounces of water to make a cherry-flavored drink. Martin mixed 5 ounces of the same cherry syrup with 42 ounces of water. Who made the drink with the stronger cherry flavor?

    a. Luis

    b. Martin

Reading

1. The next 9 questions are based on the following two passages:

Passage 1: Discourse on Woman (1849)
by Lucretia Mott

1 There is nothing of greater importance to the well-being of society at large—of man as well as woman—than the true and proper position of woman. Much has been said, from time to time, upon this subject. It has been a theme for ridicule, for satire and sarcasm. We might look for this from the ignorant and vulgar; but from the intelligent and refined we have a right to expect that such weapons shall not be resorted to,—that gross comparisons and vulgar epithets shall not be applied, so as to place woman, in a point of view, ridiculous to say the least.

2 This subject has claimed my earnest interest for many years. I have long wished to see woman occupying a more elevated position than that which custom for ages has allotted to her. It was with great regret, therefore, that I listened a few days ago to a lecture upon this subject, which, though replete with intellectual beauty, and containing much that was true and excellent, was yet fraught with sentiments calculated to retard the progress of woman to the high elevation destined by her Creator. I regretted the more that these sentiments should be presented with such intellectual vigor and beauty, because they would be likely to ensnare the young.

3 The minds of young people generally, are open to the reception of more exalted views upon this subject. The kind of homage that has been paid to woman, the flattering appeals which have too long satisfied her—appeals to her mere fancy and imagination, are giving place to a more extended recognition of her rights, her important duties and responsibilities in life. Woman is claiming for herself stronger and more profitable food. Various are the indications leading to this conclusion. The increasing attention to female education, the improvement in the literature of the age, especially in what is called the "Ladies' Department," in the periodicals of the day, are among the proofs of a higher estimate of woman in society at large. Therefore we may hope that the intellectual and intelligent are being prepared for the discussion of this question, in a manner which shall tend to ennoble woman and dignify man. . . .

4 A new generation of women is now upon the stage, improving the increased opportunities furnished for the acquirement of knowledge. Public education is coming to be regarded the right of the children of a republic. The hill of science is not so difficult of ascent as formerly represented by poets and painters; but by fact and demonstration smoothed down, so as to be accessible to the assumed weak capacity of woman. She is rising in the scale of being through this, as well as other means, and finding heightened pleasure and profit on the right hand and on the left. The study of Physiology, now introduced into our common schools, is engaging her attention, impressing the necessity of the observance of the laws of health. The intellectual Lyceum and instructive lecture room are becoming, to many, more attractive than the theatre and the ball room. The sickly and sentimental novel and pernicious romance are giving place to works, calculated to call forth the benevolent affections and higher nature

---

Passage 2: from Pioneer Work in Opening the Medical Profession to Women (1895)
by Elizabeth Blackwell

5 At this time I had not the slightest idea of how to become a physician, or of the course of study necessary for this purpose. As the idea seemed to gain force, however, I wrote to and consulted with several physicians, known to my family, in various parts of the country, as to the possibility of a lady becoming a doctor.

6 The answers I received were curiously unanimous. They all replied to the effect that the idea was a good one, but that it was impossible to accomplish it; that there was no way of obtaining such an education for a woman; that the education required was long and expensive; that there were innumerable obstacles in the way of such a course; and that, in short, the idea, though a valuable one, was impossible of execution.

7 This verdict, however, no matter from how great an authority, was rather an encouragement than otherwise to a young and active person who needed an absorbing occupation.

8 If an idea, I reasoned, were really a valuable one, there must be some way of realising it. . . .

9 Applications were cautiously but persistently made to the four medical colleges of Philadelphia for admission as a regular student. The interviews with their various professors were by turns hopeful and disappointing. . . .

10 During these fruitless efforts my kindly Quaker adviser, whose private lectures I attended, said to me: 'Elizabeth, it is of no use trying. Thee cannot gain admission to these schools. Thee must go to Paris and don masculine attire to gain the necessary knowledge.' Curiously enough, this suggestion of disguise made by good Dr. Warrington was also given me by Doctor Pankhurst, the Professor of Surgery in the largest college in Philadelphia. He thoroughly approved of a woman's gaining complete medical knowledge; told me that although my public entrance into the classes was out of the question, yet if I would assume masculine attire and enter the college he could entirely rely on two or three of his students to whom he should communicate my disguise, who would watch the class and give me timely notice to withdraw should my disguise be suspected.

11 But neither the advice to go to Paris nor the suggestion of disguise tempted me for a moment. It was to my mind a moral crusade on which I had entered, a course of justice and common sense, and it must be pursued in the light of day, and with public sanction, in order to accomplish its end.

Which phrase supports Mott's position that women's rights are "of greater importance to the well-being of society at large?"
- a. "the intelligent and refined" (paragraph 1)
- b. "intellectual vigor and beauty" (paragraph 2)
- c. "stronger and more profitable food" (paragraph 3)
- d. "the benevolent affections and higher nature" (paragraph 4)

2. What central idea about language does Mott express in Passage 1?
- a. Flattering words have failed to satisfy women's need for equality.
- b. Attempts should be made to educate those who use vulgar speech.
- c. Women must learn how to speak well before they can rise in society.
- d. Artistic words can conceal ideas that limit the progress of equal rights.

3. What does Mott cite in paragraphs 3 and 4 as evidence that the situation (Mott's central idea about language) is changing?

a. more substantial literary works
b. more accurate scientific theories
c. new opportunities for recreation
d. increased business opportunities

4. "There is nothing of greater importance to the well-being of society at large—of man as well as woman—than the true and proper position of woman." (paragraph 1)

   After stating this central claim, how does Mott structure the rest of the passage?
   a. She criticizes the immaturity of the young and then pleads for better education.
   b. She names obstacles to progress and then cites positive signs of improvement.
   c. She describes the role of men and then shows how they can help the movement.
   d. She stresses the importance of communication and then describes what it can accomplish.

5. "But neither the advice to go to Paris nor the suggestion of disguise tempted me for a moment. It was to my mind a moral crusade on which I had entered, a course of justice and common sense, and it must be pursued in the light of day, and with public sanction, in order to accomplish its end."

   Based on the phrase **public sanction**, in what way was Blackwell determined to accomplish her goals?
   a. without criticism
   b. without attention
   c. without hesitation
   d. without deception

6. Which phrase from the excerpt provides a clue to the meaning of the phrase **public sanction?**
   a. "the advice to go to Paris"
   b. "a moral crusade"
   c. "in the light of day"
   d. "to accomplish its end"

7. What is Blackwell's purpose for describing her experiences in Passage 2?
   a. to show how she handled the obstacles in the way of her goals
   b. to criticize the physicians who discouraged her interest in medicine
   c. to illustrate how effective women could be in traditional male roles
   d. to argue that medicine would benefit if more women were involved

8. Which phrase does Blackwell use to help emphasize this purpose (describing her experiences in Passage 2)?
   a. "curiously unanimous" (paragraph 6)

b. "long and expensive" (paragraph 6)

c. "absorbing occupation" (paragraph 7)

d. "cautiously but persistently" (paragraph 9)

9. How are Mott's and Blackwell's perspectives similar?

    a. Both view women's rights as an ethical issue.

    b. Both think intellect can conceal destructive ideas.

    c. Both recognize positive signs in women's progress.

    d. Both emphasize the importance of self-confidence

10. The next 8 questions are based on the following two passages:

Passage 1: from The Metamorphoses

by Ovid

Pyramus and Thisbe, the one the most beauteous of youths, the other preferred before all the damsels that the East contained, lived in adjoining houses; where Semiramis is said to have surrounded her lofty city with walls of brick. The nearness caused their first acquaintance, and their first advances in love; with time their affection increased. They would have united themselves, too, by the tie of marriage, but their fathers forbade it. A thing which they could not forbid, they were both inflamed, with minds equally captivated. There is no one acquainted with it; by nods and signs, they hold converse. And the more the fire is smothered, the more, when so smothered, does it burn. The party-wall, common to the two houses, was cleft by a small chink, which it had got formerly, when it was built. This defect, remarked by no one for so many ages, you lovers (what does not love perceive?) first found one, and you made it a passage for your voices, and the accents of love used to pass through it in safety, with the gentlest murmur. Oftentimes, after they had taken their stations, Thisbe on one side, and Pyramus on the other, and the breath of their mouths had been mutually caught by turns, they used to say, 'Envious wall, why dost thou stand in the way of lovers? what great matter were it, for thee to suffer us to be joined with our entire bodies? Or if that is too much, that, at least, thou shouldst open, for the exchange of kisses. Nor are we ungrateful; we confess that we are indebted to thee, that a passage has been given for our words to our loving ears.' Having said this much, in vain, on their respective sides, about night they said, 'Farewell'; and gave those kisses each on their own side, which did not reach the other side.

Passage 2: from Romeo and Juliet

by William Shakespeare

Romeo and Juliet meet and fall in love, but their families have an old rivalry and will not allow them to be together. In this scene, Romeo sneaks into the orchard of Juliet's family to talk with Juliet, who is at her bedroom window balcony.

2 Juliet

What man art thou that, thus bescreen'd in night,

So stumblest on my counsel?

3 Romeo

By a name

I know not how to tell thee who I am:

My name, dear saint, is hateful to myself

Because it is an enemy to thee.
Had I it written, I would tear the word.
4 Juliet
My ears have yet not drunk a hundred words
Of that tongue's utterance, yet I know the sound;
Art thou not Romeo, and a Montague?
5 Romeo
Neither, fair saint, if either thee dislike.
6 Juliet
How cam'st thou hither, tell me, and wherefore?
The orchard walls are high and hard to climb;
And the place death, considering who thou art,
If any of my kinsmen find thee here.
7 Romeo
With love's light wings did I o'erperch these walls;
For stony limits cannot hold love out:
And what love can do, that dares love attempt;
Therefore thy kinsmen are no let to me.
8 Juliet
If they do see thee, they will murder thee.
9 Romeo
Alack, there lies more peril in thine eye
Than twenty of their swords: look thou but sweet,
And I am proof against their enmity.
10 Juliet
I would not for the world they saw thee here.
11 Romeo
I have night's cloak to hide me from their sight;
And, but thou love me, let them find me here.
My life were better ended by their hate
Than death prorogued, wanting of thy love.
12 Juliet
By whose direction found'st thou out this place?
13 Romeo
By love, that first did prompt me to enquire;
He lent me counsel, and I lent him eyes.
I am no pilot; yet, wert thou as far
As that vast shore wash'd with the furthest sea,
I would adventure for such merchandise.
14 Juliet
Thou knowest the mask of night is on my face;
Else would a maiden blush bepaint my cheek
For that which thou hast heard me speak to-night.
Fain would I dwell on form, fain, fain deny
What I have spoke; but farewell compliment!
Dost thou love me, I know thou wilt say Ay;
And I will take thy word: yet, if thou swear'st,
Thou mayst prove false; at lovers' perjuries,
They say Jove laughs. O gentle Romeo,
If thou dost love, pronounce it faithfully:
Or if thou thinkest I am too quickly won,
I'll frown, and be perverse, and say thee nay,
So thou wilt woo: but else, not for the world.
In truth, fair Montague, I am too fond;
And therefore thou mayst think my 'haviour light:
But trust me, gentleman, I'll prove more true
Than those that have more cunning to be strange.
I should have been more strange, I must confess,
But that thou overheard'st, ere I was 'ware,
My true-love passion: therefore pardon me;
And not impute this yielding to light love,

Which the dark night hath so discovered.
15 Romeo
Lady, by yonder blessed moon I swear,
That tips with silver all these fruit-tree tops,—
16 Juliet
O, swear not by the moon, the inconstant moon,
That monthly changes in her circled orb,
Lest that thy love prove likewise variable.
17 Romeo
What shall I swear by?
18 Juliet
Do not swear at all;
Or if thou wilt, swear by thy gracious self,
Which is the god of my idolatry,
And I'll believe thee.
19 Romeo
If my heart's dear love,—
20 Juliet
Well, do not swear: although I joy in thee,
I have no joy of this contract to-night;
It is too rash, too unadvis'd, too sudden;
Too like the lightning, which doth cease to be
Ere one can say It lightens. Sweet, good night!
This bud of love, by summer's ripening breath,
May prove a beauteous flower when next we meet.
Good night, good night! as sweet repose and rest
Come to thy heart as that within my breast!

What two phrases does Ovid use to show that Pyramus and Thisbe experience a shared love?

    a. they were both inflamed, with minds equally captivated
    b. you lovers (what does not love perceive?) first found one
    c. Oftentimes, after they had taken their stations, Thisbe on one side, and Pyramus on the other
    d. and the breath of their mouths had been mutually caught by turns

11. Based on Pyramus and Thisbe's situation, what is a theme of Passage 1?

    a. Lasting relationships depend upon affection.
    b. True love finds ways to overcome any obstacle.
    c. The smallest defect can cause love to deteriorate.
    d. Family disapproval can lead to desperate measures.

12. Which detail from Passage 1 helps develop the theme in the question above?

    a. the setting of the city
    b. the structure of the wall
    c. the beauty of the characters
    d. the fathers of the characters

13. At the end of Passage 1, why does Ovid use the word "envious" to describe the wall?

    a. It is immune to the pain that Pyramus and Thisbe experience.
    b. It has a flaw that Pyramus and Thisbe associate with their love.

c. It hears the opinions Pyramus and Thisbe have about each other.

d. It experiences the physical contact that Pyramus and Thisbe desire.

14. In Passage 2, how do sections 6–10 increase the tension of the passage as a whole?
    a. They show that Romeo is questioning his identity.
    b. They show that Juliet misinterprets Romeo's motives.
    c. They raise the possibility that Juliet may reject Romeo.
    d. They emphasize the danger that Romeo faces if caught.

15. Romeo and Juliet retells the Pyramus and Thisbe myth in the form of a play. In the excerpt provided in Passage 2, what does the play format help Shakespeare to emphasize about his characters? Select two options.
    a. the various threats they face
    b. the physical obstacles separating them
    c. the conflicting feelings they experience
    d. the way society views their relationship
    e. the reasons for their families' disapproval
    f. the reasons they are drawn to each other

16. Which quotation from Passage 2 summarizes a theme of both passages?
    a. "The orchard walls are high and hard to climb; . . ." (section 6)
    b. "For stony limits cannot hold love out: . . ." (section 7)
    c. "Thou knowest the mask of night is on my face; . . ." (section 14)
    d. "I have no joy of this contract to-night; . . ." (section 20)

17. How does Shakespeare dramatize this theme differently than Ovid does in Passage 1?
    a. by placing the characters in a definite setting
    b. by increasing the conflict between the characters
    c. by changing the type of obstacle the characters face
    d. by allowing the characters to engage in conversation

18. The next 2 questions are based on the following passage:

How to Serve Meow-Wow Dinner
One 8-ounce cup per average-sized cat is the recommended daily amount.
Twice-a-day feeding is the general rule for most cats, so allow 1/2 cup for each meal.
Remember that some cats just naturally like to nibble often instead of having a full meal at one time. In this case, serve each cat a cupful of Meow-Wow Dinner once a day, allowing the cat to eat as much and as often as desired.
Until kittens are three months old, feed them Meow-Wow Dinner wet about three or four times a day. Let them eat all they want.
Sometimes cats lose their appetites and do not eat for a day or two. If lack of appetite continues, it may be wise to consult a veterinarian.

What should a two-month old kitten be fed?
    a. Only dry food

b. One 8-ounce cup of food a day

c. Two cups of food once in the morning and once at night

d. Wet food three or four times a day

19. If your cat doesn't finish its bowl of food one morning, what should you do?

a. Call the veterinarian.

b. Take its bowl away until evening.

c. Leave the food in the bowl for it.

d. Give its food to the kitten.

20. Read the following passage:

Travels with Charley in Search of America
Even the cabin was dismal and damp. I turned the gas mantle high, lit the kerosene lamp, and lighted two burners of my stove to drive the loneliness away. The rain drummed on the metal roof. Nothing in my stock of food looked edible. The darkness fell and the trees moved closer. Over the rain drums I seemed to hear voices, as though a crowd of people muttered and mumbled offstage. Charley was restless. He didn't bark an alarm, but he growled and whined uneasily, which is very unlike him, and he didn't eat his supper and he left his water dish untouched—and that by a dog who drinks his weight in water every day and needs to because of the outgo. I succumbed utterly to my desolation, made two peanut-butter sandwiches, and went to bed and wrote letters home, passing my loneliness around. Then the rain stopped falling and the trees dripped and I helped spawn a school of secret dangers. Oh, we can populate the dark with horrors, even we who think ourselves informed and sure, believing nothing we cannot measure or weigh. I knew beyond all doubt that the dark things crowding in on me either did not exist or were not dangerous to me, and still I was afraid. I thought how terrible the nights must have been in a time when men knew the things were there and were deadly. But no, that's wrong. If I knew they were there, I would have weapons against them, charms, prayers, some kind of alliance with forces equally strong but on my side. Knowing they were not there made me defenseless against them and perhaps more afraid.

Which of the following best describes the man's fear?

a. He was worried that his dog was becoming ill.

b. He kept having fearful thoughts even though he knew there was no danger.

c. He suspected that there were dangerous animals outside.

d. He heard voices of people trying to break into the cabin.

21. The next 2 questions are based on the following passage:

College dropout and computer whiz kid, corporate executive and philanthropist, William H. Gates (1955-) was born and raised in Seattle, Washington. His interest in computers, which began at the age of thirteen, led Gates to realize the potential of a standard operating platform for the computer era, and through the success of his company Microsoft, he became one of the world's richest men. Criticized for its monopolistic practices, Microsoft was sued by the United States government in the 1990's. In 2000, Gates established the Bill and Melinda Gates Foundation, which has become the world's largest philanthropy dedicated to improving health and education worldwide. The following essay was published in 1999.

Human beings are not the biggest animals. We're not the strongest or fastest. We're not the sharpest in sight or smell It's amazing how we survived against the many fierce creatures of nature. We survived and prospered because of our brains. We evolved to fill the cognitive niche. We learned how to use tools, to build shelter, to invent agriculture, to domesticate livestock, to develop civilization and culture, to cure and prevent disease. Our tools and technologies have helped us to shape the environment around us.

I'm an optimist. I believe in progress. I'd much rather be alive today than at any time in history—and not just because in an earlier age my skill set wouldn't have been as valuable and I'd have been a prime candidate for some beast's dinner. The tools of the Industrial Age extended the capabilities of our muscles. The tools of the digital age extend the capabilities of our minds. I'm even happier for my children, who will come of age in this new world.

By embracing the digital age, we can accelerate the positive effects and mitigate the challenges, such as privacy and have-vs.-have-not. If we sit back and wait for the digital age to come to us on terms defined by others, we won't be able to do either. The Web lifestyle can increase citizen involvement in government. Many of the decisions to be made are political and social, not technical. These include how we ensure access for everyone and how we protect children. Citizens in every culture must engage on the social and political impact of digital technology to ensure that the new digital age reflects the society they want to create.

If we are reactive and let change overwhelm us or pass us by, we will perceive change negatively. If we are proactive, seek to understand the future now, and embrace change, the idea of the unexpected can be positive and uplifting. Astronomer Carl Sagan in his last book, Billions and Billions, said: "The prediction I can make with the highest confidence is that the most amazing discoveries will be the ones we are not today wise enough to foresee."

As tough and uncertain as the digital world makes it for business—it's evolve rapidly or die—we will all benefit. We're going to get improved products and services, more responsiveness to complaints, lower costs, and more choices. We're going to get better government and social services at substantially less expense.

This world is coming. A big part of it comes through businesses using a digital nervous system to radically improve their processes.

A digital nervous system can help business redefine itself and its role in the future, but energy or paralysis, success or failure, depends on business leaders. Only you can prepare your organization and make the investments necessary to capitalize on the rapidly dawning digital age.

Digital tools magnify the abilities that make us unique in the world: the ability to think, the ability to articulate our thoughts, the ability to work together to act on those thoughts. I strongly believe that if companies empower their employees to solve problems and give them potent tools to do this with, they will always be amazed at how much creativity and initiative will blossom forth.

The author says that we can mitigate the challenges of the digital age. He is suggesting that we can:
   a. expand research studies of technological problems
   b. look forward to many technological advances
   c. lessen the problems caused by technology
   d. increase public awareness of technology

22. The author refers to the human ability to articulate thoughts. He is describing the ability to:
   a. express ideas clearly
   b. think complexly
   c. come up with new ideas
   d. think in visual images

23. Read the sentences in the paragraph below and choose the sentence that does NOT belong with the others.

> Colorado is a western state with many mountains. Colorado has more than 1,000 peaks two miles high. Gold was discovered in Colorado in 1859. A total of 54 of the 69 highest mountains in the United States are in Colorado.

    a. Colorado is a western state with many mountains.
    b. Colorado has more than 1,000 peaks two miles high.
    c. Gold was discovered in Colorado in 1859.
    d. A total of 54 of the 69 highest mountains in the United States are in Colorado.

24. The next 5 questions are based on the following passage:

> Fun is hard to have.
> Fun is a rare jewel.
>
> Somewhere along the line people got the modern idea that fun was there for the asking, that people deserved fun, that if we didn't have a little fun every day we would turn into (sakes alive!) puritans.
>
> "Was it fun?" became the question that overshadowed all other questions: good questions like: Was it moral? Was it kind? Was it honest? Was it beneficial? Was it generous? Was it necessary? And (my favorite) was it selfless?
>
> When the pleasure got to be the main thing, the fun fetish was sure to follow. Everything was supposed to be fun. If it wasn't fun, then we were going to make it fun, or else.
>
> Think of all the things that got the reputation of being fun. Family outings were supposed to be fun. Education was supposed to be fun. Work was supposed to be fun. Walt Disney was supposed to be fun. Church was supposed to be fun. Staying fit was supposed to be fun.
>
> Just to make sure that everybody knew how much fun we were having, we put happy faces on flunking test papers, dirty bumpers, sticky refrigerator doors, bathroom mirrors.
>
> If a kid, looking at his very happy parents traipsing through that very happy Disney World, said, "This ain't fun, ma," his ma's heart sank. She wondered where she had gone wrong. Everybody told her what fun family outings to Disney World would be. Golly gee, what was the matter?
> Fun got to be such a big thing that everybody started to look for more and more thrilling ways to supply it. One way was to step up the level of danger so that you could be sure that, no matter what, you would manage to have a little fun.
>
> Television commercials brought a lot of fun and fun-loving folks into the picture. Everything that people in those commercials did looked like fun: taking Polaroid snapshots, buying insurance, mopping the floor, bowling, taking aspirin. The more commercials people watched, the more they wondered when the fun would start in their own lives. It was pretty depressing.
>
> Big occasions were supposed to be fun. Christmas, Thanksgiving and Easter were obviously supposed to be fun. Your wedding day was supposed to be fun. Your honeymoon was supposed to be the epitome of fundom. And so we ended up going through every Big Event we ever celebrated, waiting for the fun to start.
>
> It occurred to me, while I was sitting around waiting for the fun to start, that not much is, and that I should tell you just in case you're worried about your fun capacity.

> I don't mean to put a damper on things. I just mean we ought to treat fun reverently. It is a mystery. It cannot be caught like a virus. It cannot be trapped like an animal. The god of mirth is paying us back for all those years of thinking fun was everywhere by refusing to come to our party. I don't want to blaspheme fun anymore. When fun comes in on little dancing feet, you probably won't be expecting it. In fact, I bet it comes when you're doing your duty, your job, or your work. It may even come on a Tuesday.
>
> I remember one day, long ago, on which I had an especially good time. Pam Davis and I walked to the College Village drug store one Saturday morning to buy some candy. We were about 12 years old. She got her Bit-O-Honey. I got my malted milk balls, chocolate stars, Chunkys, and a small bag of M & M's. We started back to her house. I was going to spend the night. We had the whole day to look forward to. We had plenty of candy. It was a long way to Pam's house but every time we got weary Pam would put her hand over her eyes, scan the horizon like a sailor and say, "Oughta reach home by nightfall," at which point the two of us would laugh until we thought we couldn't stand it another minute. Then after we got calm, she'd say it again. You should have been there. It was the kind of day and friendship and occasion that made me deeply regretful that I had to grow up.
>
> It was fun.

At the beginning of the essay, the author suggests that people are so concerned with having fun that they:

    a. try to find fun in all their experiences

    b. spend a lot of money trying to have fun

    c. join groups to learn how to have fun

    d. avoid new experiences that may not be fun

25. When the author mentions the possibility of people turning into puritans, she is using this word to refer to people who:

    a. lived a long time ago

    b. rarely make a mistake

    c. are serious and reserved

    d. dress in plain and dark clothing

26. What is the author's point about big occasions like holidays?

    a. They go by too quickly to be enjoyed.

    b. They are not as much fun as people expect them to be.

    c. They have become too centered around money.

    d. They help us to appreciate the important events in life.

27. The author assumes that the people reading her essay

    a. probably had fun going to amusement parks as children

    b. prefer dangerous experiences over fun activities

    c. may be worried that they are not having enough fun

    d. enjoy discussing the topic of fun

28. What is the author implying in this paragraph?

> Think of all the things that got the reputation of being fun. Family outings were supposed to be fun.

> Education was supposed to be fun. Work was supposed to be fun. Walt Disney was supposed to be fun. Church was supposed to be fun. Staying fit was supposed to be fun.

    a. It is possible to have fun in a wide range of activities.
    b. A person's reputation is based on how much fun the person has.
    c. Most daily activities are less important than we think.
    d. We should not expect everything in life to be fun.

29. What source should you consult to write a paper on the history of the Roman Empire?
    a. Encyclopedia
    b. Dictionary
    c. Thesaurus
    d. Almanac

30. The next 4 questions are based on the following passage.

Roosevelt:

Much has been given us, and much will rightfully be expected from us. We have duties to others and duties to ourselves; and we can shirk neither. We have become a great nation, forced by the fact of its greatness into relations with the other nations of the Earth, and we must behave as beseems a people with such responsibilities.

Toward all other nations, large and small, our attitude must be one of cordial and sincere friendship. We must show not only in our words, but in our deeds, that we are earnestly desirous of securing their goodwill by acting toward them in a spirit of just and generous recognition of all their rights.

But justice and generosity in a nation, as in an individual, count most when shown not by the weak but by the strong. While ever careful to refrain from wrongdoing others, we must be no less insistent that we are not wronged ourselves. We wish peace, but we wish the peace of justice, the peace of righteousness. We wish it because we think it is right and not because we are afraid. No weak nation that acts manfully and justly should ever have cause to fear us, and no strong power should ever be able to single us out as a subject for insolent aggression.

Our relations with the other powers of the world are important; but still more important are our relations among ourselves. Such growth in wealth, in population, and in power as this nation has seen during the century and a quarter of its national life is inevitably accompanied by a like growth in the problems which are ever before every nation that rises to greatness. Power invariably means both responsibility and danger. Our forefathers faced certain perils which we have outgrown. We now face other perils, the very existence of which it was impossible that they should foresee.

Modern life is both complex and intense, and the tremendous changes wrought by the extraordinary industrial development of the last half century are felt in every fiber of our social and political being. Never before have men tried so vast and formidable an experiment as that of administering the affairs of a continent under the forms of a democratic republic. The conditions which have told for our marvelous material well-being—which have developed to a very high degree our energy, self-reliance, and individual initiative—have also brought the care and anxiety inseparable from the accumulation of great wealth in industrial centers.

Upon the success of our experiment much depends, not only as regards our own welfare, but as regards the welfare of mankind. If we fail, the cause of free self-government throughout the world will rock to its foundations, and therefore our responsibility is heavy, to ourselves, to the world as it is today, and to the generations yet unborn.

There is no good reason why we should fear the future, but there is every reason why we should face it seriously, neither hiding from ourselves the gravity of the problems before us nor fearing to approach these problems with the unbending, unflinching purpose to solve them aright.

Yet, after all, though the problems are new, though the tasks set before us differ from the tasks set before our fathers who founded and preserved this republic, the spirit in which these tasks must be undertaken and these problems faced, if our duty is to be well done, remains essentially unchanged. We know that self-government is difficult. We know that no people needs such high traits of character as that people which seeks to govern its affairs aright through the freely expressed will of the free men who compose it.

But we have faith that we shall not prove false to memories of the men of the mighty past. They did their work, they left us the splendid heritage we now enjoy. We in our turn have an assured confidence that we shall be able to leave this heritage unwasted and enlarged to our children and our children's children. To do so we must show, not merely in great crises, but in the everyday affairs of life, the qualities of practical intelligence, of courage, of hardihood, and endurance, and above all the power of devotion to a lofty ideal, which made great the men who founded this republic in the days of Washington, which made great the men who preserved this republic in the days of Abraham Lincoln

What is the meaning of formidable in the passage?
- a. a conventional undertaking
- b. an unexpected development
- c. a lengthy process
- d. a difficult challenge

31. Roosevelt most likely refers to Washington and Lincoln at the end of the address in order to:
- a. praise the speaking styles of previous presidents
- b. encourage listeners to study history
- c. recall accomplishments from the past
- d. suggest that government was more powerful in the past

32. What is the experiment that Roosevelt describes in this paragraph?

Modern life is both complex and intense, and the tremendous changes wrought by the extraordinary industrial development of the last half century are felt in every fiber of our social and political being. Never before have men tried so vast and formidable an experiment as that of administering the affairs of a continent under the forms of a democratic republic. The conditions which have told for our marvelous material well-being—which have developed to a very high degree our energy, self-reliance, and individual initiative—have also brought the care and anxiety inseparable from the accumulation of great wealth in industrial centers.

- a. The implementation of a democratic form of government on a very large scale
- b. The successful industrialization of a country with a democratic government
- c. The resolution of social problems that come with great wealth and power

    d.   The balance between American power and the need for peaceful relations abroad

33. Which of the following best describes Roosevelt's ideas about the relationship between progress and problems?
    a.   He believes that in the future progress will not lead to problems.
    b.   He believes progress solves most problems once thought unsolvable.
    c.   He believes a nation cannot have progress without also having problems.
    d.   He believes progress can solve only certain types of problems.

34. The next 3 questions are based on the following passage:

I Start to Work

Addie, New York, Lower East Side District, 1900
My father made only four dollars a week and there were six children, so my mother took in work. She would get bundles of unfinished pants from this factory. There would be maybe twenty-five, thirty pants to a bundle. And she would bring them home and finish them, and she would keep my sister and me out of school to help. When she started this, I was eight years old.

All day we would sit in the kitchen and sew. We would turn up the bottoms and sew them, and we would put a lining in the waist and sew that. The next morning she would take the bundle back and get another one. I would go to school maybe once, twice a week.

Jess, Western Nebraska, 1906-1910
Starting when I was fourteen, I spent every summer working on farms. I packed my suitcase and took a train and would be gone for three months.

Every morning I got the team ready. Then the farmer would drive a binder through his wheat and cut it and bind it into bundles. And I would follow behind and stack the bundles on end in shocks so they wouldn't get wet. When the shocking was over, I'd help with the threshing. And when that was done, the summer was gone.

Martha, Philadelphia, 1903
When I was twelve years old my mother came to me, and she said I had to leave school and get a job. We needed the money. So I got a job makin' buttonholes in vests.

It was like nothin'. Just work. Start at seven, work till six, six days a week. I got three cents for every two buttonholes, and I made them by hand. Oh, you had to make an awful lot. The first week I made two hundred and sixty-five, and they gave me four dollars.

Joe, Northern Maine, 1895-1899
The first year I worked in the woods I was fifteen years old. This logging camp was twenty-five, thirty miles from the nearest town.

There was about eighty of us in that camp, and we all slept in log cabins. On each side there'd be bunks and in the middle there'd be a stove and a pile of wood. And they had a cook's room and an eatin' room and that sort of thing.

At night, we'd get together in the eatin' room. And some would play the mouth harp (harmonica) and

---

maybe some would sing or step dance or tell stories. And there'd always be some clown carrying on—like me. Just in fun, I'd go over and throw a dipper of water on somebody. Well, that would always start a roughhouse.

But you had to do things like that to keep your spirits up. Takin' to the woods that way all winter, you worked hard and you never got to town. That first winter I was up there two months straight. When I was eighteen, I stayed five months and eight days before I came out.

What did Martha think about her job?
    a. Her job was tiresome and uninteresting.
    b. Her job was too difficult for children.
    c. Her job was different and exciting.
    d. Her job was better than going to school.

35. Which person had a job at home?
    a. Addie
    b. Jess
    c. Martha
    d. Joe

36. What was one thing Joe found hard about his work?
    a. Getting along with the loggers, who liked to roughhouse
    b. Learning how to cook food on a wood stove
    c. Staying in the woods for several months without going to town
    d. Showing the men on the job that he was strong enough to work

37. Add the numbers 1 and 2. Multiply the resulting sum by 2. Then, before multiplying the result by 4, subtract 1. What is the resulting number?
    a. 20
    b. 23
    c. 24
    d. 5

38. The school offers 7 courses: English, Math, Biology, Chemistry, Physics, Spanish, and French.
If you choose Spanish, you cannot also choose French.
If you choose Biology, you must also choose Chemistry.
If you choose English, you must also choose Math.
Which of the following combinations of classes corresponds to the directions?

    a. English, Math, Biology, Spanish, French
    b. English, Biology, Chemistry, Physics, Spanish
    c. English, Math, Biology, Chemistry, Spanish
    d. English, Math, Biology, Physics, Spanish

39.

> **Vines**
> Grapes
> Kiwi
> Passion fruit
>
> **Bushes**
> Blueberries
> Tomatoes
>
> **Trees**
> Peaches
> Plums
> Apples

Which of the following statements is correct based on the outline above?
- a. Vines and bushes are similar.
- b. Blueberries are more related to tomatoes than peaches.
- c. There are more types of trees than vines.
- d. Peaches are more related to passion fruit than apples.

40. The next two questions are based on the following chart:

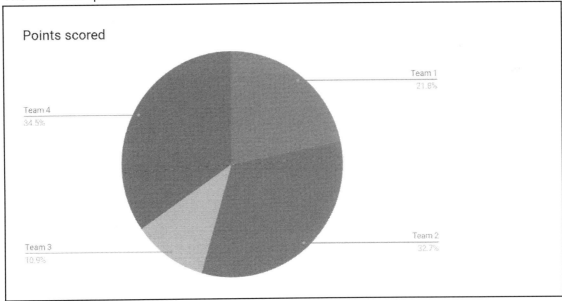

Points scored

Team 1 21.8%
Team 4 34.5%
Team 2 32.7%
Team 3 10.9%

Which combination of team scores is the highest?
- a. Team 1 and Team 4
- b. Team 1, Team 2, and Team 3
- c. Team 2 and Team 4
- d. Team 1 and Team 3

41. Based on the points scored, Team 4's biggest competitor is?
- a. Team 1

b. Team 2

c. Team 3

42. Read the following letter.

Hi Mom,

Your Christmas tree looks beautiful. The kids are really excited about all the presents under the tree and cannot wait to visit you guys next week and open the presents for Christmas. See you soon. Love you!

This letter was most likely written in what month?
   a. January
   b. February
   c. March
   d. December

43. You are writing a research paper on how melatonin affects a person's sleep cycle. Which source should you consult?
   a. An academic study on the number of hours people slept after taking melatonin.
   b. An academic study on how insomnia affects people.
   c. An academic study on how melatonin affects skin color.
   d. A blog post about one person's experience with taking melatonin to treat insomnia.

44. She is very fair skinned.
   Which of the following definitions of "fair" is correct as used in the sentence above?
   a. Beautiful
   b. Light
   c. Just
   d. None of the above

45. I would _____ you to seek a second opinion. Fill in the blank.
   a. advice
   b. advise

46. It is hard to sleep with a guilty _____. Fill in the blank.
   a. conscience
   b. conscious

47.

```
1 2 3 4 5
```
1. Increment each even number by 1.
2. Any time a number repeats, increment the second occurrence of that number by 1.

What is the result?
- a. 1 3 3 5 5
- b. 1 3 4 5 6
- c. 1 4 3 6 5
- d. 2 3 4 5 6

48. Read the following drug label.

Directions:
Take this medicine on an empty stomach, preferably before breakfast.
Take this medication at least 4 hours before taking antacids.

Warning:
Not for children under 5 years old.

Which of the following statement should be a cause for concern?
- a. I gave my 5 year old daughter the medication this morning.
- b. I took the medication right before bedtime.
- c. I took the medication with breakfast.
- d. All of the above.

49. To boil eggs, you need to put a pot, filled with 2 cups of water, on top of the stove. Turn the heat to high and wait for the water to boil. Put the eggs in the pot and cook for 15 minutes.

What is the first step?
- a. Put the pot on top of the stove.
- b. Fill the pot with water.
- c. Put the egg in the pot.
- d. Turn on the stove.

50. He warned that an attack was _____.
- a. eminent
- b. imminent

51. The next 2 questions are based on the following:

Climbing Roses: Lady of Shalott, The Generous Gardener, The Pilgrim

Tree Roses: Charlotte, Mary Rose, Darcy Bussell
Shrub Roses: Mrs. Red, Bonica, The Fairy

Which rose should choose to grow over a trellis?
   a. Lady of Shalott
   b. Charlotte
   c. Mrs. Red
   d. Not enough information

52. Which rose is red?
   a. Mrs. Red
   b. Mary Rose
   c. The Pilgrim
   d. Not enough information

53. The library is 5 miles east of your house. The grocery store is 3 miles west of your house. Starting from your house, you walked to the library. Then you walked to the grocery store and then walked home. How many miles did you walk?
   a. 8 miles
   b. 13 miles
   c. 16 miles
   d. None of the above

English and Language Usage

1. Which of these words indicate contrast?
   a. Furthermore
   b. Moreover
   c. Nevertheless
   d. Additionally

2. I was grounded for skipping school - someone ratted on me. The word "ratted" is an example of
   a. sensory language
   b. informal language
   c. technical language
   d. academic language

3. Those things which are sacred, are to be imparted only to sacred persons; and it is not lawful to impart them to the profane until they have been initiated in the mysteries of the science.
   Based on the paragraph, what is the relationship between the words "sacred" and "profane"?
   a. The two words are antonyms.
   b. The two words are synonyms.
   c. "Sacred" is the root word of "profane."
   d. "Profane" is an outdated word for "sacred."

4. They were left standing upon the corner, staring; down a side street there were two rows of brick houses, and between them a vista: half a dozen chimneys, tall as the tallest of buildings. What is the meaning of vista?
   a. scene
   b. wreck
   c. illusion
   d. fragment

5. She waved back to the man _____ had waved to her.
   a. that
   b. whom
   c. which
   d. who

6. She wheedled and pleaded, but he could not be swayed. Based on the sentence, wheedling is a kind of
   a. Apology
   b. Persuasion
   c. Aggression
   d. Entertainment

7. The class was excited to attend _____ first pep rally.
   a. they're
   b. there
   c. it's
   d. its

8. It is _____ to pack your suitcase the night before a trip.
   a. adviseable
   b. advisable
   c. advizable
   d. advisabel

9. _____ responsible for bringing donuts to the potluck.
   a. There
   b. Their
   c. They're
   d. We

10. Apple trees are deciduous perennials. They lose their leaves and go dormant during the winter. Apple trees fruit in the summer. Everyone loves to eat apples.
    Which of the following sentence does not belong in a well-organized paragraph?
    a. Apple trees are deciduous perennials.
    b. They lose their leaves and go dormant during the winter.
    c. Apple trees fruit in the summer.
    d. Everyone loves to eat apples.

11. Which of the following words is spelled incorrectly?
    a. Absence
    b. Accomodate
    c. Achieve
    d. Acquire

12. Which of the following sentences is correct?
    a. Jacob, along with a couple of friends, have decided to go see a movie tonight.
    b. Jacob, along with a couple of friends, has decided to go see a movie tonight.
    c. Jacob along with a couple of friends has decided to go see a movie tonight.
    d. Jacob along with a couple of friends have decided to go see a movie tonight.

13. The girls gossipped about Alicia in her abcence. Which of the following words are misspelled in the sentence?
    a. Gossipped
    b. Abcence
    c. There are no spelling errors in the sentence.

  d. Both gossipped and abcence are spelled incorrectly.

14. He is very anal, every item in his drawer must be color coded. What is the meaning of "anal" in the sentence?
  a. Near the anus
  b. Uptight
  c. Loose
  d. Fashionable

15. The next 4 questions are based on the following passage:

> People often talk about the beauty of a sunset or sunrise. The Sun is able to inspire many feelings in <u>people</u> awe, wonder, and even delight. Some of the Sun's optical phenomena are so rare and mysterious that for centuries they were believed to have mystical associations. But knowing the scientific explanations for these natural light shows doesn't make them any less Breathtaking.
>
> Rainbows, among the most common optical effects, are caused by a process known as refraction. Refraction takes place when the Sun's light rays are bent, reflected, and <u>split</u> into an arc of color as they pass through drops of water in the atmosphere. This happens because light bends at different angles depending on its wavelength.
>
> Other optical effects are rarer because they require more specific circumstances. One such phenomenon is variously called a parhelion, a mock sun, or <u>referred to as a sundog</u>. Sundogs are caused when flat, hexagonal ice crystals are present in the atmosphere. As the crystals move, light is refracted through the crystals to create a circular effect called a halo. If the crystals are being pushed in one direction by the wind, the light will be concentrated in spots on either side of the halo these bright spots are known as sundogs.

 Choose the correct word or phrase.
 The Sun is able to inspire many feelings in <u>people</u> awe, wonder, and even delight.
  a. people:
  b. people,
  c. people;
  d. correct as is

16. Choose the correct word or phrase.
 One such phenomenon is variously called a parhelion, a mock sun, or <u>referred to as a sundog</u>.
  a. is also called a sundog
  b. a sundog
  c. Sundogs
  d. correct as is

17. Choose the correct word or phrase.

If the crystals are being pushed in one direction by the wind, the light will be concentrated in spots on either side of the <u>halo</u> these bright spots are known as Sundogs.

    a. halo,

    b. halo;

    c. halo/

    d. correct as is

18. Choose the correct word or phrase.

    Refraction takes place when the Sun's light rays are bent, reflected, and <u>split</u> into an arc of color as they pass through drops of water in the atmosphere.

    a. they split

    b. it splits

    c. splits

    d. correct as is

19. The students _____ planning to go to the library tomorrow.

    a. Will

    b. Is

    c. Are

    d. Be

20. Jason was the one that chose the Marriott Hotel. (There was a cheaper hotel nearby.) What is the purpose of the parentheses?

    a. To highlight a belief

    b. To present a contrast

    c. To transition to a new idea

    d. To provide additional information.

21. Martin made a quick tour of the attic to make sure nothing was amiss. What is the meaning of amiss?

    a. Stolen

    b. Shocking

    c. Out of order

    d. Broken into pieces

22. He died of cardiac arrest. What is the meaning of arrest in the sentence?

    a. to slow or stop

    b. to seize or enclose

    c. to manage or direct

    d. to notice or consider

23. Suddenly, away on our left, I saw a faint flickering blue flame.

    In the above sentence, "flickering" is used as

a. A verb
b. A noun
c. An adverb
d. An adjective

24. How can such a humble person hold such sway? Which of the following would best replace the phrase "hold such sway" in the sentence?
    a. Be so confident
    b. Be so modest
    c. Have so much influence
    d. Have so much to say

25. She went to the grocery store.
    What kind of sentence is this?
    a. Simple
    b. Compound
    c. Complex
    d. Compound Complex

26. Which of the following sentences is correct?
    a. My favorite uncle is uncle Jason.
    b. My favorite uncle is Uncle Jason.
    c. My favorite uncle is, uncle Jason.
    d. My favorite uncle is, Uncle Jason.

27. The dog had a tenacious grip on the intruder. What is the meaning of tenacious?
    a. Scary
    b. Not easily pulled apart
    c. Loose
    d. None of the above

28. You must provide a citation when
    a. Using information that is common knowledge
    b. Using information that is not well known
    c. Using information that cannot be attributed to a specific person or group
    d. None of the above

Practice Exam 1 Answers

Science

1. A. 8. The atomic mass (A) is equal to Z (the number of protons) plus N (the number of neutrons). Based on the equation A = Z + N, if you know any two of the following values: atomic mass, number of protons, or number of neutrons, you can solve for the missing value. For example, the atomic number of oxygen is 8 which means it has 8 protons and its atomic mass is 16, so oxygen has 8 neutrons (16 = 8 + N).
2. A. circulatory, muscular, and nervous.
3. C. 50%. Since Dog W's dad had brown coating (bb) and Dog W's mother had black coating (Bb or BB), Dog W must be Br. Since Dog X has brown coating, it must be bb. From the punnett square below, 50% of Dog W and Dog X's offspring would have brown coating.

	B	b
b	Bb	bb
b	Bb	bb

4. C. Chlorine (Cl) with 17 protons, 18 neutrons, and 18 electrons. All the other choices are neutral (same number of protons and neutrons) or positively charged (more protons than neutrons).
5. B. The liver. The appendix is unnecessary for survival. You have two lungs and two kidneys so you can survive the loss of one lung or kidney.
6. A. DNA Sequences
7. B. Nervous and endocrine
8. A. Elements to molecules to cells to tissues to organs. B is wrong because cells are simpler than tissues. C is wrong because elements are simpler than molecules. D is wrong because tissues are simpler than organs.
9. A. Dilate blood vessels. When nerves in the skin detect that the body is overheated (hyperthermia), the integumentary system will trigger blood vessels to dilate and sweat glands to produce and release sweat. Sweat evaporating from the skin surface cools the body. Dilated blood vessels allow more blood to travel to the surface of the skin where excess heat is released to the environment through thermal radiation. Answers B and C occur when the body is cold.
10. B. Heart and lungs.
11. A. The offspring show genetic variation from the parents.
12. B. A hormone. Antibodies are used by the immune system to fight illness. Nucleic acid is involved with protein synthesis. Sugar is broken down to provide energy.

13. D. It receives signals from the internal and external environments.

14. D. Both the chemical and physical properties of a compound are different from the properties of the elements of which it is composed.
15. A. Mutations in the genes regulating limb development led to gradual changes in structure, which provided a selective advantage to the organisms.
16. D. The two birds mate and produce fertile offspring.
17. C. The diaphragm muscle contracts to expand the chest and draw air into the respiratory system.
18. B. Water molecules attract ions and the charged parts of molecules.
19. B. Stomach and small intestine
20. A.
21. C. Malaria reduces oxygen transport to cells.
22. A. Heart rate increases when a person exercises.
23. A. 26. Gametes contain half the number of chromosomes of the parent cell.
24. C. An electrical signal. Dendrites branch from the soma, receive information from other neurons, and carry that information to the soma. When dendrites receive information or an impulse, it generates an action potential (electrical signal) that travels to the soma and then, through the axon. Action potentials are like switches, they are either triggered on or off; there is no in between. Most neurons receive signals through the dendrites and send out signals through the axon. Neurons communicate with other neurons or cells through junctions or spaces called synapses. Communication in synapses can occur chemically (most of the time) or electrically.
25. D. A section of mRNA with the base sequence AUCCUCGUA. Answer choice A is wrong because amino acids are produced during translation, not transcription. Answer choice B is wrong because DNA sequences are transcribed into mRNA, not tRNA. See section on transcription and translation for more detail.
26. C. Transmission of nerve impulses. Neurons are nerve cells that transmit information to other nerve, muscle, or gland cells of the body; so damage to neurons would interfere with transmission of nerve impulses.
27. B. Lack of energy. As oxygen levels decrease, energy levels will decrease as well.
28. D. to push food toward an organ that breaks down macromolecules
29. C. Cushioning and resisting compression at joints. Ligaments are fibrous connective tissue that connect bone to bone. Tendons connect muscles to bones. Cartilage is connective tissue that acts as a cushion between bones. A joint is where two bones meet.
30. B. Body cells will receive less oxygen than usual. Red blood cells contain hemoglobin. Hemoglobin is a protein that is rich in iron and helps with transporting oxygen. Less blood means less oxygen.
31. C. Removing toxins from blood. The liver filters the blood coming from the digestive tract, detoxifies chemicals, and metabolizes drugs. It also produces bile and stores it in the gallbladder.
32. D. More growth hormone is released from the pituitary gland when the level of growth hormone in the blood falls too low.
33. D. Sensory neurons. The sensory neurons sends sensory information from the body to the CNS.

34. A. Fallopian tubes. Fertilization occurs in the fallopian tubes. If an egg is fertilized, it will travel to the uterus and implant in the endometrium.

35. B. Pancreas. The pancreas secretes hormones that control blood glucose levels. It releases insulin when blood glucose levels are high; insulin increases cell uptake of glucose, reducing the levels of glucose in blood. The pancreas releases glucagon when blood glucose levels are low; glucagon causes cells to release glucose into the blood. The pineal gland releases melatonin to regulate sleep cycles.

36. B. Innate immune system. The innate immune system responds to pathogens by causing inflammation and/or fever. The adaptive immune system triggers an immune response when it detects pathogens with specific antigens.

37. A. Concentration of sugar water. An independent variable stands alone and is not affected by other variables. A dependent variable depends on or is affected by the independent variable.

38. C. Covalent. Covalent bonds occur when atoms share electrons instead of gaining or losing electrons. Ionic bonds are bonds between ions with opposite charges. An ionic bond occurs when an atom gives up one or more electrons (becoming positively charged) and another atom accepts one or more electrons (becoming negatively charged); the positively charged atom and negatively charged atom bond because opposite charges attract. An example of an ionic bond is sodium chloride (table salt).

39. C. Alveoli. The lower away includes the trachea (tube that connects the pharynx to the bronchi), bronchi (tubes that lead to the lungs), and alveoli. The alveoli are tiny air sacs of the lungs where oxygen and carbon dioxide are exchanged. Alveoli diffuse oxygen to the red blood cells and pulmonary capillaries diffuse carbon dioxide from the body to the alveoli.

40. A. Sagittal plane. The sagittal plane or midline is a vertical line that divides the body into left and right sections. The transverse plane is a horizontal line, parallel to the ground, at the level of the navel and divides the body into superior (top) and inferior (bottom) sections. The coronal plane is a vertical line that divides the body into anterior (front) and posterior (back) sections.

41. B. Poor. Blood flows through the body in a closed circulatory system of two loops: the pulmonary and systemic loop. Blood actually flows through the heart twice: once when oxygen-rich blood flows through the heart to the body and once more when oxygen-poor blood flows through the heart to the lungs.

42. A. Control Group.

43. B. 10. 10 decimeters = 1 m

44. B. Heart muscles relax. During systole, the heart muscles contract. During diastole, the heart muscles relax. Blood pressure is a measure of the pressure during systole (systolic pressure) and diastole (diastolic pressure).

45. A. Group of plants given no sugar. The control group is a group in the experiment that does not receive any treatment or changes; the control group is the standard or benchmark to which comparisons are made.

46. B. Temperature and pressure. The state of matter is most affected by temperature and pressure. Temperature and pressure influence the state of matter by affecting intramolecular forces between particles.
47. B. Lipids. There are 4 major types of macromolecules: carbohydrates, lipids, proteins, and nucleic acids. Carbohydrates, such as sugars and starches, are composed of carbon, hydrogen, and oxygen. Lipids or fats consist mainly of hydrocarbon chains.
48. A. The adrenal glands are divided into two parts: the cortex (outer part) and medulla (inner part). The medulla regulates hormones associated with the "fight or flight" or stress response such as epinephrine (adrenaline), noradrenaline, etc. The cortex regulates hormones such as cortisol (which helps regulate metabolism and helps your body respond to stress) and aldosterone (which helps control blood pressure).
49. A. Frontal lobe. The frontal lobe is responsible for key functions such as decision making, problem solving, emotional expression, voluntary movement, memory, and personality. The parietal lobe is mainly responsible for processing sensory information such as taste, temperature, touch, spatial awareness, etc. The occipital lobe is mainly responsible for processing visual input. The temporal lobe is mainly responsible for processing auditory input.
50. C. The bladder. The kidneys filter blood, produce urine, and help regulate blood pressure. The ureters carry waste from the kidneys to the bladder. The bladder stores urine and the urethra is where urine exits out of the body.
51. B. Most neurons receive signals through the dendrites and send out signals through the axon. Neurons communicate with other neurons or cells through junctions or spaces called synapses.
52. A. The heart contains one-way valves that ensures blood flows in the correct direction.
53. C. Multiple sclerosis. The axon is covered with a layer of myelin sheath (made from glial cells); the myelin sheath increases the speed at which electrical impulses travel through the axon. Demyelinating disorders, such as multiple sclerosis, reduce the speed at which signals travel through the axon.

Mathematics

1. A. 2. Using PEMDAS, $\frac{((40) + (20))}{(30)} = \frac{60}{30} = 2$.

2. B. The data shows a positive correlation; as x increases, y also increases.

3. C. 180.8 cubic inches. The equation to find the volume of a cylinder is $V = \pi r^2 *$ height. The height is 6.4 inches. The radius is 6 inches/2 = 3 inches. $V = 3.14 * 3^2 * 6.4 = 180.8$.

4. C. Many solutions. One solution is x = 1 and y = ½. Another solution is x=0 and y= 3/2.

5. C. 240. 210 + 160 = 370 girls were surveyed. 30 + 100 = 130 boys were surveyed. 370 - 130 = 240.

6. B. Kim. Speed is distance/time. See graph below for the calculated speeds.

	Interval A Speed	Interval B Speed	Interval C Speed
Mary	(0.2 - 0)/(4-0) = 0.2/4=0.05	(0.6 - 0.2)/(7-4) = 0.4/3 = 0.13	(0.7 - 0.6)/(15-7) = 0.1 /8 = 0.01
Kim	(0.3 - 0)/(4-0) = 0.3 /4 = 0.08	(0.3 - 0.3)/(7-4) = 0 /3 = 0	(0.7 - 0.3)(15-7) = 0.4 /8 = 0.05

7. B. Kim stopped during interval B.

8. A. Mary rode slower in interval C than in interval B. Kim rode 0 miles/min in interval B and 0.05 miles/min in interval C, so she rode faster in interval C than in interval B.

9. C. Both Mary and Kim live 0.7 miles from school since that is the distance they both travel in 15 minutes.

10. B. 42 degrees. If the transversal line crosses two or more parallel lines, all acute angles are equal to each other and all obtuse angles are equal to each other, as shown in the diagram below. Since the angles of a triangle add up to 180 degrees, you can solve for b using the following equation: 48 + 90 + b = 180. B = 42.

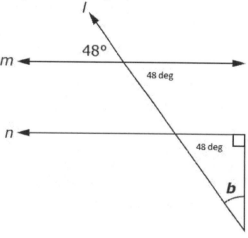

11. B. 49% liked mint. 86 people out of 175 people like mint, so 86/175 = 0.49. 100 * 0.49 = 49%

12. D. 60% like strawberry. 105 out of 175 people like strawberry, so 105/175 = 0.6. 100 * 0.6 = 60%

13. D. Surveying employees from each sales department at each location would provide the most reliable results.

14. C. 4/3 cups per teaspoon. We have to solve for $\dfrac{\text{cups}}{\text{teaspoon}}$ and since there is ⅔ cup of sugar per ½ teaspoon of vanilla, the equation is: $\dfrac{2/3\ \text{cup}}{1/2\ \text{teaspoon}}$. To divide fractions, you multiply the top fraction, by the reciprocal of the bottom fraction. $\dfrac{2}{3} * \dfrac{2}{1} = \dfrac{4}{3}$.

15. B. 16 pint water jug.

16. D. Between 8 and 10 months. The truck is driven at a rate of 40,000 miles/ 52 weeks, which equals 769 miles/week. The truck currently has 119,866 miles on it, so will need to driven 30,134 miles (150,000 - 119,866) before it needs a new engine. The truck will need to be driven 39.2 weeks (30134 miles * $\dfrac{1\ \text{week}}{769\ \text{miles}}$ = 39.2 weeks). There are 4 weeks in a month, so 39.2/4 = 9.8 months.

17. B. $\dfrac{n - 4 - 5}{3}$. After giving her brother 4 apples and keeping 5 for herself, the number of apples she has left is n - 4 - 5. She then divides the number of apples she has left by 3.

18. C. 77 cents. Since fractions of an ounce are rounded up, we have to pay for 3 ounces. 33 + 2(22) = 77.

19. B. 6. The formula for calculating the area of a rectangle or square is A = L * W. The area of the rectangle is 2 * 18 = 36. Since squares have equal length sides, 36 = L * L = L². L = $\sqrt{36}$ = 6.

20. B. 1/12. There are 2 out of 8 slices left, so 2/8. You then divide the 2/8 slice by 3, so $\dfrac{2/8}{3}$. When dividing fractions, you multiply the top fraction by the reciprocal of the bottom fraction, so $\dfrac{2}{8} * \dfrac{1}{3} = \dfrac{2}{24}$ which reduces to $\dfrac{1}{12}$.

21. A. 4x² + 30x + 56. Since f(x) = x² + x, f(g(x)) = (g(x))² + g(x) = (2x + 7)² + (2x+7) = (2x + 7)(2x + 7) + 2x + 7 = 4x² + 14x + 14x + 49 + 2x + 7 = 4x² + 30x + 56.

22. D. 36. 48 - 12 = 36.

23. B. 3.6 in. The conversion ratio is $\dfrac{3/4 \text{ inch}}{10 \text{ feet}} = \dfrac{3 \text{ inch}}{40 \text{ feet}}$. Then multiply the measurement you want to convert by the conversion ratio. $48 \text{ feet} * \left(\dfrac{3 \text{ inch}}{40 \text{ feet}}\right) = 3.6$ inches.

24. C. 5. 40% of those scheduled do not keep their reservations. To find 40% of 13, multiply 13 by $0.40 = 5.2$.

25. A. The number has been decreased by 990. After increasing the digit in the tens place by 1 and decreasing the digit in the thousands place by 1, the resulting number is 36,251. $37241 - 36251 = 990$.

26. C. x = 3. From the first equation, x = 1 - 2y. From replacing x with 1 - 2y in the second equation, we get 2(1 - 2y) = 7 which resolves to 2 - 5y = 7. Y = -1. Now, solve for x by substituting y with -1. X = 1 - 2y = 1 - 2(-1) = 1 + 2 = 3.

27. 8. From the graph, 20 out of 100 people have a pulse rate above 80 which means that 20% of the group have a pulse rate over 80. Out of a group of 40, 8 people (40 * 0.2 = 8) are expected to have a pulse rate over 80.

28. ¼. From the graph, there is a total of 4 brown puppies. Of the 4 brown puppies, 1 is male; so the probability is ¼.

29. D. 11. The sequence is as follows: ½, 2, 5, 11.

30. C. 2(F - 1) and F - 1

31. C. $125,000. The rate of taxation is $\dfrac{\$42}{\$1000}$. If x represents the value of the property, then $x * \dfrac{\$42}{\$1000} = \$5250$. Solving for x, x = $125,000.

32. A. $5. Calculate the cost for y= 0 and y=2 and then find the difference.
C = 2.50(0) + 13 = 13.
C = 2.50 (2) + 13 = 18.
18 - 13 = 5.

33. C. 2x. The problem states the length is two times the width and the width is represented by x.

34. D. 2x². The problem states the length is two times the width and the width is represented by x. The area of a rectangle is length * width; so $2x * x = 2x^2$.

35. C. Centimeter.

36. B. Martin. Luis' mixture contains a ratio of $\dfrac{6 \text{ oz cherry}}{53 \text{ oz water}} = 0.11$. Martin's mixture contains a ratio of $\dfrac{5 \text{ oz cherry}}{42 \text{ oz water}} = 0.12$. Since 0.12 is greater than 0.11, Martin's mixture contains more cherry syrup.

Reading

1. D. Mott's emphasis on the "higher nature" in written works shows her belief that forms of popular entertainment should have a moral component.

2. D. Mott objects to the lecture she attends because its apparent eloquence conceals ideas she sees as damaging to women's progress.

3. A. In paragraph 4, Mott makes a point that the sentimental novels previously marketed to women are giving way to more substantial fare.

4. B. Mott names the lecture she attends as an example of how much there still is to combat but proceeds to discuss a number of ways in which the women's movement has made positive strides.

5. D. The phrase and subsequent surrounding text indicate that Blackwell wishes to accomplish her goals without having to disguise herself or study elsewhere. She wants the public to know what she intends to accomplish.

6. C. The phrase "in the light of day" indicates that Blackwell wishes to accomplish her goals with everyone knowing about it.

7. A. Blackwell mentions that she applied to many medical colleges without gaining entry, but that did not deter her from accomplishing her goal of becoming a doctor.

8. D. This phrase describes how Blackwell approached the obstacles she faced gaining entry into a medical college.

9. A. Mott's repeated appeals for achieving an "elevated position" for women and Blackwell's pronouncement that she is on a "moral crusade" support this interpretation.

10. A,D. Answer choice 'a' describes Thisbe's and Pyramus's behavior and state of mind, revealing how they experience the same love for one another. Answer choice 'd' shows that both Thisbe and Pyramus share their affection for one another.

11. B. True love finds ways to overcome any obstacle. Despite the obstacle of the wall, the love of Pyramus and Thisbe remains strong

12. B. The structure of the wall. Pyramus and Thisbe use a defect in the wall (which otherwise is an obstacle) in order to communicate, which they would not otherwise be able to do.

13. D. The use of the word "envious" refers to the idea that the wall is keeping Pyramus and Thisbe physically apart.

14. D. The details about Juliet's kinsmen and the violence they would perhaps inflict on Romeo pervade the rest of the passage, giving an underlying tension to the exchanges that follow.

15. A,C. Option A: Although Ovid only says that Pyramus's and Thisbe's fathers forbid their marriage, Shakespeare dramatizes the family disapproval by suggesting that they may kill Romeo if they find him there. Option C: While Passage 1 presents the characters as having nearly identical sentiments, Romeo and Juliet's exchanges are full of questions and mixed emotions.

16. B. This quote reveals the theme in both passages that love can overcome obstacles.

17. C. Shakespeare removes the physical barrier that Ovid leaves between his characters and replaces it with the cover of darkness, thus opening up more dramatic possibilities in the scene.

18. D. Wet food three or four times a day. The instructions say: "Until kittens are three months old, feed them Meow-Wow Dinner wet about three or four times a day".

19. C. Leave the food in the bowl for it. The instructions say to consult the veterinarian if the cat's lack of appetite continues for more than a couple of days, so answer 'a' is incorrect. The instructions do not mention anything about taking bowls away or giving the food to kittens instead, so answers c and d are wrong. The instructions do say that cats like to nibble often instead of having a full meal at one time, so answer 'c' makes sense.

20. B. He kept having fearful thoughts even though he knew there was no danger. In the passage, the man says: "Knowing they were not there made me defenseless against them and perhaps more afraid.", which tells us he was fearful of things that weren't physically there. There was no mention of hearing voices or dangerous animals outside. The man did mention that his dog wasn't behaving as usual, but did not mention being worried that the dog was sick.

21. C. Lessen the problems caused by technology. Mitigate means to make less grave.

22. A. Express ideas clearly. Articulate means expressing ideas clearly.

23. C. The paragraph is about mountains in Colorado. When gold was discovered in Colorado does not relate to mountains in Colorado.

24. A. Try to find fun in all their experiences. The author doesn't mention anything about the amount of money spent on fun nor does the author discuss how to have fun (joining groups, new experiences, etc.), so answers b, c, and d are incorrect.

25. C. Are serious and reserved. Looking at the sentence: " if we didn't have a little fun every day we would turn into (sakes alive!) puritans", suggests that puritans are people who don't have "a little fun every day"; serious and reserved are very different or opposite of fun.

26. B. They are not as much fun as people expect them to be. The author does not discuss how quickly time passes by, how much money is spent, or what is important in life so answers a, c, and d are wrong.

27. C. May be worried that they are not having enough fun. In the passage, the author writes: "It occurred to me, while I was sitting around waiting for the fun to start, that not much is, and that I should tell you just in case you're worried about your fun capacity.", which suggests the author thinks readers may be worried about their fun capacity.

28. D. We should not expect everything in life to be fun. The fact that the author uses the term "supposed to be fun" suggests expectations of fun that were not fulfilled. The paragraph does not discuss the importance of fun or work nor a person's reputation so answers b and c are wrong. The paragraph states activities that are "supposed to be fun" suggesting that they are not fun, so answer 'a' is incorrect.

29. An encyclopedia. A dictionary is used to find the definition of words. A thesaurus is used to find synonyms and antonyms for words. An almanac is used to find information about the weather.

30. D. A difficult challenge.

31. C. recall accomplishments from the past. The passage does not mention anything about speaking styles, studying history, or whether the government had more power in the past, so answers a, b, and d are wrong.

32. A. The implementation of a democratic form of government on a very large scale. Roosevelt says "an experiment as that of administering the affairs of a continent under the forms of a democratic republic", "the affairs of a continent" are not restricted to industrialization, social problems, or balance of power so answers b, c, and d are incorrect.

33. C. He believes a nation cannot have progress without also having problems. Roosevelts says: "There is no good reason why we should fear the future, but there is every reason why we should face it seriously, neither hiding from ourselves the gravity of the problems before us nor fearing to approach these problems with the unbending, unflinching purpose to solve them aright.", so clearly he believes there will be problems in the future so answer 'a' is incorrect. He does not mention any problems that were once or are unsolvable, so answer b and d are incorrect.

34. A. Her job was tiresome and uninteresting. B and C are wrong because Martha says the work was like "nothin", which likely means the work was not difficult or exciting. D is wrong because there is nothing in the paragraph that suggests Martha preferred her job better than going to school.

35. A. Addie. In the passage, Addie says: "And she would bring them home and finish them, and she would keep my sister and me out of school to help."

36. C. Staying in the woods for several months without going to town. The author says: "But you had to do things like that to keep your spirits up. Takin' to the woods that way all winter, you worked hard and you never got to town.", the "but" keyword tells us that his spirit wasn't always up or good and the statement that follows (working hard and never going to town) brought his spirit down.

37. 20. First, 1 + 2 = 3. Then multiply by 2 (3*2) = 6. Then subtract 1 (6-1) = 5. Then multiply by 4 (5 *4) = 20.

38. C. Answer A violates the rule that Spanish and French cannot be chosen together. Answer B violates the rule that English must be chosen with Math. Answer D violates the rule that Biology must be chosen with Chemistry.

39. B. Blueberries and tomatoes grow on bushes, whereas peaches grow on trees. From the outline above, we cannot determine if vines and bushes are similar.

40. C. The combined scores of Team 2 and Team 4 is 32.7% + 34.5% = 67.2% which is the highest of all the combination choices listed as options.

41. C. Team 3 scored the second highest number of points, so they are most likely Team 4's biggest competitor.

42. D. In the letter, it says they will visit next week to open Christmas presents, so this letter was most likely written in December.

43. A. An academic study on the number of hours people slept after taking melatonin is the most relevant and reliable information to use for the research paper. A single person's account on a blog post would not be considered reliable information for a research paper. How insomnia affects people or their skin color is not directly relevant to how melatonin affects a person's sleep cycle.

44. B. As used in the sentence, "fair" means light skinned.

45. B. Advise means to give someone a recommendation or advice.

46. A. Conscience means a sense of right and wrong. Conscious means to be awake or aware of your surroundings.

47. B. 1 3 4 5 6. First, increment each even number by 1, which gets you 1 3 3 5 5. Then increment the second occurrence of each repeated number, which gets you 1 3 4 5 6.

48. C. "I took the medication with breakfast" should be cause for concern since the directions say to take the medicine on an empty stomach. The label says "not for children under 5 years old", but the daughter is 5 (not under 5), so that is not a cause for concern. Though the medication should preferably be taken before breakfast, taking the medication before bedtime is not necessarily a concern; we do not know if the person's stomach was or was not empty before bedtime, so we cannot definitively determine that the statement was concerning.

49. B. The first step is to fill the pot with water.

50. B. Imminent means about to happen. Eminent means prominent or distinguished.

51. A. Lady of Shalott is a climbing rose; climbing roses grow over trellises.

52. D. There is not enough information to answer this question. Just because a rose is named "Mrs. Red" does not necessarily mean it is red in color.

53. C. 16 miles. Walking to the library from the house is 5 miles. Walking from the library to the grocery store is 8 miles. Walking from the grocery store, back to the house is 3 miles. 8 + 5 + 3 = 16.

English and Language Usage

1. C. Nevertheless indicates that what follows is in contrast with the previous sentence fragment.
2. B. informal language
3. A. The two words are antonyms.
4. A. scene.
5. D. Who. "That" and "Which" refer to things, not a person. "Whom" should be used to refer to the object of a verb or preposition.
6. B. Persuasion. Wheedle means to try and persuade using flattery.
7. D. its. The subject of the sentence is "the class," which is singular, so requires a singular pronoun. They is a plural pronoun. "There" refers to a location. "It's" means "it is" and does not imply possession.
8. B. advisable.
9. C. They're. "Their" implies possession, which would not be appropriate for this sentence. "There" refers to a place. "They're" is a contraction of "they" and "are".
10. D. All of the sentences relate to how apple tree grow, except for sentence D.
11. B. "Accomodate" should be spelled "accommodate".
12. B. Jacob, along with a couple of friends, has decided to go see a movie tonight. Jacob is the subject and is singular, so the singular verb "has" is required. The phrase "along with a couple of friends" does not change the subject.
13. B. The correct spelling is absence.
14. B. Uptight.
15. A. This option shows the correct use of a colon in a sentence to precede a list of ideas.
16. B. This option shows the correct use of parallelism in a sentence.
17. B. This option shows the correct use of a semicolon to join two closely related independent clauses.
18. D. This option shows the correct use of the verb in the sentence.
19. C. The subject "students" is plural, so the plural verb "are" should be used.
20. D. To provide additional information.
21. C. Out of order.
22. A. to slow or stop
23. D. adjective. "Flickering" was used to describe the flame (a noun), so it is an adjective.
24. C. Have so much influence. Sway means to influence or control.
25. A. Simple. Simple sentences contain one independent clause. Compound sentences contain two or more independent clauses. The two clauses are usually joined using a coordinating conjunction (for, and, nor, but, or, yet, and so). Complex sentences contain an independent clause and at least one dependent clause. Compound-Complex sentences contain two or more independent clauses and one or more dependent clauses.
26. B. My favorite uncle is Uncle Jason. Titles are capitalized if they immediately precede the name. A comma is not needed in the sentence.

27. B. Not easily pulled apart.

28. B. Using information that is not well known. You must provide citations when: using direct quotes, using ideas from another author or source, and using information that is not well known. You do not need to provide citations when: using information that is common knowledge and using information that cannot be attributed to a specific person or group.

Practice Exam 2

Science

1. Which part of the digestive system eliminates solid wastes from the human body?
    a. kidneys
    b. liver
    c. pharynx
    d. Rectum

2. Carbon monoxide is a poisonous gas because it competes with the gas that binds to hemoglobin in red blood cells. Which of the following would be most directly affected by carbon monoxide poisoning?
    a. fat digestion
    b. cellular respiration
    c. synthesis of proteins
    d. breakdown of wastes

3. Which characteristic is shared by all cells?
    a. They need energy.
    b. They reproduce sexually.
    c. They make their own food.
    d. They move from place to place.

4. When the equation below is balanced and all coefficients are reduced to their lowest whole-number values, the coefficient for H2O is

    $$C_3H_8 + O_2 \rightarrow H_2O + CO_2$$

    a. 2
    b. 3
    c. 4
    d. 6

5. When sulfuric acid, H_2SO_4, is broken down into separate elements, how many different elements result?
    a. Two
    b. Three
    c. Six
    d. Seven

6. The table below lists some problems associated with four organs of the human digestive system.

Organ	Problem
1	Acid inside this organ begins to dissolve some of its tissue lining.
2	An infection prevents the movement of nutrients through this organ's walls into the bloodstream.
3	Inflamed tissue prevents the smooth passage of food through this organ after swallowing.
4	Swelled-up veins make eliminating wastes from this organ difficult.

Which organ is most likely the stomach?
- a. organ 1
- b. organ 2
- c. organ 3
- d. organ 4

7. Which of the following describes how a large mouse population with high genetic diversity will most likely be affected by a sudden, significant environmental change?
- a. All of the individuals within the population will reproduce at a higher rate, leading to a decrease in genetic diversity.
- b. New traits will arise as a result of new selective pressures in the environment, leading to an increase in genetic diversity.
- c. Only those individuals best adapted to the new environment will survive and reproduce, leading to a decrease in genetic diversity.
- d. Only some individuals will develop traits to help them survive in the new environment, leading to an increase in genetic diversity.

8. In which of the following ways does the respiratory system help to maintain homeostasis during exercise?
- a. Reserves of oxygen are built up in the alveoli.
- b. The pharynx supplies glucose so that the muscles can produce ATP.
- c. Breathing rate is increased to exchange oxygen and carbon dioxide more rapidly.
- d. The lungs release hemoglobin so that the blood can carry more oxygen to tissues.

9. Which of the following is a reason for DNA replication in skin cells?
- a. to produce identical daughter skin cells
- b. to enable the skin cells to make more proteins
- c. to allow the skin cells to adapt to a changing environment
- d. to ensure daughter skin cells will have higher genetic diversity

10. Which of the following is the chemical formula for an element?
    a. H_2O
    b. NaCl
    c. Cl_2
    d. NH_3

11. The feather color of Andalusian chickens is controlled by a single gene with two alleles. A cross between a true-breeding, white-feathered Andalusian hen and a true-breeding, black-feathered Andalusian rooster results in 100% blue-feathered Andalusian offspring. Which of the following describes the inheritance pattern for feather color in these chickens?
    a. It is a polygenic pattern because more than two phenotypes are possible.
    b. It is a dominant-recessive pattern because both parents are true breeding.
    c. It is a sex-linked pattern because the hen and the rooster have different feather colors.
    d. It is a codominant pattern because the heterozygous offspring have a different phenotype than either parent.

12. In the presence of the enzyme CPK, the reaction below can occur in muscle cells.

    $$\text{Phosphocreatine} + \text{ADP} \xrightarrow{\text{CPK}} \text{Creatine} + \text{ATP}$$

    Based on this information, when should the CPK enzyme be the most active?
    a. during sleep, when body temperature is low
    b. during exercise, when the need for energy is high
    c. during digestion, when the need for glucose is high
    d. during periods of growth, when nutrient levels are low

13. Secretions from the pancreas contain compounds called lipases. Lipases increase the rate of digestion of lipids. Lipases are an example of which of the following?
    a. enzymes
    b. hormones
    c. nucleic acids
    d. simple sugars

14. Which of the following is always part of normal sexual reproduction?
    a. The male produces gametes by mitosis.
    b. An offspring looks identical to the parents at birth.
    c. The female carries only one fertilized egg at a time.
    d. An offspring receives half its chromosomes from each parent.

15. The stored information in DNA codes for which of the following?
    a. proteins
    b. simple sugars

c. mitochondria when energy is needed

d. large vacuoles when nutrients are abundant

16. During exercise, a person's muscles need a constant supply of ATP. To meet this need, the rate of which of the following processes increases?
    a. cellular respiration
    b. mitosis
    c. protein synthesis
    d. transcription

17. T-cells are responsible for?
    a. Detecting antigens
    b. Storing information for creating antibodies
    c. Producing antibodies
    d. None of the above

18. Which of the following represents a path that a nerve impulse can travel in the nervous system?
    a. brain → motor neuron → spinal cord
    b. brain → sensory neuron → motor neuron
    c. sensory neuron → spinal cord → brain
    d. motor neuron → spinal cord → sensory neuron

19. The atomic number of oxygen is 8. How many protons does oxygen have?
    a. 8
    b. 16
    c. 24
    d. Cannot be determined.

20. What hormone is released when blood sugar levels are low?
    a. Insulin
    b. Glucagon
    c. Thyroxine
    d. None of the above

21. Anna is setting up an experiment to study how time spent studying affects student test scores. The student test scores are an example of:
    a. A control variable
    b. An independent variable
    c. A dependent variable
    d. A placebo

22. Which valve closes over the trachea during swallowing to prevent choking?
    a. Nasopharynx
    b. Oropharynx
    c. Larynx
    d. Epiglottis

23. Muscle fiber cells have a lot of _____ to provide the cells with energy.
    a. Ribosomes
    b. Mitochondria
    c. Vesicles
    d. Centrosomes

24. What divides the body into anterior and posterior sections?
    a. Sagittal plane
    b. Transverse plane
    c. Coronal plane
    d. None of the above

25. Oxygen poor blood enters the heart through
    a. The open circulatory system
    b. The pulmonary loop
    c. The systemic loop
    d. None of the above

26. The most populous blood vessels in the body are
    a. Arteries
    b. Capillaries
    c. Veins

27. Which layer of the skin contains nerve endings and hair follicles?
    a. Epidermis
    b. Dermis
    c. Subcutaneous
    d. None of the above

28. An experiment should only have 1 independent variable.
    a. True
    b. False

29. The fact that phospholipids are both hydrophilic and hydrophobic is important to the function of
    a. The cell wall
    b. The cell membrane
    c. Ribosomes

d. Cell plasma

30. What type of muscles are typically found in the intestines?
    a. Cardiac
    b. Smooth
    c. Skeletal
    d. Striated

31. Damage to what lobe would affect your hearing?
    a. Frontal lobe
    b. Parietal lobe
    c. Occipital lobe
    d. Temporal lobe

32. What are the functional units of the kidney?
    a. Ureters
    b. Renal arteries
    c. Nephrons
    d. Bladder

33. _____ transmits signals faster than _____.
    a. Electrical synapses, chemical synapses
    b. Chemical synapses, electrical synapses

34. If blood calcium levels are low, the parathyroid glands sense the decrease and secrete more parathyroid hormone to increase calcium release from the bones and increase calcium uptake into the bloodstream. This is an example of
    a. A negative feedback loop
    b. A positive feedback loop

35. The inability for heart muscles to respond to electrical impulse will result in
    a. A faster heartbeat
    b. A slower heartbeat
    c. No changes to the heartbeat
    d. Cardiac arrest

36. _____ is where all the nerve synapses in the brain are located and where the actual processing of signals happen.
    a. Grey matter
    b. White matter

37. In the periodic table, the atomic radius
    a. Increases as you move up
    b. Increases from left to right

c. Decreases from left to right

d. Decreases as you move down

38. What hormone stimulates the uterus to contract during labor?
    a. Prolactin
    b. Oxytocin
    c. Luteinizing hormone
    d. Vasopressin

39. What connects muscles to bones?
    a. Ligaments
    b. Tendons
    c. Cartilage
    d. Joints

40. The pulmonary arteries contain
    a. Oxygen poor blood
    b. Oxygen rich blood

41. Muscles work in group; one muscle will contract, while the other relaxes. The muscle that relaxes is called
    a. The agonist
    b. The antagonist

42. Where are most nutrients absorbed in the body?
    a. Mouth
    b. Stomach
    c. Small intestine
    d. Large intestine

43. Phagocytes
    a. Eat bacteria
    b. Bind to antigens
    c. Only kills host cells that display specific antigens
    d. Release interferon which causes nearby cells to increase their defense

44. The pituitary gland controls the hypothalamus.
    a. True
    b. False

45. Osmosis is important for
    a. Maintaining cellular water levels
    b. Transporting nutrients

c. Cell to cell diffusion

d. All of the above.

46. As electronegativity increases, ionization energy
   a. Increases
   b. Decreases

47. What would be affected if the parathyroid gland was damaged?
   a. Blood sugar levels
   b. Sleep cycles
   c. Secondary sex characteristics
   d. Bone density

48. The peripheral nervous system is divided into the sympathetic and parasympathetic systems.
   a. True
   b. False

49. Which duct carries sperm from the scrotum to the urethra?
   a. Testes
   b. Epididymis
   c. Vas deferens
   d. Prostate gland

50. In which of the following would blood pressure be the lowest?
   a. Aorta
   b. Renal artery
   c. Pulmonary artery
   d. Pulmonary vein

51. A _____ causes the uterine lining to shed.
   a. Drop in progesterone levels
   b. Increase in estrogen levels
   c. Increase in oestrogen levels
   d. Increase in FSH levels

52. Which of the following is a flat bone?
   a. Femur
   b. Tarsal bones
   c. Sternum
   d. Kneecap

53. Two identical cups contain water at 30°C. Cup A contains 20 grams (g) of water, and Cup B contains 40 grams of water. Which cup of water will release more thermal energy when it is allowed to reach the room temperature of 25°C?
    a. Cup A
    b. Cup B
    c. Both cups will release the same amount of thermal energy.

Mathematics

1. The population of each of four towns is predicted to increase or decrease at a constant rate. The equations shown in this table can be used to predict the population, P, of each town t years from today.

    Population Predictions

Town	Equation
Pinehill	$P = 800 - 20t$
Rye	$P = 500 + 15t$
Smithfield	$P = 10t + 950$
Troy	$P = -50t + 600$

    Based on the equations in the table, which statements about the populations of these towns are true?

    Select two true statements.
    a. The population of Troy is decreasing.
    b. The population of Pinehill is increasing.
    c. The populations of Rye and Smithfield are each increasing.
    d. The populations of Smithfield and Troy are each decreasing.
    e. The populations of all four of the towns are each increasing.

2. Which of the following lists the towns, based on their populations today, from least to greatest population?
    a. Pinehill, Rye, Smithfield, Troy
    b. Rye, Troy, Pinehill, Smithfield
    c. Smithfield, Pinehill, Rye, Troy
    d. Troy, Pinehill, Smithfield, Rye

3. A storage rack has two wires that help support the sides of the rack. Each wire connects the top of one side to the base of the rack. The sides form right angles with the base of the rack. The rack and its interior dimensions are shown in this diagram. Which of the following is closest to the length, in feet, of each wire?

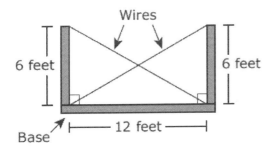

    a. 9
    b. 10.4

c. 13.4

d. 18

4. On a map, 1 inch equals 0.75 mile. The actual distance between the library and a bus stop is 3 miles. What is the distance, in inches, between the library and the bus stop on the map?

    a. 1.5 in

    b. 2 in

    c. 3 in

    d. 4 in

5. A factory worker loaded some boxes onto a cart. Each box has the same weight. This expression represents the total weight, in pounds, of the cart and n boxes.

      10n + 25

Based on the expression, what is the weight, in pounds, of the cart?

    a. 2.5

    b. 10

    c. 25

    d. Cannot be determined.

6. A sphere and one of its dimensions are shown in this diagram. Which of the following is closest to the volume of the sphere?

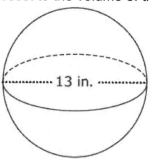

13 in.

    a. 9203 in.^{3}

    b. 1150 in.^{3}

    c. 163 in.^{3}

    d. 82 in.^{3}

7. A rectangular garden that is $16\frac{1}{4}$ feet wide and $11\frac{3}{4}$ feet long will be covered with soil. If a bag of soil covers an area of 20 square feet, which of the following is closest to the number of bags of soil needed to cover the garden?

    a. 2

    b. 3

    c. 8

    d. 10

8. A waiter recorded the amount of money he earned in tips each weekday for a two-week period. His data is shown in this table. Which statement about the data in the table is true?

Money Earned in Tips

Week	Monday	Tuesday	Wednesday	Thursday	Friday
1	$25	$44	$48	$63	$75
2	$35	$35	$48	$62	$75

    a. The median and the range for week 1 are equal to the median and the range for week 2.

    b. The median and the mode for week 1 are equal to the median and the mode for week 2.

    c. The mean and the median for week 1 are equal to the mean and the median for week 2.

    d. The mean and the range for week 1 are equal to the mean and the range for week 2.

9. Which of the following is equivalent to this expression?

$$-5x(-6x^2 + 1)$$

    a. $30x^3 - 4x$

    b. $30x^3 - 5x$

    c. $-11x^3 - 4x$

    d. $-11x^3 - 5x$

10. Which of the following is closest to the height of the door to your classroom?
    a. 1 meter
    b. 2 meters
    c. 4 meters
    d. 7 meters

11. 1 gallon = 4 quarts
1 quart = 2 pints
The number of pints in 10 gallons could be determined by performing which of the following operations?
    a. Multiplying 10 by 2
    b. Dividing 10 by 6
    c. Multiplying 10 by 6
    d. Dividing 40 by 2
    e. Multiplying 40 by 2

12. Carol wanted to estimate the distance from A to D along the path shown on the map above. She correctly rounded each of the given distances to the nearest mile and then added them. Which of the following sums could be hers?

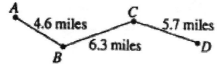

    a. 4 + 6 + 5 = 15
    b. 5 + 6 + 5 = 16
    c. 5 + 6 + 6 = 17
    d. 5 + 7 + 6 = 18

13. Which of the following pieces of information would NOT be useful in deciding what type of car is the most economical to drive?
    a. Median income of drivers
    b. Range of insurance costs
    c. Average miles per gallon
    d. Typical cost of repairs per year
    e. Cost of routine maintenance

14. A certain machine produces 300 nails per minute. At this rate, how long will it take the machine to produce enough nails to fill 5 boxes of nails if each box will contain 250 nails?
    a. 4 min
    b. 4 min 6 sec
    c. 4 min 10 sec
    d. 4 min 50 sec

15. A rectangular pool 24 feet long, 8 feet wide, and 4 feet deep is filled with water. Water is leaking from the pool at the rate of 0.40 cubic foot per minute. At this rate, how many hours will it take for the water level to drop 1 foot?
    a. 4
    b. 8
    c. 12
    d. 16

16. In a recent election between Candidates A and B, 48 percent of the male voters and 55 percent of the female voters voted for Candidate A. Did Candidate A receive more votes than Candidate B?
    a. YES
    b. NO
    c. CANNOT TELL

17. From a shipment of 500 batteries, a sample of 25 was selected at random and tested. If 2 batteries in the sample were found to be dead, how many dead batteries would be expected in the entire shipment?
    a. 10
    b. 20
    c. 30
    d. 40

18. Debbie runs 0.6 of a mile every day. How many miles will Debbie run in 45 days?
    a. 27
    b. 75
    c. 270
    d. None of the above

19. The graph best conveys information about which of the following situations over a 40-minute period of time?

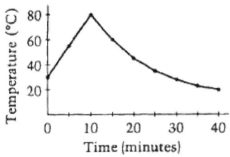

    a. Oven temperature while a cake is being baked
    b. Temperature of water that is heated on a stove, then removed and allowed to cool
    c. Ocean temperature in February along the coast of Maine
    d. Body temperature of a person with a cold

20. It takes 64 identical cubes to half fill a rectangular box. If each cube has a volume of 8 cubic centimeters, what is the volume of the box in cubic centimeters?
    a. 1,024
    b. 512
    c. 128
    d. 16

21. If k can be replaced by any number, how many different values can the expression k plus 6 have?
    a. One
    b. None
    c. Infinitely many
    d. Cannot be determined

22. If the pattern in the list below continues, what will be the next number after 56?

42, 51, 49, 58, 56, . . .

    a. 54
    b. 63
    c. 64
    d. 65

23. What is the difference between the smallest positive 3-digit number and the largest positive 2-digit number?

    a. 1
    b. 9
    c. 10
    d. 90
    e. 900

24. The entire circle shown represents a total of 2,675 radios sold. Of the following, which is the best approximation of the number of radios represented by the shaded sector of the circle?

RADIO SALES

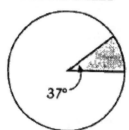

    a. 70
    b. 275
    c. 985
    d. 25,880
    e. 98,420

25. Ken bought a used car for $5,375. He had to pay an additional 15 percent of the purchase price to cover both sales tax and extra fees. Of the following, which is closest to the total amount Ken paid?

    a. $806
    b. $5,510
    c. $5,760
    d. $5,940
    e. $6,180

26. The area of rectangle BCDE shown below is 60 square inches. If the length of AE is 10 inches and the length of ED is 15 inches, what is the area of trapezoid ABCD, in square inches?

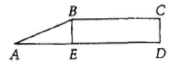

a. 70
b. 80
c. 90
d. Cannot be determined.

27. Which of the following is both a multiple of 3 and a multiple of 7?
    a. 7,007
    b. 8,192
    c. 21,567
    d. 22,287

28. In the figure below, a circle with center O and radius of length 3 is inscribed in a square. What is the area of the shaded region?

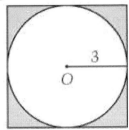

    a. 3.86
    b. 7.73
    c. 28.27
    d. 32.86

29. Raymond must buy enough paper to print 28 copies of a report that contains 64 sheets of paper. Paper is only available in packages of 500 sheets. How many whole packages of paper will he need to buy to do the printing?
    a. 2
    b. 3
    c. 4
    d. 5

30. Tracy said, "I can multiply 6 by another number and get an answer that is smaller than 6." Pat said, "No, you can't. Multiplying 6 by another number always makes the answer 6 or larger." Who is correct?
    a. Tracy
    b. Pat

31. Which of these numbers represents 1.75?

a. 5/4
b. 4/3
c. 7/4
d. None of the above

32. In a group of 1,200 adults, there are 300 vegetarians. What is the ratio of nonvegetarians to vegetarians in the group?
    a. 1 to 3
    b. 1 to 4
    c. 3 to 1
    d. 4 to 1

33. What is the least whole number x for which 2x > 11 ?
    a. 5
    b. 6
    c. 9
    d. 22

34. If a measurement of a rectangular box is given as 48 cubic inches, then the measurement represents the
    a. distance around the top of the box
    b. length of an edge of the box
    c. surface area of the box
    d. volume of the box

35. What is the distance between the midpoint of MN and the midpoint of PQ shown below?

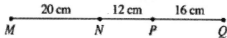

    a. 24 cm
    b. 26 cm
    c. 28 cm
    d. 30 cm

36. A fruit stand sells apples, oranges, and bananas. The cost of 1 apple is $0.50, and the cost of 1 orange is $0.60.
    Ronald bought 4 apples and 1 banana.
    Madison bought 2 oranges and 3 bananas.
    The total cost of the fruit Ronald bought was the same as the total cost of the fruit Madison bought.
What is the cost of 1 banana at the fruit stand?
    a. $0.20
    b. $0.40
    c. $0.55
    d. $0.80

Reading

1. Read the following passage:

> The scent of honeysuckle seemed to linger in the air and joined itself with the sweet odor of freshly cut grass. I slipped out of my bright red sweats and flung them to the base of the tree. I picked up the javelin, stuck point down in the turf. I stretched my arms with the javelin behind my neck. Out of habit, I stood and held the javelin in my left hand, and with the thumb of my right forced small clumps of dirt from the tip. I searched for a target. Picking a spot in a cloud moving towards me I cocked the javelin above my shoulder and regulated my breathing. My right foot was placed on the first mark and my left foot rested behind. My eyes were focused on one abstract point in the sky. Pierce it. I built up energy. Slowly, my legs flowed in motion, like pistons waiting for full power and speed. I could feel my legs churning faster, the muscles rippling momentarily, only to be solidified when foot and turf met like gears. Hitting the second mark, I escaped from the shadow of the tree and was bathed in sunlight . . . . Left foot forward . . . javelin back, straight back, . . . turn now, five steps . . . three, four . . . stretch, the clouds, the point . . . turn back, throw the hips . . . chest out . . . explode through the javelin . . . terminate forward motion, release.
>
> The muscles of my right leg divided in thirds just above my knee, as the full weight of my body in motion was left to its support. Skipping, I followed through and watched the quivering javelin climb as it floated in the oncoming wind. For a moment, it reflected the sunlight and I lost sight of the javelin. The javelin landed quickly, piercing the ground. I heaved in exhaustion, and perspiration flowed from my face and hands. Before me the field stretched and I attempted to evaluate my throw. I was pleased. The smell of honeysuckle again drifted into my senses and somehow, I had a feeling of accomplishment I could just as easily have experienced had I thrown poorly.

What is the main reason the writer wrote this story?
   a. To express an athlete's feeling of failure
   b. To provide information about javelin throwing
   c. To describe how it feels to throw the javelin
   d. To encourage people to take up javelin throwing

2. The next 5 questions are based on the following passage:

> Voting Rights for Women
> One of the greatest victories of the Progressive movement has not yet been mentioned. This victory came when women won the right to vote.
>
> The battle for woman's suffrage was a long one. Ever since the 1840's, some women had demanded the right to vote. They had hoped to get the vote after the Civil War, but the Fifteenth Amendment gave voting rights only to Black men. A few women ran for President, but they got very few votes.
>
> After these defeats, many women turned their attention to getting suffrage laws passed by the states. These women were then called suffragettes. Their first success came in 1869 when women won the right to vote in the territory of Wyoming. When the Wyoming legislature asked to become a state in 1889, it said that Wyoming women must be allowed to keep that right. The state legislature telegraphed Congress, "We may stay out of the Union a hundred years, but we will come in with our women." Congress finally agreed to admit Wyoming to statehood, women voters and all.
>
> Women across the country were encouraged by the victory in Wyoming. In campaigning to get the vote, suffragists sang the following song:
>
> In Wyoming, our sisters fair
> Can use the ballot well.
> Why can't we do so everywhere,

Can anybody tell?

By 1900 women in Colorado, Utah, and Idaho had joined Wyoming women in gaining the right to vote. Others followed. Within a few years every state west of the Rocky Mountains had passed woman-suffrage laws. In 1917 New York followed the example of the western states. In that same year Jeannette Rankin of the state of Montana took office as the first United States congresswoman.

Women leaders were getting involved in many fields. Women were active in the settlement-house movement. Settlement houses were centers that helped poor people, and thousands of women became involved with settlement houses. The poverty and crime they saw made them think men had not done a good job of running the nation.

Suffragists also paid attention to the problems of working women. Many women had become members of unions. One of the best-known organizations was the International Ladies' Garment Workers Union (ILGWU). Working conditions were harsh for people who made clothes for a living. Workers had to sit on boxes. They had to buy their own needles. They even had to pay for the electricity they used. Workers often had to buy the clothes on which they had made mistakes.

In 1909 the ILGWU called a strike to protest working conditions. Over 20,000 union members refused to work. When the strike ended, the union had won a 52-hour workweek and four paid holidays a year. Employers also promised to pay for electricity and needles.

The success of the garment workers encouraged working women in other unions. But serious problems remained. In 1911 a terrible fire broke out at the Triangle Shirtwaist Factory in New York City. There were no sprinklers in the factory and the doors were locked. Trapped workers crowded into the top floors of the building. Others jumped to the streets below. More than a hundred women were killed.

After the Triangle fire, many working women joined the fight for voting rights. They argued that once they had gained the vote, women could work to get laws passed that would prevent such disasters.
Union speakers joined suffragists in trying to convince state legislators to pass voting rights bills. One popular speaker was Rose Schneiderman. When a state senator said that women would lose their beauty and charm if they were allowed to vote, she reported the following exchange:

I had to point out to him that women were working in factories, but he said nothing about their losing their charm. Nor had he mentioned the women in laundries who stood for thirteen hours in terrible heat and steam with their hands in hot starch. I asked him if he thought they would lose more of their beauty and charm by putting a ballot in the ballot box than by standing all day in factories or laundries.

The suffrage movement was given a boost when American troops went to Europe in 1917 to fight in the First World War. Thousands of women took over jobs that had been held by men. National leaders began to think that women should be repaid for their work during the war. President Wilson had once felt that the question of woman's suffrage should be decided by the states. After the war he changed his mind. In 1919 Congress passed the Nineteenth Amendment. By 1920 enough states ratified the amendment so that women could vote in the presidential election that year. American women had taken a big step toward participating fully in national life.

What is the main purpose of this article?
- a. To suggest that women should not work in the garment industry
- b. To inform the reader about the problems of women
- c. To argue that women need to vote for better working conditions
- d. To give the history of how women got the right to vote

3. The passage says, "The battle for woman's suffrage was a long one." What does the word "suffrage"mean in this sentence?
- a. Right to vote
- b. Settlement houses

c. Progressive movement

d. Victories

4. According to the passage, how did the disaster at the Triangle shirtwaist factory affect the suffrage movement?

a. The company endorsed the suffrage movement.

b. Men as well as women began to join the suffrage movement.

c. The Triangle Company tried to fire suffragists who worked there.

d. Many working women joined in the fight for woman's suffrage.

5. A state senator said that women would lose their beauty and charm if they were allowed to vote. What did Rose Schneiderman say?

a. She argued that working conditions were more likely than voting rights to lead to the loss of a woman's beauty and charm.

b. She agreed with him but insisted on voting rights for women anyway.

c. She showed him that beautiful and charming women were voting in some western states.

d. She responded that women with beauty and charm probably did not need to vote.

6. According to the passage, how did the First World War help the cause of the suffragists?

a. It gave garment workers an opportunity to get better jobs.

b. It helped union leaders to get better conditions for their members.

c. It encouraged women to protest the war.

d. It drew national attention to the contributions of women.

7. The next 3 questions are based on the following passage:

The Battle of Lexington
Passage A
In April 1775, General Gage, the military governor of Massachusetts, sent out a body of troops to take possession of military stores at Concord, a short distance from Boston. At Lexington, a handful of "embattled farmers," who had been tipped off by Paul Revere, barred the way. The "rebels"were ordered to disperse. They stood their ground. The English fired a volley of shots that killed eight patriots. It was not long before the swift riding Paul Revere spread the news of this new atrocity to the neighboring colonies. The patriots of all of New England, although still a handful, were now ready to fight the English. Even in faraway North Carolina, patriots organized to resist them.
Samuel Steinberg, The United States:
Story of a Free People (1963)

Passage B
At five o'clock in the morning the local militia of Lexington, seventy strong, formed up on the village green. As the sun rose the head of the British column, with three officers riding in front, came into view. The leading officer, brandishing his sword, shouted, "Disperse, you rebels, immediately!"
The militia commander ordered his men to disperse. The colonial committees were very anxious not to fire the first shot, and there were strict orders not to provoke open conflict with the British regulars. But in the confusion someone fired. A volley was returned. The ranks of the militia were thinned and there was a general melee. Brushing aside the survivors, the British column marched on to Concord.
Winston Churchill,History of
the English Speaking Peoples (1957)

Passage C
The British troops approached us rapidly in platoons, with a General officer on horse-back at their head. The officer came up to within about two rods of the centre of the company, where I stood.—The first platoon being about three rods distant. They there halted. The officer then swung his sword, and said, "Lay down your arms, you damn'd rebels, or you are all dead men—fire." Some guns were fired by the British at us from the first platoon, but no person was killed or hurt, being probably charged only with powder. Just at this time, Captain Parker ordered every man to take care of himself. The company immediately dispersed; and while the company was dispersing and leaping over the wall, the second platoon of the British fired, and killed some of our men. There was not a gun fired by any of Captain Parker's company within my knowledge.
Sylvanus Wood, Deposition (June 17, 1826)

Passage D
I, John Bateman, belonging to the Fifty-Second Regiment, commanded by Colonel Jones, on Wednesday morning on the nineteenth day of April instant, was in the party marching to Concord, being at Lexington, in the County of Middlesex; being nigh the meeting-house in said Lexington, there was a small party of men gathered together in that place when our Troops marched by, and I testify and declare, that I heard the word of command given to the Troops to fire, and some of said Troops did fire, and I saw one of said small party lay dead on the ground nigh said meeting-house, and I testify that I never heard any of the inhabitants so much as fire one gun on said Troops.
John Bateman, Testimony (April 23, 1775)

The "someone" referred to in Passage B is most probably:
   a. a colonist
   b. a British soldier
   c. Captain Parker
   d. Paul Revere

8. Which statement about the author of Passage C is best supported by the information in that passage?
   a. He was an eyewitness to the battle.
   b. He knew Paul Revere.
   c. He leapt over the wall with the other men.
   d. He sympathized with the British.

9. The author of Passage A has a point of view that favors the colonists because he
   a. mentions the contributions of General Gage
   b. says that no shots were fired
   c. mentions that Paul Revere tipped off the colonists
   d. says that news of the atrocity was spread to neighboring colonies

10. The next 4 questions are based on the following passage:

"My aunt will be down presently, Mr. Nuttel," said a very self-possessed young lady of fifteen; "in the meantime you must try and put up with me."

Framton Nuttel endeavored to say the correct something which should duly flatter the niece of the moment without unduly discounting the aunt that was to come. Privately he doubted more than ever whether these formal visits on a succession of total strangers would do much towards helping the nerve cure which he was supposed to be undergoing.

"I know how it will be," his sister had said when he was preparing to migrate to this rural retreat; "you will bury yourself down there and not speak to a living soul, and your nerves will be worse than ever from moping. I shall just give you letters of introduction to all the people I know there. Some of them, as far as I can remember, were quite nice."

Framton wondered whether Mrs. Sappleton, the lady to whom he was presenting one of the letters of introduction, came into the nice division.

"Do you know many of the people round here?" asked the niece, when she judged that they had had sufficient silent communion.

"Hardly a soul," said Framton. "My sister was staying here, at the rectory, you know, some four years ago, and she gave me letters of introduction to some of the people here."

He made the last statement in a tone of distinct regret.

"Then you know practically nothing about my aunt?" pursued the self-possessed young lady.

"Only her name and address," admitted the caller. He was wondering whether Mrs. Sappleton was in the married or widowed state. An undefinable something about the room seemed to suggest masculine habitation.

"Her great tragedy happened just three years ago," said the child; "that would be since your sister's time."

"Her tragedy?" asked Framton; somehow in this restful country spot tragedies seemed out of place.

"You may wonder why we keep that window wide open on an October afternoon," said the niece, indicating a large French window that opened onto a lawn.

"It is quite warm for the time of the year," said Framton; "but has that window got anything to do with the tragedy?"

"Out through that window, three years ago to a day, her husband and her two young brothers went off for their day's shooting. They never came back. In crossing the moor to their favorite snipe-shooting ground they were all three engulfed in a treacherous piece of bog. It had been that dreadful wet summer, you know, and places that were safe in other years gave way suddenly without warning. Their bodies were never recovered. That was the dreadful part of it." Here the child's voice lost its self-possessed note and became falteringly human. "Poor aunt always thinks that they will come back someday, they and the little brown spaniel that was lost with them, and walk in at that window just as they used to do. That is why the window is kept open every evening till it is quite dusk. Poor dear aunt, she has often told me how they went out, her husband with his white waterproof coat over his arm, and Ronnie, her youngest brother, singing, 'Bertie, why do you bound?' as he always did to tease her, because she said it got on her nerves. Do you know, sometimes on still, quiet evenings like this, I almost get a creepy feeling that they will all walk in through that window—"

She broke off with a little shudder. It was a relief to Framton when the aunt bustled into the room with a whirl of apologies for being late in making her appearance.

"I hope Vera has been amusing you?" she said.

"She has been very interesting," said Framton.

"I hope you don't mind the open window," said Mrs. Sappleton briskly; "my husband and brothers will be home directly from shooting, and they always come in this way. They've been out for snipe in the marshes today, so they'll make a fine mess over my poor carpets. So like you menfolk, isn't it?"

She rattled on cheerfully about the shooting and the scarcity of birds, and the prospects for duck in the winter. To Framton it was all purely horrible. He made a desperate but only partially successful effort to turn the talk onto a less ghastly topic; he was conscious that his hostess was giving him only a fragment of her attention, and her eyes were constantly straying past him to the open window and the lawn beyond.

It was certainly an unfortunate coincidence that he should have paid his visit on this tragic anniversary.

"The doctors agree in ordering me complete rest, an absence of mental excitement, and avoidance of anything in the nature of violent physical exercise," announced Framton, who labored under the tolerably widespread delusion that total strangers and chance acquaintances are hungry for the least detail of one's ailments and infirmities, their cause and cure. "On the matter of diet they are not so much in agreement," he continued.

"No?" said Mrs. Sappleton, in a voice which only replaced a yawn at the last moment. Then she suddenly brightened into alert attention-but not to what Framton was saying.

"Here they are at last!" she cried. "Just in time for tea, and don't they look as if they were muddy up to the eyes!"

Framton shivered slightly and turned towards the niece with a look intended to convey sympathetic comprehension. The child was staring out through the open window with a dazed horror in her eyes. In a chill shock of nameless fear Framton swung round in his seat and looked in the same direction.
In the deepening twilight three figures were walking across the lawn towards the window; they all carried guns under their arms, and one of them was additionally burdened with a white coat hung over his shoulders. A tired brown spaniel kept close at their heels. Noiselessly they neared the house, and then a hoarse young voice chanted out of the dusk: "I said, Bertie, why do you bound?"

Framton grabbed wildly at his stick and hat; the hall door, the gravel drive, and the front gate were dimly noted stages in his headlong retreat. A cyclist coming along the road had to run into the hedge to avoid imminent collision.

"Here we are, my dear," said the bearer of the white mackintosh, coming in through the window; "fairly muddy, but most of it's dry. Who was that who bolted out as we came up?"

"A most extraordinary man, a Mr. Nuttel," said Mrs. Sappleton; "could only talk about his illnesses, and dashed off without a word of goodbye or apology when you arrived. One would think he had seen a ghost."

"I expect it was the spaniel," said the niece calmly; "he told me he had a horror of dogs. He was once hunted into a cemetery somewhere on the banks of the Ganges by a pack of pariah dogs, and had to spend the night in a newly dug grave with the creatures snarling and grinning and foaming just above him. Enough to make anyone lose their nerve."

Romance at short notice was her specialty.

Which of the following best describes what happens in the story?
    a. A young man visits his aunt and tells her about a recent tragedy.
    b. A young girl amuses her family by telling them scary stories.
    c. A young girl makes up a story and frightens a nervous visitor.
    d. A family plays a trick on a young man from out of town.

11. Why does Framton Nuttel visit the countryside?
    a. To cure his nervous condition
    b. To take a tour of the area
    c. To meet his sister's friends
    d. To visit his aunt, Mrs. Sappleton

12. The narrator says Framton has the **delusion** that total strangers are interested in his nervous condition. This means Framton:
    a. has a common illness related to his nerves

b. is worried about what people think of him

c. dreams that he is constantly being watched

d. has a mistaken idea about how others view him

13. What is the main strategy the author uses in the story?

    a. He creates conflict among the important characters.

    b. He adds romance to the relationship between the two main characters.

    c. He withholds information from the reader until the story's conclusion.

    d. He creates suspense by disguising the identity of a character.

14. The next 4 questions are based on the following two passages:

Passage 1: Odysseus and the Sirens
by Homer
In this excerpt from Homer's Odyssey, the Greek king Odysseus tells of his encounter with a group of dangerous creatures called the Sirens. He begins with the warnings given by the witch Circe before he and his men leave her island.

1 "'Now, then, stay here for the rest of the day, feast your fill, and go on with your voyage at daybreak tomorrow morning. In the meantime I will tell Ulysses1 about your course, and will explain everything to him so as to prevent your suffering from misadventure either by land or sea.'

2 "We agreed to do as she had said, and feasted through the livelong day to the going down of the sun, but when the sun had set and it came on dark, the men laid themselves down to sleep by the stern cables of the ship. Then Circe took me by the hand and bade me be seated away from the others, while she reclined by my side and asked me all about our adventures.

3 "'So far so good,' said she, when I had ended my story, 'and now pay attention to what I am about to tell you—heaven itself, indeed, will recall it to your recollection. First you will come to the Sirens who enchant all who come near them. If any one unwarily draws in too close and hears the singing of the Sirens, his wife and children will never welcome him home again, for they sit in a green field and warble him to death with the sweetness of their song. . . . Therefore pass these Sirens by, and stop your men's ears with wax that none of them may hear; but if you like you can listen yourself, for you may get the men to bind you as you stand upright on a cross piece half way up the mast, and they must lash the rope's ends to the mast itself, that you may have the pleasure of listening. If you beg and pray the men to unloose you, then they must bind you faster.

4 "Here she ended, and dawn enthroned in gold began to show in heaven, whereon she returned inland. I then went on board and told my men to loose the ship from her moorings; so they at once got into her, took their places, and began to smite the grey sea with their oars. Presently the great and cunning goddess Circe befriended us with a fair wind that blew dead aft, and staid steadily with us, keeping our sails well filled, so we did whatever wanted doing to the ship's gear, and let her go as wind and helmsman headed her.

5 "Then, being much troubled in mind, I said to my men, 'My friends, it is not right that one or two of us alone should know the prophecies that Circe has made me, I will therefore tell you about them, so that whether we live or die we may do so with our eyes open. First she said we were to keep clear of the Sirens, who sit and sing most beautifully in a field of flowers; but she said I might hear them myself so long as

no one else did. Therefore, take me and bind me to the crosspiece half way up the mast; bind me as I stand upright, with a bond so fast that I cannot possibly break away, and lash the rope's ends to the mast itself. If I beg and pray you to set me free, then bind me more tightly still.'

6 "I had hardly finished telling everything to the men before we reached the island of the two Sirens, for the wind had been very favourable. Then all of a sudden it fell dead calm; there was not a breath of wind nor a ripple upon the water, so the men furled the sails and stowed them; then taking to their oars they whitened the water with the foam they raised in rowing. Meanwhile I took a large wheel of wax and cut it up small with my sword. Then I kneaded the wax in my strong hands till it became soft, which it soon did between the kneading and the rays of the sun-god son of Hyperion. Then I stopped the ears of all my men, and they bound me hands and feet to the mast as I stood upright on the cross piece; but they went on rowing themselves. When we had got within earshot of the land, and the ship was going at a good rate, the Sirens saw that we were getting in shore and began with their singing.

7 "'Come here,' they sang, 'renowned Ulysses, honour to the Achaean name, and listen to our two voices. No one ever sailed past us without staying to hear the enchanting sweetness of our song—and he who listens will go on his way not only charmed, but wiser, for we know all the ills that the gods laid upon the Argives and Trojans before Troy, and can tell you everything that is going to happen over the whole world.'

8 "They sang these words most musically, and as I longed to hear them further I made signs by frowning to my men that they should set me free; but they quickened their stroke, and Eurylochus and Perimedes bound me with still stronger bonds till we had got out of hearing of the Sirens' voices. Then my men took the wax from their ears and unbound me."

Passage 2: The Sirens
by James Russell Lowell
1 The sea is lonely, the sea is dreary,
The sea is restless and uneasy;
Thou seekest quiet, thou art weary,
Wandering thou knowest not whither;—
5 Our little isle is green and breezy,
Come and rest thee! O come hither,
Come to this peaceful home of ours,
Where evermore
The low west-wind creeps panting up the shore
10 To be at rest among the flowers;
Full of rest, the green moss lifts,
As the dark waves of the sea
Draw in and out of rocky rifts,
Calling solemnly to thee
15 With voices deep and hollow,—
"To the shore
Follow! O, follow!
To be at rest forevermore!
Forevermore!"
20 Look how the gray old Ocean
From the depth of his heart rejoices,
Heaving with a gentle motion,
When he hears our restful voices;
List how he sings in an undertone,
25 Chiming with our melody;

And all sweet sounds of earth and air
Melt into one low voice alone,
That murmurs over the weary sea,
And seems to sing from everywhere,—
30 "Here mayst thou harbor peacefully,
Here mayst thou rest from the aching oar;
Turn thy curvèd prow ashore,
And in our green isle rest for evermore!
Forevermore!"

What advice from Circe is essential for Ulysses and his men to prepare for the Sirens in Passage 1?

    a. The Sirens are few in number.

    b. The Sirens can predict the future.

    c. The Sirens enjoy flattery and praise.

    d. The Sirens never let anyone leave their island.

15. Which detail from the Sirens' song in Passage 1 contradicts what Circe tells the men?

    a. "'Come here,' they sang,'renowned Ulysses, honour to the Achaean name, and listen to our two voices.

    b. No one ever sailed past us without staying to hear the enchanting sweetness of our song

    c. and he who listens will go on his way not only charmed, but wiser

    d. for we know all the ills that the gods laid upon the Argives and Trojans before Troy, and can tell you everything that is going to happen over the whole world

16. Which ideas are contrasted throughout Passage 2?

    a. the harshness of the sea and the peace of the island

    b. the ugliness of the ship and the beauty of the island

    c. the comfort of home and the toughness of the open sea

    d. the excitement of the battlefield and the dullness of the sea

17. Ancient Greece was a seagoing culture that made important explorations. Ancient Greeks also believed the sea to be a dangerous place. How is this aspect of ancient Greek culture symbolized in Passage 1?

    a. The Sirens appear enchanting, but they are lethal.

    b. Circe enjoys the adventures of Ulysses but warns him of the Sirens.

    c. The Sirens reveal important knowledge to sailors who listen to them.

    d. Ulysses follows Circe's instructions, but he is tempted by the Sirens' song.

18. The next 5 questions are based on the following passage:

Radio Address about the National Energy Crisis, January 19, 1974
by Richard Nixon
President Nixon spoke to the American people about the energy crisis
multiple times during this period. This speech was made several weeks later.

1 Good afternoon:

2 Ten weeks ago, I reported to the Nation on the energy crisis. I asked all Americans to accept some sacrifices in comfort and convenience so that no American would have to suffer real hardship.

3 Today, I want to report to you on our progress and answer the basic questions that many Americans have asked about this crisis.

4 On the positive side, I am glad to be able to report that we are making solid progress in facing up to this challenge. There are several reasons for this:

5 Far more important than anything else is what every American has done voluntarily. It is your response—the actions you take to save energy on a personal, voluntary, day-in, day-out basis—that is now the single most important reason for our success so far.

6 For the past 7 weeks, we have observed "gasless Sundays" across the country. Your cooperation with this program helped to make it possible for me to announce today that during the month of December, the total consumption of gasoline in the United States was nearly 9 percent below expectations.

7 Americans are also responding to the call for lower temperatures at home and at work. A recent report from New England shows that 19,000 homes surveyed there have reduced heating oil consumption by more than 16 percent under last year, and that is after making adjustments for warmer weather.

8 Utilities are reporting that the consumption of natural gas across the country has been reduced by approximately 6 percent over last year, while the consumption of electricity—in homes, offices, factories, and elsewhere—is down by about 10 percent.

9 Beyond the progress we have made because of voluntary conservation, we have also been fortunate because the weather in the last quarter of 1973 was warmer than usual, so we did not consume so much for fuel for heating as we expected. Even though the oil embargo continues in the Middle East, we have also received some oil we did not expect at the time the embargo was imposed.

10 Finally, let me tell you what your Government has been doing to meet this crisis.

11 A fuel allocation program has been set up so that no area of the Nation is being subjected to undue hardship. We have begun the process of converting oil-burning utilities to the use of coal wherever possible, freeing some 200,000 barrels of oil a day for use in other areas.

12 At my request, laws governing energy conservation, such as year-round daylight savings time, have been enacted by the Congress and are now in effect. Teams of Federal inspectors have been sent to investigate fuel prices at gasoline stations and truck stops. Where price gouging is discovered, it is being stopped.

13 Within the Government, where we have a special obligation to set an example, I first directed that energy consumption be cut by at least 7 percent. That goal has now been met, and it has been exceeded. Consumption of energy by the Federal Government has been cut by more than 20 percent under anticipated demands.

14 These are just some of the steps we have taken to meet the problem head-on, and you can expect more in the future.

15 Nothing which the Federal Government might do could be successful, however, without the full cooperation of the American people. It is your sacrifice that is making the difference. You deserve the credit.

****

16 America is a rich, a strong, and a good country. We must set for ourselves this goal: We must never again be caught in a foreign-made crisis where the United States is dependent on any other country, friendly or unfriendly, for the energy we need to produce our jobs, to heat our homes, to furnish our transportation for wherever we want to go.

17 Late last year, I announced the beginning of Project Independence, a full-scale effort to provide the capacity to meet American energy needs with American energy resources by 1980. As an important part of that project, the head of the Federal Energy Office, William Simon, will mount a major effort this year to accelerate the development of new energy supplies for the future.

18 Most of the money and the work for Project Independence must come from private enterprise. But the Federal Government also has a vital role to play. It must be a catalyst for industrial initiative. It must clear away the red tape that lies in the way of expanding our supplies, and it must provide the seed money for research and development.

19 Many of these Federal responsibilities can only be met with new legislation. That is why, over the next few weeks, I shall submit to the Congress a broad legislative package of energy initiatives and urge it to place these requests at the very top of the Congressional agenda for 1974. If we are to be successful in dealing with our long-term energy needs, the Congress must play its part, and I believe that the Congress, after returning from their districts over the Christmas holidays, will agree that the people want them to play their part along with the Administration.

20 The burden of energy conservation, of cutbacks and inconvenience, of occasional discomfort, continued concern is not, I can assure you, an artificial one. It is real. During the Second World War, Winston Churchill was once asked why England was fighting Hitler. He answered, "If we stop, you will find out."

21 If we should choose to believe that our efforts in fighting the energy crisis are unnecessary, if we permit ourselves to slacken our efforts and slide back into the wasteful consumption of energy, then the full force of the energy crisis will be brought home to America in a most devastating fashion, and there will be no longer any question in anyone's mind about the reality of the crisis.

22 The distance between the winter of 1974 and the springtime of energy independence for the United States remains great. We must proceed with confidence in our ability to do the job. Far more importantly, we must act now, as one people, to do the job that must be done.

Select two ideas that show how President Nixon develops the idea of responsibility in the passage.

    a. by highlighting areas for continued improvement

    b. by outlining roles for different parts of society

    c. by minimizing the influence of outside factors

    d. by summarizing government successes

    e. by using the opinions of expert

19. "But the Federal Government also has a vital role to play. It must be a catalyst for industrial initiative. It must clear away the red tape that lies in the way of expanding our supplies, and it must provide the seed money for research and development." (paragraph 18)

Why does Nixon use the word "catalyst" in describing the role of the federal government?

    a. to show that the government needs to initiate change

b. to describe how the government has caused the crisis

c. to argue that the government must solve the crisis alone

d. to highlight how the government will work with the American people

20. How does President Nixon's allusion to World War II reflect the purpose of his speech?
    a. It highlights the historical causes of the crisis.
    b. It emphasizes the importance of dealing with the crisis.
    c. It reassures people that the crisis is coming to an end.
    d. It shows that problems are best solved through strong leadership.

21. Which sentence supports the argument that people must make sacrifices to help the government deal with the crisis?
    a. "For the past 7 weeks, we have observed 'gasless Sundays' across the country." (paragraph 6)
    b. "These are just some of the steps we have taken to meet the problem head-on, and you can expect more in the future." (paragraph 14)
    c. "Nothing which the Federal Government might do could be successful, however, without the full cooperation of the American people." (paragraph 15)
    d. "Late last year, I announced the beginning of Project Independence, a full-scale effort to provide the capacity to meet American energy needs with American energy resources by 1980." (paragraph 17)

22. What two sentences provide evidence that government action lessens the burdens of the crisis for Americans?
    a. A fuel allocation program has been set up so that no area of the Nation is being subjected to undue hardship.
    b. We have begun the process of converting oil-burning utilities to the use of coal wherever possible, freeing some 200,000 barrels of oil a day for use in other areas.
    c. At my request, laws governing energy conservation, such as year-round daylight savings time, have been enacted by the Congress and are now in effect.
    d. Teams of Federal inspectors have been sent to investigate fuel prices at gasoline stations and truck stops.

23.

> You have the following numbers: 1 2 3 4 5.
> Switch the second and fourth number.
> Increment each number by 1.
> Switch the second and fifth number.

What is the result?
    a. 1 4 3 2 5
    b. 2 5 4 3 6
    c. 2 6 4 3 5

d. 5 2 4 3 6

24.

> You are creating a seating chart. Each table seats 4 people. There are 8 people, named: Anna, Bella, Cindy, Donna, Emma, Fred, Greg, Henry.
> Anna cannot sit with Bella, unless Donna is also seated at the same table.
> Bella must sit with either Cindy or Fred.
> Fred must sit with Greg or Henry.

Which one of these seating charts corresponds to the rules?
   a. Anna, Bella, Cindy, Donna
   b. Anna, Bella, Cindy, Fred
   c. Anna, Bella, Donna, Henry
   d. Anna, Bella, Greg, Henry

25.

> **Carnivores**
> Wolves
> Lions
> Hawks
>
> **Omnivores**
> Humans
> Bears
>
> **Herbivores**
> Cows
> Elk
> rabbits

Which of the following statements is correct based on the outline above?
   a. Omnivores are humans
   b. Cows are herbivores
   c. Bears are carnivores and herbivores
   d. Lions and hawks have the same diet.

26. The next three questions are based on the following chart:

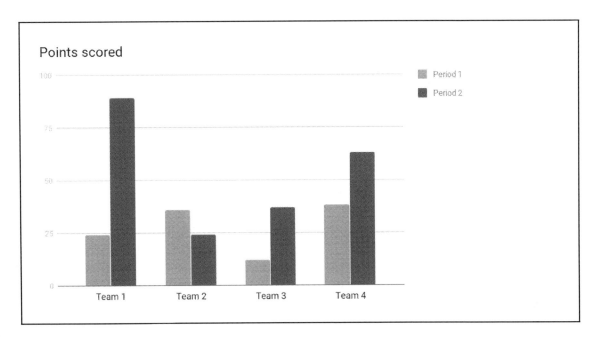

Which team scored the most during period 2?
- a. Team 1
- b. Team 2
- c. Team 3
- d. Team 4

27. Which team's performance suffered during period 2?
- a. Team 1
- b. Team 2
- c. Team 3
- d. Team 4

28. Who is Team 1's biggest competitor?
- a. Team 2
- b. Team 3
- c. Team 4

29. What is the tone of the passage:

The children crowded around the birthday boy and began singing "Happy Birthday". The sound of laughter and clapping filled the air as the birthday boy blew out the candles. The kids jumped up and down when it was announced that it was time to open the presents.

- a. Serene
- b. Fearful
- c. Exciting
- d. Suspenseful

30. You are writing a paper on the life of John Smith. Which is your best source?
   a. A biography
   b. An autobiography
   c. An encyclopedia
   d. Wikipedia

31. She was a person with good moral _____.
   a. principle
   b. principal

32.

> 2 4 3 6 8 7
> Increment each number by 1.
> Replace all odd numbers with the letter A.
> Replace all even numbers with the letter B.
> If there are any consecutive odd or even numbers, replace each number with an X.

What is the result?
   a. A X B A X A
   b. A A B X X A
   c. X X B X X B

33. The next 2 questions are based on the following drug label.

> Active Ingredient: Hydrocortisone 1%
>
> Directions:
> * For itching of skin irritation, inflammation, and rashes
> * Adults and children 2 years of age and older: apply to affected area not more than 3 to 4 times daily
> * Children under 2 years of age: do not use, ask a doctor.
>
> Warnings:
> * For external use only.
> * Do not use in the genital area if you have a vaginal discharge. Ask a doctor.
> * Do not use for the treatment of diaper rash. Ask a doctor.

You have not had a chance to see a physician, but your 1 year old baby has a diaper rash. Is it okay for you to use hydrocortisone on your baby until you can see the physician?
   a. Yes
   b. No

34. Your physician said it was okay for you to use hydrocortisone in the genital area even though you have vaginal discharge. Does this violate the warnings on the drug label?

    a. Yes

    b. No

35.

Types of Real Estate Investing
- Single Family Homes
- Land
- Apartment Buildings
- Loans

Which of the following is out of place?

    a. Single family homes

    b. Land

    c. Apartment buildings

    d. Loans

36. The next two questions are based on the following:

Anna is standing between Ethan and Jacob.
Jacob is standing next to Jared.
Jared is standing next to Charlize.
Charlize is the last in line.

Who is the first in line?

    a. Anna

    b. Ethan

    c. Jacob

    d. Jared

37. The next 5 questions are based on the following passage:

Advancements in Modern Clothing
by Anthony Kazanjian

Rapid advancements in computer technology during the late 20th and early 21st centuries have given today's fashion designers unprecedented freedom to express their creativity. In previous generations, garments were designed by hand, using pencil sketches and traditional math-based pattern sizing. Today, designers often have computer-aided design (CAD) software at their disposal to determine textile weaves and sizing designs. CAD software allows them to view designs of clothing on virtual models of various shapes and sizes. This makes for a much more efficient garment design process, saving companies both time and resources that would have otherwise been spent on manually creating and adjusting prototypes.

The impact of CAD software on everyday clothing is becoming more prevalent as the software is linked to 3-D printing technology. While other industries, such as aerospace or architecture, have been using this technology for decades, it has now started to spread to the world of fashion. Designers have been experimenting with 3-D printed apparel, and this could revolutionize the experience of buying clothes for the average consumer. For example, a swimwear company can now offer custom-designed bathing suits on its website, using nylon and a 3-D printer to print out each order to a customer's body shape and measurements. In addition to the use of 3-D printers by industry specialists, machines for home printing are becoming more and more affordable. If this trend continues, it will allow consumers to print out objects like bracelets in a matter of minutes from the comfort of their homes. Though it may be a while before anyone can print out his or her own complete wardrobe, the ability to create customized clothing is becoming more of a reality as technology evolves. One day, we may all be wearing our own one-of-a-kind, perfectly tailored clothes.

What is the author's purpose?
   a. To inform
   b. To persuade
   c. To advertise
   d. To warn

38. What is the main idea of the passage?
   a. 3-D printing will soon take over the world
   b. Clothing is now very easy to make
   c. Advancements in CAD and 3-D printing has and will revolutionize the clothing industry.
   d. Consumers will be able to create customized clothing.

39. "The ability to create customized clothing is becoming more of a reality as technology evolves."
   What is the meaning of evolve in this sentence?
   a. Develops
   b. Spreads
   c. Rises
   d. Subjugates

40. What can be inferred from the passage?
   a. Advancement in the clothing industry will provide consumers with more choices.
   b. Advancement in the clothing industry will put clothing industry workers out of jobs.
   c. Clothing designers love CAD and 3D printing for making their jobs easier.
   d. CAD software is very easy to use.

41. "For example, a swimwear company can now offer custom-designed bathing suits on its website, using nylon and a 3-D printer to print out each order to a customer's body shape and measurements."
   The above sentence is best described as?
   a. A theme
   b. A topic
   c. A main idea
   d. A supporting detail

42. The recent rains made the hillside appear all the more _____.
    a. ubiquitous
    b. rampant
    c. verdant
    d. xenophobic

43. Who is Jacob standing between?
    a. Anna and Jared
    b. Ethan and Anna
    c. Jared and Charlize
    d. It cannot be determined

44. The next 3 questions are based on the following:

Bulb Type	Bulb Cost
tulips	3 for 9.99 Each additional bulb is 0.99
lilies	5 for 10.99 10 for 14.99
freesias	1.99 per bulb

How much would it cost to buy 1 tulip bulb?
    a. 0.99
    b. 9.99
    c. 2.49
    d. You cannot purchase a single tulip bulb

45. If you wanted to purchase 5 bulbs, which bulb type would be the cheapest?
    a. Tulips
    b. Lilies
    c. Freesias

46. How much would 20 lily bulbs cost?
    a. 36.97
    b. 29.98
    c. None of the above.

47. Please ensure your seat belts are fastened.
    a. Ensure
    b. Insure

48. Which of these do not belong?
    a. Square

b. Triangle

c. Trapezoid

d. Circle

49. You have a 5 gallon bucket of water. You dump out 2 gallons of water and add 1 gallon of water. How many gallons of water are in the bucket?

    a. 1 gallon

    b. 2 gallon

    c. 3 gallons

    d. 4 gallons

50. Reading the dictionary is so boring, it borders on soporific. What is the meaning of soporific in this sentence?

    a. Make one sleepy

    b. Challenging

    c. Illness inducing

    d. Stressful

51. The next 3 questions are based on the following passage:

This is English at its most colorful—a language spoken by multitudes, able and willing to assimilate any words it finds useful.

"It's always been a vacuum cleaner of a language. It sucks in words from everywhere," said David Crystal, author of the Cambridge Encyclopedia of the English Language.

Places, peoples, tongues from around the world: all are hidden in the folds of English's lexicons, co-existing in a polyglot that makes its vocabulary more malleable and gives a sense of belonging to those who speak it as a second or foreign language.

Consider this unlikely but perfectly serviceable sentence: "You've got some chutzpah taking the ketchup I was going to use on my barbecued hamburger, you skunk!"

Flawless English. Yet "chutzpah" is Yiddish, "ketchup" originally Chinese, "barbecue" Caribbean, "hamburger" German and "skunk" Native American. All folded into English.

From all corners they come, these words. From Swedish (ombudsman and dynamite) and Basque (bizarre). From Yiddish (meshuganeh and kibbitzing) and Spanish (siesta and coyote). From Finnish (sauna), Russian (apparatchik), Hindi (juggernaut), Sri Lankan Sinhala (anaconda) and Malay (amok).

From Japanese (judo), Filipino Tagalog (boondocks) and Arabic via Swahili (safari). According to the Oxford English Dictionary, English contains words from more than 350 living languages.

"English is a free market," said Allan Metcalf, author of The World in So Many Words, a freewheeling exploration of English's imports. "Other languages are homogeneous enough that you can notice foreign words coming in and say, 'That's a terrible thing; keep them out.' But English is multicultural."

Viking languages contributed words and grammar to Old English in England's earliest days, but linguists trace the real dawn of importation to 1066, when King William, a Norman from what is now France, conquered England. That meant English speakers were being ruled by French speakers, and the subjugated language had to adjust.

The conquerors considered themselves more genteel than the low-country Anglo-Saxons. Animal words—cow, pig, sheep—are out-in-the-barn Anglo-Saxon. Food words for the same beasts—beef, pork, mutton—come from dress-up-for-dinner Norman.

By Chaucer's time, 300 years later, Middle English had swelled with French terms such as "reign," "jurisprudence" and "reason," setting a precedent: new words could be foreign and still sound English. During the Renaissance, words flowed in from Latin—not that different from French—and Greek. The Age of Exploration introduced novel terms from all corners. English was becoming a polyglot.

And the United States changed everything. Here was an English-speaking land molded by successive generations of immigrants, each bringing new ideas and new expressions. Irish, Italians, Germans, Eastern Europeans, Latinos, Africans, Asians—all changed English in ways minuscule and momentous.

The passage describes English vocabulary as malleable. This means that English
- a. is constantly changing
- b. is a rich and colorful language
- c. sounds familiar to speakers of other languages
- d. is difficult for most students to learn

52. The passage refers to "novel terms." This means that the terms were:
- a. used in Renaissance texts
- b. formed from Greek or Latin roots
- c. new to the English language
- d. shared by many languages

53. The passage says that after the year 1066, English was the "subjugated language." This means that English was
- a. being taught to people in France
- b. no longer used by scholars in France
- c. more difficult to learn than French
- d. considered inferior to French

English and Language Usage

1. I think the book was good.
   The above sentence is grammatically correct.
   a. True
   b. False

2. Diagrams often help elucidate information made in text. What is the meaning of elucidate?
   a. To obscure
   b. To make clear
   c. To provide additional detail
   d. To emphasize

3. Which of the following is correct?
   a. Jason said let's go to Disneyland.
   b. Jason said "let's go to Disneyland."
   c. Jason said "Let's go to Disneyland."
   d. Jason said, "Let's go to Disneyland."

4. I bought eggs and milk, but I forgot to buy bread.
   What kind of sentence is this?
   a. Simple
   b. Compound
   c. Complex
   d. Compound complex

5. Which of the following sentences are correct?
   a. Green eggs and ham are my favorite dish.
   b. Green eggs and ham is my favorite dish.

6. The word "rivulet," which means a river that is small in size, was adapted from the word "river." Which of the following words has undergone a similar adaptation?
   a. pellet
   b. triplet
   c. scarlet
   d. droplet

7. "To survive in baseball in that era, professionals needed more than talent. Cunning and fearlessness were prerequisites." Which word from the sentences provides a context clue for the meaning of the word prerequisites?
   a. "needed"
   b. "limited"
   c. "profits"
   d. "customers"

8. "My stipend was fifty cents a day, but because I came early and stayed late, Mr. Ferguson upped my wage to seventy-five cents." What is the meaning of the word stipend.
    a. Salary
    b. Training
    c. Position
    d. Schedule

9. Which of the following sentences is correct?
    a. Neither Claire nor Charlize want to go to her room.
    b. Neither Claire nor Charlize wants to go to their room.
    c. Neither Claire nor Charlize wants to go to her room.
    d. Neither Claire nor Charlize want to go to their room.

10. Which of the following words is spelled incorrectly?
    a. Basicly
    b. Beginning
    c. Ceiling
    d. Cemetery

11. The next 4 questions are based on the following passage:

> Food was always important to my family, although no one could ever agree about what good food really meant. To my mother, good food meant fresh ingredients; to my father, good food meant that there was a lot of it; <u>and my grandmother thought</u> good food meant that you had taken the time to do all of the little details yourself. I never argued with my parents about it, but secretly I thought that my grandmother was right, and that's why I always enjoyed helping her make bread.
>
> My grandmother was of French <u>ancestry therefore</u>, her bread reflected that heritage. It was neither the light, fluffy, supermarket sandwich bread, nor the puffed rolls so common at dinner, nor the thin, crusty baguettes that people call French bread. This was pain de campagne (French for "country bread"), a giant, round loaf of chewy, crunchy sourdough.
>
> In the evening, my grandmother would make a sticky, shaggy mess out of the most basic mix of <u>ingredients</u>: water, salt, flour, and starter. The starter was a glob taken from a bowl of fermenting dough that my grandmother always had ready. There was nothing <u>glamorus</u> about the work, but the transformation of those simple ingredients seemed like magic.

Choose the correct word or phrase.
To my mother, good food meant fresh ingredients; to my father, good food meant that there was a lot of it; <u>and my grandmother thought</u> good food meant that you had taken the time to do all of the little details yourself.
    a. to my grandmother,
    b. my grandmother always said

    c. but for my grandmother,

    d. correct as is

12. Choose the correct word or phrase.
    In the evening, my grandmother would make a sticky, shaggy mess out of the most basic mix of <u>ingredients:</u> water, salt, flour, and starter.
    a. ingredients
    b. ingredients;
    c. ingredients,
    d. correct as is

13. There was nothing <u>glamorus</u> about the work, but the transformation of those simple ingredients seemed like magic.
    a. glamorous
    b. glamerus
    c. glamerous
    d. correct as is

14. Is the following grammatically correct?
        I had so much fun at the festival. Best festival ever!
    a. Yes
    b. No

15. What is the meaning of surreptitious?
    a. Kept secret
    b. By chance
    c. Serendipitous
    d. Suspicious

16. I went to the grocery store I bought milk.
    How should the above sentence be rewritten?
    a. I went to the grocery store to buy milk.
    b. I went to the grocery store, and I bought milk.
    c. I went to the grocery store; milk was bought.
    d. The sentence is correct as is.

17. Which word is misspelled?
    a. Inoculate
    b. Occasion
    c. miniature
    d. Exilerate

18. Fashion is often ephemeral. What does ephemeral mean?
    a. Thin

        b. Short-lived
        c. Cyclical
        d. Flamboyant

19. Which of the following sentences is correct?
        a. I have travelled to: San Diego, CA, Miami, FL, and Austin, TX.
        b. I have travelled to: San Deigo CA, Miami FL, and Austin TX.
        c. I have travelled to: San Diego, CA; Miami, FL; and Austin, TX.
        d. I have travelled to: San Diego, CA: Miami, FL: and Austin, TX.

20. What is the meaning of dissonance?
        a. A lack of agreement
        b. To be in agreement
        c. Concordance
        d. Peace

21. I bought peanut butter cupcakes, but Ethan did not eat any cupcakes because he is
    allergic to peanuts.
    What kind of sentence is this?
        a. Simple
        b. Compound
        c. Complex
        d. Compound complex

22. There are many beautiful _____ in the sea.
        a. Kind of fish
        b. Kinds of fishes
        c. Fish
        d. Fishes

23. Which of the following sentences is correct?
        a. Every living person has a beating heart.
        b. Every living person have a beating heart.
        c. Every living person have beating hearts.

24. What is the meaning of acquiesce?
        a. To attain
        b. A person you know, but who is not a close friend
        c. To give in
        d. To comfort

25. Which of the following sentences is correct?
        a. The two best things about San Diego is the beaches and the weather.
        b. The two best things about San Diego is: the beaches and the weather.

c. The two best things about San Diego is, the beaches and the weather.

d. The two best things about San Diego are the beaches and the weather.

26. When Michael saw his father, he was so happy.
    How should the above sentence be rewritten?
    a. When Micheal saw his father, he was very happy.
    b. Michael was so happy when he saw his father.
    c. Michael and his father are so happy.
    d. The sentence is correct as is.

27. What is the meaning of capricious?
    a. Stable
    b. Unpredictable
    c. Risky
    d. Relating to the sea

28. Choose the correct word or phrase.
    My grandmother was of French <u>ancestry therefore</u>, her bread reflected that heritage.
    a. ancestry; therefore
    b. ancestry therefore
    c. ancestry; therefore,
    d. correct as is

Practice Exam 2 Answers

Science

1. D. rectum. Kidneys help eliminate liquid waste.
2. B. cellular respiration
3. A. They need energy.
4. C. 4. Start out by listing the reactants and products.

Reactants	Products
C=3	C=1
H=8	H=2
O=2	O=3

Balance the carbons.

$$C_3H_8 + O_2 \rightarrow 3CO_2 + H_2O$$

Reactants	Products
C=3	C=3
H=8	H=2
O=2	O=7

Balance the hydrogen.

$$C_3H_8 + O_2 \rightarrow 3CO_2 + 4H_2O$$

Reactants	Products
C=3	C=3
H=8	H=8
O=2	O=10

Balance the oxygen.

$$C_3H_8 + 5O_2 \rightarrow 3CO_2 + 4H_2O$$

Reactants	Products
C=3	C=3
H=8	H=8

O=5	O=10

5. B. Three (Hydrogen, Sulfur, Oxygen).
6. A. organ 1. The stomach releases gastric juice, which consists of highly acidic hydrochloric acid, pepsin (an enzyme), and mucus.
7. C. Only those individuals best adapted to the new environment will survive and reproduce, leading to a decrease in genetic diversity.
8. C. Breathing rate is increased to exchange oxygen and carbon dioxide more rapidly.
9. A. to produce identical daughter skin cells.
10. C. Cl_2. All other answers are molecules.
11. D. It is a codominant pattern because the heterozygous offspring have a different phenotype than either parent.
12. B. during exercise, when the need for energy is high. ATP is the primary source of energy for a cell.
13. A. Enzymes.
14. D. An offspring receives half its chromosomes from each parent.
15. A. Proteins. In transcription, information in DNA is used to produce a complementary messenger RNA (mRNA).In translation, messenger RNA (mRNA) is decoded in a ribosome to produce a protein (an amino acid chain).
16. A. Cellular respiration. Cellular respiration is the process that takes place in cells to convert nutrients into ATP and release waste products.
17. A. Detecting antigens. The main cells involved in the immune response are: B lymphocytes (B-cells) and T lymphocytes (T-cells). T-cells are responsible for detecting antigens. There are two types of B-cells: plasma cells and memory cells. Plasma cells produce antibodies and memory cells remember the antigen and stores information for creating the antibody.
18. C. sensory neuron → spinal cord → brain. Neurons send information to the brain through the spinal cord, so answer choices A and B are wrong. Motor neurons do not communicate with sensory neurons through the spinal cord so answer D is wrong.
19. A. 8. The atomic mass (A) is equal to Z (the number of protons) plus N (the number of neutrons). Based on the equation A = Z + N, if you know any two of the following values: atomic mass, number of protons, or number of neutrons, you can solve for the missing value. For example, the atomic number of oxygen is 8 which means it has 8 protons and its atomic mass is 16, so oxygen has 8 neutrons (16 = 8 + N).
20. B. Glucagon. The pancreas releases insulin when blood glucose levels are high; insulin increases cell uptake of glucose, reducing the levels of glucose in blood. The pancreas releases glucagon when blood glucose levels are low; glucagon causes cells to release glucose into the blood.
21. C. A dependent variable. An independent variable stands alone and is not affected by other variables. A dependent variable depends on or is affected by the independent variable.

22. D. Epiglottis. The upper airway consists of the nose, mouth, nasopharynx, oropharynx, larynx (voice box), epiglottis (valve that closes over the trachea during swallowing to prevent choking).

23. B. Mitochondria.

24. C. Coronal plane. The sagittal plane or midline is a vertical line that divides the body into left and right sections. The transverse plane is a horizontal line, parallel to the ground, at the level of the navel and divides the body into superior (top) and inferior (bottom) sections. The coronal plane is a vertical line that divides the body into anterior (front) and posterior (back) sections.

25. B. The pulmonary loop. In the pulmonary loop, when oxygen-poor blood enters the heart's right atrium, the atria contracts and pumps blood to the right ventricle. When the ventricles contract, blood is pumped from the right ventricle, through the pulmonary arteries, to the lungs where the blood becomes oxygenated (carbon dioxide is exchanged for oxygen). The now oxygen-rich blood is pumped through the pulmonary veins and into the heart's left atrium and then to the left ventricle. In the systemic loop, oxygen-rich blood is pumped from the heart's left ventricle to the aorta and the blood vessels of the body. Oxygen-poor blood is then transported back to the heart's right atrium by veins.

26. B. Capillaries. Arteries carry blood away from the heart and have thick, muscular, and elastic walls to withstand the high pressure of blood leaving the heart. Veins carry blood back to the heart and have one way valves to prevent backflow. They have thinner and less elastic walls than arteries because they do not have to withstand as high of a blood pressure. Capillaries are the smallest and most populous blood vessels. They have thin walls to allow substances and gases to be exchanged or diffused between the blood and cell tissues.

27. B. Dermis. The skin is the largest organ of the body and protects the body from pathogens. The skin also helps regulate body temperature and serves our sense of heat, cold, pain, and pressure. It consists of the epidermis (outermost layer); dermis (contains blood vessels, nerve endings, hair follicles, sweat/oil glands); and subcutaneous layer (fatty tissue below the dermis and above the muscles). The epidermis also contains melanocytes; melanocytes are responsible for producing skin pigmentation and protecting the skin from ultraviolet rays.

28. A. True. All experiments must have an independent variable (it should only have 1 independent variable), dependent variable(s), and control variable(s).

29. B. The cell membrane. The fact that phospholipids are both hydrophilic and hydrophobic is important to the function of the cell membrane; this is what allows a cell to be semi-permeable and create a barrier between its contents and its environment.

30. B. Smooth muscles. Smooth muscles are not under voluntary control and are typically found in the digestive tract, blood vessels, and other internal organs.

31. D. Temporal lobe. The frontal lobe is responsible for key functions such as decision making, problem solving, emotional expression, voluntary movement, memory, and personality. The parietal lobe is mainly responsible for processing sensory information such as taste, temperature, touch, spatial awareness, etc. The occipital lobe is mainly

responsible for processing visual input. The temporal lobe is mainly responsible for processing auditory input.

32. C. Nephrons. Nephrons, which are tiny tubes in a kidney, are the functional units of the kidney; each kidney contains millions of nephrons. The nephron is responsible for filtering blood as well as reabsorbing valuable proteins, salts, water, and glucose.

33. A. In electrical synapses, ions flow directly between cells through a channel called a gap junction. The main advantage of electrical synapses is that they transmit signals faster than chemical synapses.

34. A. A negative feedback loop. In negative feedback loops, when conditions deviate from normal or ideal values, a response is triggered to bring conditions back to normal. In positive feedback loops, deviation from normal values are increased.

35. D. Cardiac arrest. Contractions in the heart are caused by electrical impulses. . The inability to generate an electrical impulse or for heart muscles to respond to electrical impulse will result in cardiac arrest.

36. A. Grey matter. The brain consists of gray matter and white matter. Grey matter is where all the nerve synapses are located and where the actual processing of signals happen. White matter mainly consists of neuron axons and is mainly responsible for transmitting signals between gray matter regions and between the brain and spinal cord.

37. C. Decreases from left to right. The atomic radius is the distance between the nucleus and the outermost electron shell. The atomic radius decreases from left to right, this is because as you move right, the elements have more protons to attract/pull the electrons toward the center of the atom. The atomic radius increases as you move down because of the addition of a new energy level.

38. B. Oxytocin. Oxytocin stimulates the uterus to contract during labor. Prolactin stimulates milk production. Luteinizing hormone (LH) induces ovulation and testosterone production. Vasopressin causes kidneys to reabsorb water.

39. B. Tendons. Ligaments are fibrous connective tissue that connect bone to bone. Tendons connect muscles to bones. Cartilage is connective tissue that acts as a cushion between bones. A joint is where two bones meet.

40. A. Oxygen poor blood. Arteries carry oxygen-rich blood away from the heart to body tissues, and veins carry oxygen-poor blood back to the heart. The only exceptions are the pulmonary artery (which carries oxygen-poor blood) and the pulmonary vein (which carries oxygen-rich blood).

41. B. The antagonist.

42. C. Small intestine. The small intestine is where digestion ends and absorption begins.

43. A. Eat bacteria. Neutrophils are a type of white blood cell that phagocytize (eat) bacteria. Cytotoxic T-cells only kills host cells that display specific antigens.

44. B. False.The hypothalamus and pituitary gland can be considered the "master" or "command center" of the endocrine system. The hypothalamus is the link between the nervous system and the endocrine system. Located at the base of the brain near the pituitary gland, it secretes hormones that control the pituitary gland. The pituitary gland, when triggered by the hypothalamus, secretes hormones that control multiple body functions.

45. D. All of the above. In organisms, osmosis is important for maintaining cellular water levels, transporting nutrients, and cell to cell diffusion. Diffusion helps in the exchange of gases during respiration.

46. A. Increases. Ionization is the process by which an atom or a molecule acquires a negative or positive charge by gaining or losing electrons. Ionization energy, measured in joules, is the amount of energy needed to remove an electron from an atom. The lower the attraction (electronegativity) between an atom and electron, the easier it is to remove the electron. Ionization energy increases as you move right and as you move up the periodic table.

47. D. Bone density. The parathyroid glands release parathyroid hormones to control calcium and phosphorus levels in the body.

48. B. False. The PNS motor system is divided into somatic (voluntary) and autonomic (involuntary) portions. The autonomic system is further divided into the sympathetic and parasympathetic systems. The sympathetic division controls the "fight or flight" response and prepares the body for emergencies. The parasympathetic portion returns the body functions back to normal after a sympathetic "fight or flight" response.

49. C. Vas deferens. The reproductive system consists of sex organs that aid in sexual reproduction. The penis is the male external sexual organ. In males, sperm is produced in the testes (specifically, in the seminiferous tubules) and stored in the scrotum (specifically, in the epididymis). The prostate gland produces seminal fluid; it is located below the bladder and surrounds the urethra. The vas deferens is a duct that carries ejaculated sperm from the epididymis to the urethra. The urethra is the duct through which semen exits the body.

50. D. Pulmonary vein. Arteries carry blood away from the heart and have thick, muscular, and elastic walls to withstand the high pressure of blood leaving the heart. Veins carry blood back to the heart and have one way valves to prevent backflow. They have thinner and less elastic walls than arteries because they do not have to withstand as high of a blood pressure.

51. A. A drop in progesterone levels causes the uterine lining to shed. FSH stimulates the ovaries to release estrogen. Estrogen causes an ovarian follicle to mature and the uterine wall/lining (also called endometrium) to thicken. The corpus luteum releases progesterone and oestrogen to maintain a thickened uterine lining.

52. C. Sternum. Long bones are longer than they are wide and make up the bones of the limbs (femur, tibia, ulna, humerus, etc.). They provide strength, structure, and mobility. Short bones are wider than they are long. They are found in the carpal bones (wrist) and tarsal bones (foot). Flat bones are thin bones that protect internal organs and provide a surface for muscles to attach to. The sternum, ribs, and pelvis are made of flat bones. Sesamoid bones are bones embedded within a tendon or muscle. The kneecap is a sesamoid bone. Irregular bones are bones that do not fit into the other categories. The vertebral column, skull, and elbow are examples of irregular bones.

53. B. Cup B. The amount of thermal energy released depends on the mass of the material and its change in temperature. Since the temperature change is the same in both cups of water, Cup B, with the greater mass, releases more thermal energy.

Mathematics

1. A, C.
2. B. Rye, Troy, Pinehill, Smithfield. The current populations are Rye: 500, Troy: 600, Pinehill: 800, Smithfield: 950.
3. C. 13.4 ft. Since there is a right triangle, we can use the Pythagorean theorem to solve for the hypotenuse (the length of the wires).

$a^2 + b^2 = c^2$

$6^2 + 12^2 = c^2$

$36 + 144 = c^2$

$180 = c^2$

$13.4 = c$

4. D. 4 inches. The conversion ratio is $\frac{1\text{ inch}}{0.75\text{ miles}}$. 3 miles $* \frac{1\text{ inch}}{0.75\text{ miles}}$ = 4 inches.
5. C. 25. Since the total weight of the cart plus n boxes is 10n + 25, the weight of 1 box is 10 lbs and the weight of the cart is 25 lbs.
6. B. 1150 in.^{3}. The formula for calculating the volume of a sphere is $(4/3)\pi r^3$. Since the diameter of the sphere is 13 in., the radius is 6.5 in. $V = (4/3)\pi(6.5)^3 = 1150$ in.^{3}
7. D. 10. The area of a rectangle is length * width, so multiply $16\frac{1}{4} * 11\frac{3}{4}$. Convert the mixed numbers into improper fractions before multiplying them. $16\frac{1}{4} = \frac{(16 * 4) + 1}{4} = \frac{65}{4}$

$11\frac{3}{4} = \frac{(11 * 4) + 3}{4} = \frac{47}{4}$

$\frac{65}{4} * \frac{47}{4} = \frac{3055}{16} = 190$ sq ft.

190 / 20 = 9.5 = ~10.

8. C. The mean and the median for week 1 are equal to the mean and the median for week 2.

Week 1:

Mean: (25 + 44 +48 + 63 + 75)/5 = 51

Median: {25, 44, 48, 63, 75}, the middle/median of the set is 48

Mode: There is no mode since all numbers appear equally frequently.

Range: The smallest amount is 25 and the largest amount is 75, so the range is 75 - 25 = 50.

Week 2:

Mean: (35 + 35 + 48 + 62 +75)/5 = 51

Median: {35, 35, 48, 62, 75}, the middle/median of the set is 48.

Mode: The number 35 appears most frequently

Range: The smallest amount is 35 and the largest amount is 75, so the range is 75 - 35 = 40

9. B. $30x^3 - 5x$
10. B. 2 meters. 1 meter = 3.28 feet. 2 meters = 6.56 feet.
11. E. Multiplying 40 by 2.

$$10 \text{ gallons} * \left(\frac{4 \text{ quarts}}{1 \text{ gallon}}\right) = 40 \text{ quarts}.$$

$$40 \text{ quarts} * \left(\frac{2 \text{ pints}}{1 \text{ quart}}\right) = 40 * 2 = 80 \text{ pints}.$$

12. C. 5 + 6 + 6 = 17. 4.6 rounds to 5; 6.3 rounds to 6, 5.7 rounds to 6.

13. A. Median income of drivers.

14. C. 4 min 10 sec. To fill 5 boxes of nails with 250 nails each, requires 5 * 250 = 1250 nails.

$$1250 \text{ nails} * \left(\frac{1 \text{ minute}}{300 \text{ nails}}\right) = 4.16 \text{ minutes}.$$

$$0.16 \text{ minute} * \left(\frac{60 \text{ seconds}}{1 \text{ minute}}\right) = 9.6 = \sim 10 \text{ seconds}$$

Answer: 4 minutes and 10 seconds

15. B. 8. The volume of water that is leaked, in order to have the water level dropped 1 foot, is

$$24 * 8 * 1 = 92 \text{ ft}^3.$$

$$92 \text{ cubic ft} * \left(\frac{1 \text{ minute}}{0.40 \text{ cubic ft}}\right) = 480 \text{ minutes}$$

$$480 \text{ minutes} * \left(\frac{1 \text{ hour}}{60 \text{ minutes}}\right) = 8 \text{ hours}$$

16. C. Cannot tell. In order to tell, you need to know the number of males and the number of females that voted in the election.

17. D. 40. 2 out of 25 batteries are dead. We should expect the same ratio of dead batteries in the shipment of 500.

$$\frac{2}{25} = \frac{x}{500}$$

25x = 1000

X = 40

18. A. 27. 45 * 0.6 = 27.

19. B. Temperature of water that is heated on a stove, then removed and allowed to cool.

20. A. 1024. Since 64 cubes fill up half the box, 64 *2 = 128 cubes fill up the entire box. Since each cube has a volume of 8 cubic centimeters and it takes 128 cubes to fill up the box, the volume of the box is 8 * 128 = 1024.

21. C. Infinitely many.

22. D. 65. The pattern is 42+9=51, 51-2=49, 49+9=58, 58-2=56, 56+9=65

23. A. 1. The smallest positive 3 digit number is 100. The largest positive 2 digit number is 99. 100 - 99 = 1.

24. B. 275. There are 360 degrees in a circle, so the ratio of the shaded portion to the circle

    is $\dfrac{37}{360}$

The entire circle represents 2675 radios.

$$\dfrac{37}{360} = \dfrac{x}{2675}$$

X = 275.

25. E. $6,180. 15% of 5375 = 0.15 * 5375 = 806. 5375 + 806 = 6181.

26. B. 80. The area of the rectangle is equal to the length of ED multiplied by the length of BE.

    ED * BE = 60

    15 * BE = 60

    BE = 4

    The area of the triangle is ½ * AE * BE. We are given that the length of AE is 10 and we figured out the length of BE above.

    ½ * 10 * 4 = 20

    The area of the trapezoid is equal to the area of the triangle + area of the square.

    20 + 60 = 80.

27. C. 21,567.

28. B. 7.73. The area of the circle is $\pi * r^2$ = 3.14 * 3^2 = 28.26. The width of the square is 6 and so is the length of the square. The area of the square is 6*6 = 36. The shaded area is equal to the area of the square minus the area of the circle. 36 - 28.26 = 7.74.

29. C. 4. Raymond must be 28 * 64 = 1792 pages of paper. He needs at least 1792/500 = 3.6 packages. Since you can only buy whole packages, he needs to buy 4 packages.

30. A. Tracy. If you multiply 6 by 0, the answer is 0.

31. C. 7/4 is equal to 1.75.

32. C. 3 to 1. There are 300 vegetarians and 900 (1200 - 300) non-vegetarians, so the ratio is 900 to 300, which reduces to 3 to 1.

33. B. 6. 2 * 5= 10 which is less than 11, so we have to go up one. 2 * 6 = 12 which is greater than 11, so 6 is the least whole number for which 2x > 11.

34. D. Volume of the box. The volume of a rectangle is represented by cubic inches.

35. D. 30 cm. The midpoint of MN is 10 cm. The midpoint of PQ is 8 cm. 10 + 12 + 8 = 30 cm.

36. B. $0.40. Assign the following variables: A = cost of an apple, B = cost of a banana, C = cost of an orange. A = 0.5 and C = 0.6.

    4A + 1B = 2C + 3B

    4(0.5) + 1B = 2(0.6) + 3B

    2 + 1B = 1.2 + 3B

    2 = 1.2 + 2B

    0.8 = 2B

    0.4 = B

Reading

1. C. To describe how it feels to throw the javelin.
2. D. To give the history of how women got the right to vote.
3. A. Right to vote. Suffrage means the right to vote.
4. D. Many working women joined in the fight for woman's suffrage. The passage says: "After the Triangle fire, many working women joined the fight for voting rights. "
5. A. She argued that working conditions were more likely than voting rights to lead to the loss of a woman's beauty and charm. In the passage, Rose says: "I asked him if he thought they would lose more of their beauty and charm by putting a ballot in the ballot box than by standing all day in factories or laundries."
6. D. It drew national attention to the contributions of women. The passage says: "Thousands of women took over jobs that had been held by men. National leaders began to think that women should be repaid for their work during the war. ".
7. A. A colonist. The passage says: "The colonial committees were very anxious not to fire the first shot, and there were strict orders not to provoke open conflict with the British regulars. But in the confusion someone fired.", the "but" keyword tells us that someone who was told NOT to fire, fired a shot. The colonial committees were under strict orders to not fire shots, so someone on the colonial committee (a colonist) fired a shot. Passage B does not mention Captain Parker or Paul Revere so answers c and d are wrong.
8. A. He was an eyewitness to the battle. The passage says: "The officer came up to within about two rods of the centre of the company, where I stood.", suggesting that the author was an eyewitness to the battle. There was no mention of Paul Revere, so answer B is incorrect. The author says: "The company immediately dispersed; and while the company was dispersing and leaping over the wall, the second platoon of the British fired, and killed some of our men.", the author mentions that the "British fired, and killed some of our men" tell us that he was not on the British side, so answer d is wrong.
9. D. Says that news of the atrocity was spread to neighboring colonies. The fact that the author refers to the colonists being shot as an atrocity tells us that he favors the colonists. Shots were fired so answer b is wrong. Mentioning the contributions of General Gage or that Paul Revere tipped off the colonists tells us nothing about the author's feelings, so answers c and a are wrong.
10. C. A young girl makes up a story and frightens a nervous visitor. In the passage, the man is not visiting his aunt so answer 'a' is incorrect. The family does not know why Mr. Nuttel dashed off without a word, so they do not appear to be in on the "joke" nor do they appear to be amused, so answers b and d are incorrect.
11. A. To cure his nervous condition. In the passage, it says: "Privately he doubted more than ever whether these formal visits on a succession of total strangers would do much towards helping the nerve cure which he was supposed to be undergoing." which suggests that he is trying to cure his nervous condition.
12. D. Has a mistaken idea about how others view him. A delusion is a false belief.

13. C. He withholds information from the reader until the story's conclusion. There are no major conflicts or romances between characters, so answer a and b are incorrect. The identities of the characters are revealed as we meet them, so answer 'd' is incorrect.

14. D. In paragraph 3, Circe clearly warns Ulysses about the dangers associated with encountering the Sirens, remarking that "If any one unwarily draws in too close and hears the singing of the Sirens, his wife and children will never welcome him home again . . ."

15. C. Circe warns the men that the Sirens' intention is to keep them on the island, whereas this detail contradicts Circe's warning and describes the benefits of the Sirens' influences.

16. A. Throughout Passage 2, the Sirens contrast the harshness of the sea and the eternal peace of their Island, remarking that "The sea is restless and uneasy . . . Come to this peaceful home of ours."

17. A. The ancient Greeks were attracted to the sea and made important explorations and discoveries, but Greek culture also acknowledged that the sea was dangerous. This simultaneous allure and danger represented by the Sirens reflects this aspect of ancient Greek culture.

18. B, C. Answer 'B': . President Nixon spends much of the speech thanking the American people for taking the necessary actions to weather the crisis; he also outlines plans of action for the people, the government, Congress, and industry to take in the future. Answer 'C': President Nixon mentions the fact that some outside forces (warmer temperatures and unexpected oil) made things easier on the country, but he deliberately minimizes these contributions in favor of the voluntary actions of the American people.

19. A. Nixon uses the word "catalyst" to show that the government must instigate and initiate changes that will help solve the crisis.

20. B. Churchill's quotation emphasizes the importance of the outcome of World War II. Nixon quotes Churchill to highlight the importance of the energy crisis.

21. C. President Nixon reiterates that the success of his various plans relies on voluntary cooperation as much as new laws and regulations.

22. B,D. Answer B: This option describes how resources are being allocated by the government to lessen the burden of the crisis for Americans. Answer D: This option describes how the government is protecting its citizens from price gouging, therefore lessening the crisis for Americans.

23. C. 2 6 4 3 5. You start with the numbers: 1 2 3 4 5. After switching the second and fourth number, you have: 1 4 3 2 5. After incrementing each number by 1, you have: 2 5 4 3 6. Aftering switching the second and fifth number, you have: 2 6 4 3 5.

24. A. Anna, Bella, Cindy, Donna. Option B violates the rule that Anna cannot sit with Bella unless Donna is at the same table. Option C and D violates the rule that Bella must sit with either Cindy or Fred.

25. B. Cows are herbivores. Humans are omnivores, but not all omnivores are humans. While bears eat both meat and plants, they are not carnivores (animals that only eat meat) and are not herbivores (animals that only eat plants). Both lions and hawks are carnivores, but that does not necessarily mean they have the same diet.

26. A. Team 1 scored the most during period 2.

27. B. Team 2 performed better during the first period.

28. C. Among Teams 2, 3, and 4, Team 4 has the highest combined score, so they are Team 1's biggest competitor.

29. C. The mood of the passage is exciting.

30. B. An autobiography is considered a primary source and is usually more reliable than secondary sources.

31. A. Principle means a code of conduct. Principal is a person in a lead position in an organization.

32. C. X X B X X B. After incrementing each number by 1, we have: 3 5 4 7 9 8. After replacing all odd numbers with A, we have: A A 4 A A 8. After replacing all even numbers with B, we have: A A B A A B. After replacing consecutive odd numbers (represented by the letter 'A') with 'X', we have: X X B X X B.

33. B. No. The directions say "Do not use for the treatment of diaper rash. Ask a doctor."

34. B. No. The directions say to not use in the genital area if you have vaginal discharge, but says to "Ask a doctor", which would mean that the doctor has the final say.

35. D. Loans. Single family homes, apartment buildings, and land are all types of real estate that you can buy.

36. B. Ethan is first in line. The order is as follows: Ethan, Anna, Jacob, Jared, Charlize.

37. A. The author's purpose is to inform the reader about advancements in modern clothing. The author does not try to persuade the user into action. The author does not warn the user, not advertise to the user.

38. C. The main idea is that advancements in CAD and 3-D printing will revolutionize the clothing industry. Answer choice 'A' is wrong because the author doesn't mention anything about 3D printing affecting industries other than clothing. Though the author mentions that clothing will be easier to make and consumers will be able to create customized clothing, they are not the main idea of the passage.

39. A. Evolve means to develop gradually.

40. A. Advancement in the clothing industry will provide consumers with more choices. The passage does not discuss the ease or difficulty of using CAD software, nor does it discuss clothing industry employment. Though advancements in CAD has made designers' jobs easier, it does not necessarily mean they love CAD.

41. D. The sentence is an example of a supporting detail. It supports the main idea that advancements in 3D printing are changing the clothing industry.

42. A. Verdant means green. Ubiquitous means everywhere. Rampant means spreading unchecked. Xenophobic means prejudice againsts others from different countries.

43. A. Jacob is standing between Anna and Jared. The order is as follows: Ethan, Anna, Jacob, Jared, Charlize.

44. D. You cannot purchase a single tulip bulb; you must purchase at least 3 or more.

45. C. Freesias (1.99 * 5 = 9.95). Lilies (5 for 10.99). Tulips (9.99 + (2 * 0.99)) = 11.97.

46. B. 20 lily bulbs would cost 14.99 * 2 = 29.98.

47. A. Ensure. Ensure means to make certain. Insure is to protect the financial value of something.

48. D. Circle. Squares, triangles, and trapezoids are made of straight lines.

49. D. 4 gallons of water. You start out with 5 gallons. After dumping out 2 gallons of water, you have 3 gallons of water. Then you add 1 gallon of water, resulting in 4 gallons of water.
50. A. Soporific means to make one sleepy.
51. A. Is constantly changing. Malleable means easily influenced or changed, and pliable.
52. C. New to the English language. "Novel" means new. Looking at the sentence: "The Age of Exploration introduced novel terms from all corners.", the use of the word "introduced" should have clued you into thinking novel means something that was new or previously unknown.
53. D. Considered inferior to French. Subjugate means to bring under control or domination. The passage says: "That meant English speakers were being ruled by French speakers, and the subjugated language had to adjust." which means that English speakers were dominated by French speakers. The passage does not talk about whether or not French was taught, how difficult French was to learn, or what language scholars used, so answers a, b, and c are wrong.

English and Language Usage

1. B. False. This is incorrect because 'was' is a past tense word, but 'think' is a present tense word.
2. B. The meaning of elucidate is to make clear.
3. D. Jason said, "Let's go to Disneyland." Use quotation marks to identify direct quotes. The first word in a quotation that is a complete sentence is capitalized, but the first word in a partial quotation is not. You should use a comma to introduce quoted material or dialogue.
4. B. Compound. Compound sentences contain two or more independent clauses. The two clauses are usually joined using a coordinating conjunction (for, and, nor, but, or, yet, and so). "I bought eggs and milk" is one independent clause. "I forgot to buy bread" is another independent clause.
5. B. Green eggs and ham is my favorite dish. When two subjects are joined by "and" and they both refer to the same thing, a singular verb form is required. Green eggs and ham refers to a single dish.
6. D. droplet. A rivulet is a small river; a droplet is a small drop of liquid.
7. A. needed.
8. A. Salary.
9. C. Neither Claire nor Charlize wants to go to her room. Two nouns joined by the words neither-nor take a singular verb and a singular pronoun in reference. The verb should be "wants" and the possessive pronoun should be "her".
10. A. "Basicly" should be spelled "basically".
11. B. This option shows the correct use of parallelism and sentence structure after a semicolon.
12. D. This option shows the correct use of a colon to precede a list of items.
13. A. This option shows the correct spelling of the word "glamorous."
14. B. No. Sentence fragments are incomplete sentences (they are missing a subject or verb or both) and should be avoided. "Best festival ever" is a sentence fragment.
15. A. Surreptitious means kept secret.
16. B. I went to the grocery store, and I bought milk. Two independent clauses can be joined by a comma and a conjunction. Option "D" is incorrect because the sentence is a run-on sentence and needs to be corrected. Option "A" is incorrect because it changes the meaning of the sentence; just because the subject bought milk at the grocery, it does not mean that was the purpose of going to the grocery store. Option "C" is incorrect because "milk was bought" is not an independent clause.
17. D. Exilerate is spelled incorrectly. The correct spelling is exhilirate.
18. B. Ephemeral means short-lived.
19. C. I have travelled to: San Diego, CA; Miami, FL; and Austin, TX. Semicolons are used to separate list items that have commas.
20. A. Dissonance means a lack of agreement.

21. D. compound complex. Compound-Complex sentences contain two or more independent clauses and one or more dependent clauses. "I bought peanut butter

cupcakes" is an independent clause. "Ethan did not eat any cupcakes" is another independent clause. "Because he is allergic to peanuts" is a dependent clause.

22. C. Fish. Option 'A' is wrong because "kind" is singular, but the plural form is needed. Option 'B' and 'D' are wrong because the plural form of "fish" is "fish", not "fishes".

23. A. Every living person has a beating heart. If "each", "every" or "no" precedes a subject, a singular verb is required.

24. C. Acquiesce means to give in.

25. D. The two best things about San Diego are the beaches and the weather. The subject is "two best things", so a plural verb should be used.

26. B. Michael was so happy when he saw his father. Options "A" and "D" are incorrect because the sentences are ambiguous; was Michael happy or was the father happy? Option "C" is incorrect because it changes the meaning of the sentence.

27. B. Capricious means unpredictable.

28. C. This option shows the correct use of a semicolon with conjunctive adverbs.

Thank You For Your Purchase

Thank you for your purchase. If you found this study guide helpful, please leave a review for us on Amazon; we would truly appreciate it.

If you have any questions or concerns, please contact us at hut8testprep@gmail.com.

Bibliography

Miller, Kenneth and Joseph Levine. Miller and Levine Biology Foundation Edition. New Jersey, 2014.

Kaplan Incorporated. Kaplan ATI TEAS. New York, 2017.

Allen, John. ATI TEAS Crash Course. New Jersey, 2017.

Trivium Test Prep. ATI TEAS Test Study Guide 2018-2019. 2018.

https://en.wikipedia.org/wiki/Cell_theory

https://en.wikipedia.org/wiki/Cell_(biology)

https://en.wikipedia.org/wiki/Organelle

https://en.wikipedia.org/wiki/Ribosome

https://en.wikipedia.org/wiki/Cell_nucleus

https://www.rnasociety.org/about/what-is-rna/

https://www.khanacademy.org/science/biology/cellular-molecular-biology/mitosis/a/cell-cycle-phases

https://en.wikipedia.org/wiki/Cell_cycle

https://en.wikipedia.org/wiki/Mitosis

https://medium.com/countdown-education/8-chemistry-trends-across-the-periodic-table-explained-537b035371d5

https://biodifferences.com/difference-between-osmosis-and-diffusion.html

https://www.wikihow.com/Balance-Chemical-Equations

https://grammar.yourdictionary.com/sentences/20-rules-of-subject-verb-agreement.html

Made in the
USA
Columbia, SC

82346159R00157